The Certainty of Uncertainty

The Certainty of Uncertainty

The Way of Inescapable Doubt and Its Virtue

Mark Schaefer

WIPF & STOCK · Eugene, Oregon

THE CERTAINTY OF UNCERTAINTY
The Way of Inescapable Doubt and Its Virtue

Wipf & Stock
An Imprint of Wipf and Stock Publishers
199 W. 8th Ave., Suite 3
Eugene, OR 97401

www.wipfandstock.com

PAPERBACK ISBN: 978-1-5326-5343-8
HARDCOVER ISBN: 978-1-5326-5344-5
EBOOK ISBN: 978-1-5326-5345-2

For Rania

Contents

Illustrations and Tables

Tables

Illustrations

Author's Preface

THE WORLD HAS A certainty problem.

Right now, all around the world, there are all kinds of people who are very certain about things: certain that their political ideologies are the right ones, certain that their religious beliefs are absolutely correct, certain that their understanding of the world is entirely accurate. Such people are less inclined to compromise with others, less inclined to tolerate differing points of view, and less inclined to embrace the humility that makes community in a diverse world possible.

This certainty has a number of ill effects. It is dividing our communities into ever more rigid camps, who are quick to condemn each other as "heretics" or "traitors" or "unbelievers," but mostly as "other." It causes otherwise good people to resist hearing what others might say for fear that they will be branded unfaithful or, worse, might begin to doubt what they had previously believed with such certainty. And this certainty becomes a source of harm—emotional, psychological, and spiritual—to anyone who admits even the slightest doubt.

This last point is the one I am concerned about the most. I am a United Methodist pastor and have served nearly two decades in campus ministry working with college students, faculty, and staff, exploring issues of meaning, purpose, and identity. I have seen how people can feel such great pain at the very idea that they don't know something. They're not sure what they believe. They don't know what they want to do with their lives. They don't know who they are. And worst of all, they feel bad because they feel this way. Especially over questions of faith.

In religious communities that place a high priority on faith, admitting doubt can feel like failure. Especially when everyone else seems so sure. *If I am having these doubts*, they think, *what is wrong with me? Why don't I believe like everyone else?* My usual response is to reassure them that doubt and questioning are perfectly natural—and healthy—religious responses. But it has become clear that the struggle with doubt in the face of the expectation of certainty is not an isolated occurrence, it's a systemic problem.

And so, I have set out to address that problem. I have preached on it. I have taught about it. And now I have come to write this book about it.

It has occurred to me that very often books that seek to explore some question of faith or belief are written in a very "insider" way. That is, they are written using religious language for people who are religious themselves. Rarely do they bring in insight from other realms, especially the scientific realms. But the problem of uncertainty is not limited to the religious; it is a universal problem that affects every single one of us. The book I wanted to write was one that would set out to address uncertainty not simply as a religious issue, but as a human one, and in so doing would explore the insights that other disciplines had to offer, especially those of philosophy, science, and linguistics.

And so, I have set out to write this exploration of uncertainty and to do so in a way that takes on the reality of our world, the medium we use to communicate about it, and, in religion, the systems we construct to help find meaning for our experiences. In doing so, I hope to address a universal problem from a universal perspective, rather than from a narrow, religiously oriented one.

Having said that, I am both a teacher and a pastor. My purpose in this book is not simply to explore the bases for uncertainty in our world, language, and religion, but to find a way for people to be okay with that uncertainty. The final portion of the book looks at the ways we can see uncertainty as an opportunity: for wonder, for mystery, for a deeper, more meaningful faith, and for building bridges with others. I write so that those who are struggling to hold on to their rigid certainties, living in a perpetual state of cognitive dissonance, might be able to let go of those certainties for something better. And I write so that those who feel like they have failed at the task of faith because they have doubt will instead come to see that through their doubt they have come into a more powerful and more meaningful faith than they might ever have imagined.

As Christianity is the tradition in which I was raised and in which I am ordained, it is, obviously, the one with which I am the most familiar. The fact that a larger percentage of illustrations in this work come from Christianity rather than from Judaism or Islam, and that likewise illustrations from the Abrahamic faiths will outweigh illustrations from the Eastern traditions, should not be read as a statement that the phenomena I describe are limited to Christianity or to the Abrahamic traditions. Anyone with any familiarity with a religious tradition will no doubt see the phenomena described in this book manifested in that tradition. In my own experience, whenever I have a conversation on these questions with a Muslim friend and describe anything in Christianity, she will usually say something like, "Oh, that's just like the *hadith* where the Prophet said . . ." No doubt readers can find examples in all the faiths to illustrate the propositions made herein and I hope you do so.

I invite you to go on this journey with me as together we explore the world we live in, the language we use to share our experiences of that world, and the systems that give meaning to those experiences. Through a careful examination of religion, language, and science, we'll see that there are unavoidable uncertainties in these great domains of human experience. But we will also come to see that there is great potential and promise in embracing uncertainty and that by doing so we might come to a more honest engagement with the world we live in, and a more powerful and transformative faith that can change our uncertainty-filled world of fear into a mystery-filled world of hope.

* * *

About the Conventions Used in This Book

Unless otherwise noted, all scriptural translations are my own.

With regard to those translations, I wish to clarify my treatment of the Name of God. In the Hebrew Bible, the sacred Name of God is rendered יהוה *yod-he-waw-he*. By the first century of the Common Era, it had long become Jewish practice not to pronounce the Name out of fear of profaning it. When the Masoretic scribes added vowels to the text in the Early Middle Ages, they added the vowels of a different word—אדני *Adonai* ("my Lord")—to the Name to indicate what word should be pronounced instead. This led one hapless Latin scholar to suppose that the Name of God was *Iehovah*, fusing the consonants *Y-h-w-h* and the vowels of *Adonai*. (Many scholars believe the Name to have actually been pronounced *Yahweh*—though that is by no means certain.) In this book, I render the Name as *Yhwh*, preserving the mystery of the Name as found in the original Hebrew texts. If you should have occasion to read this book aloud, or want to give a pronunciation to the word for the silent inner voice as you read, feel free to substitute *Lord*, *Adonai, Yahweh, Jehovah*, or some other term as you feel appropriate.

Throughout this book, a good deal of attention is paid to language. In that treatment, a couple of conventions will be observed. When words are discussed as words, those words will be in italics, as seen in this example:

> In fact, the word *creed* comes from the Latin *credo*, meaning "I believe."

Likewise, when metaphors are discussed as metaphors, they will appear in small capitals:

> The Sinai Covenant, the centerpiece of the Old Testament Law,
> is built on the metaphor GOD IS A KING.

This follows a convention used in linguistics to distinguish between the ordinary use of a metaphor and the discussion of one.

In direct quotations, I have not usually edited the dated, sexist language of other writers except for clarity. In paraphrases and in my own writing, I aspire to gender-neutral and inclusive terminology when it comes to the divine, but feel strongly about not unduly altering another person's art. So, there will be quotes that refer to "religious men," "men of faith," and the like that will remain in that phrasing unless the phrasing or the excerpting thereof creates confusion.

And finally, I endeavor to use the word *they* throughout the text as a gender-neutral third-person pronoun, the way we all already do but our grammar teachers tell us is impermissible. I may also, from time to time and style permitting, use other grammatical constructions like split infinitives and prepositions at the end of sentences. Both of these constructions are perfectly permissible in English and were only prohibited by academics who believed that English grammar should more resemble Latin's. But as English has its own perfectly respectable grammar, I prefer to go with that.

Acknowledgments

THIS BOOK IS THE result of a lifetime of reflection and study, of conversation and discovery. A lot of people have been a part of that process and I will endeavor to thank as many of them as I can, recognizing that a true listing of all the people responsible for contributions to this book would be longer than the text itself.

Firstly, I thank my parents and my sister, who gave me a household full of love that informed my earliest understandings of God. My mother's steadfast love, my father's openness (and ability to sniff out religious hypocrisy), and my sister's abiding compassion were the earliest lessons of faith that I received. As no theologian can be separated from their theology, those lessons lie at the core of who I am and thus the theology I espouse.

I likewise owe a great debt to my teachers, too numerous to name with any hope that I'd include them all. They kindled my interest in language learning and helped me turn that interest into two degrees and a lifelong passion. They cast me in dramatic roles that unwittingly sparked my deep and abiding interest in linguistics. They indulged my intellectual curiosity and nurtured a lifelong interest in diverse disciplines. They introduced me to the concept of religion as art, a concept that has been with me ever since and long before I ever even dreamed of a career in religion. They taught me how to think like a lawyer and to seek to uncover the unspoken presumptions of any argument. They gave me the language to talk about theology and faith, informed my understandings of poetry, symbol, and metaphor, and helped me to see the beauty of the mysteries of faith. I hope this book is worthy of their instruction and guidance.

I am likewise indebted to my pastors, friends, and colleagues in the church, especially to J. Philip Wogaman, Dean Snyder, and Ginger Gaines-Cirelli of Foundry United Methodist, my church home these past twenty-three years. To Joe Eldridge, University Chaplain Emeritus at American University, and to the students on the interview committee, Chris, Kate, and Amber, who took a chance on me as a seminary intern all those years ago and put me on the collegiate ministry track that has been my vocational home ever since. Because of you, I have had the tremendous privilege of working in a thriving intellectual and spiritual environment where many of the ideas in this book took shape and where the need to address questions of faith and doubt became apparent.

Among those who are more directly responsible for helping this book to come into existence, thanks first must go to Sarah Ryan, whose initiative and drive made it possible for me to take the sabbatical leave that allowed me to write. Without her energies, I would not have had the opportunity to reflect, renew, and create. Likewise, thanks must also go to David Finnegan-Hosey, whom I was able to trust completely to shepherd the campus ministry in my absence. Knowing the ministry was in good hands freed me to take the time apart necessary for the work.

Thanks are due also to Amy Oliver, chair emeritus of the Department of Philosophy and Religion at American University, whose guidance and encouragement were extremely helpful. It was Amy who, having heard about my project, recommended Unamuno's *The Tragic Sense of Life in Men and Nations*. Thanks are likewise due to Ellen Feder, the current chair of the department, whose support in finding resources to assist in the manuscript preparation and in the promotion of the book were invaluable.

To Naomi Baron, for her comments on the language section of the book, her feedback on tone, her support and encouragement that I had something worth reading, and for her friendship and invaluable guidance in navigating the unfamiliar waters of preparing a book proposal.

To Lesley Pink for editing the initial draft of my manuscript and getting it so much closer to something publishable. Having someone you trust with this process is vital and I'm grateful to her for being that person.

To my students and colleagues at American University, whose interest in what I was writing and constant questions about when it would be done were a great motivator to finish.

To the library staff at the Georgetown University library, my academic residence in exile during my sabbatical leave.

To the service staff at Soho Tea & Coffee, the M Street Starbucks, and Saxby's Coffee in Georgetown, where the bulk of the writing of this book took place.

To Matthew Wimer at Wipf & Stock, whose guidance and help throughout this publishing process—and patience in responding to my constant stream of questions—have been so greatly appreciated. From the moment I entered into a publishing relationship with Wipf & Stock, I have truly been made to feel that I and the book had found a home.

To Hannah Shows, my publicist intern, whose initiative, energy, and creativity have helped greatly to get the word about this book out.

To Steven Pinker for his kindness in engaging in correspondence with me over the years, even though the returns he got from our exchanges had to have been greatly outweighed by those I received. His writing and example have been incredibly influential on me and I hope, in some small way, to have done honor to that gift by producing something that others will likewise find informative, thought provoking, and enjoyable.

And finally, to Rania Tarboush, for the conversations that inspired this book and continued throughout its writing (the reason I keep referring to it as "our" book), for serving as my scientific advisor, and for your insights into the nature of science. And mostly for the moral support and encouragement without which the project could never have been finished.

Over the course of the fall 2015 semester, when this book was written, one of my goals for that time was to visit a different house of worship every week and to reflect on the metaphors that I encountered in those places. I expected all of these places to be rich with symbol and metaphor, and many of them were places I had been wanting to visit for a very long time. Each place I visited was wonderful and I want to offer special thanks to the spiritual leaders of those congregations for their hospitality and for the meaningful ways in which they lead their people into the mystery of faith: Rev. Ginger Gaines-Cirelli, Foundry United Methodist Church, Washington, DC; Rev. Fr. Dimitri Lee, St. Sophia Greek Orthodox Cathedral, Washington, DC; Rev. Msgr. W. Ronald Jameson, VF, Cathedral of Saint Matthew the Apostle, Washington, DC; Rev. John Ferree and Pat Konoloheskie, Cherokee United Methodist Church, Cherokee, North Carolina; Rev. Fr. Joseph Rahal, St. George Antiochian Orthodox Christian Church, Washington, DC; Rabbi Mark Novak, Minyan Oneg Shabbat, Washington, DC; Rev. D. Andrew Olivo and Rev. Sarah Taylor Miller, St. John's Episcopal Church, Washington, DC; Very Rev. Fr. George Rados, St. Peter & Paul Antiochian Orthodox Church, Potomac, Maryland; Archpriest George Kokhno and Fr. Valery Shemchuk, St. Nicholas Russian Orthodox Cathedral, Washington, DC; Mr. Abbassie, The Islamic Center of Washington, Washington, DC; Rev. Nancy McDonald Ladd, River Road Unitarian Universalist Church, Bethesda, Maryland; and Rev. Tom Omholt, St. Paul's Lutheran Church, Washington, DC.

It was my privilege to sojourn in your metaphors.

Abbreviations

1–2 Kgs	1–2 Kings
1–2 Sam	1–2 Samuel
BDB	Francis Brown, S. R. Driver, and Charles A. Briggs, *Hebrew and English Lexicon of the Old Testament* (Oxford: Clarendon, 1907)
Exod	Exodus
Gen	Genesis
Hos	Hosea
Isa	Isaiah
Jas	James
Jer	Jeremiah
Mal	Malachi
Matt	Matthew
NRSV	New Revised Standard Version

Part I

The Quest for Certainty

Chapter 1

The One Thing Certain

BY THE TIME YOU finish reading this book, you could be dead.

It's not that long a book, but even so, a car accident, a slip and fall, a random crime, a plane crash, a sudden and devastating disease, a heart attack, a brain aneurysm, or any other random lethal misfortune could claim your life before you get to the final page. Or not. The problem is that you don't know which fate awaits you.

We, perhaps alone among the creatures that inhabit the globe with us, can contemplate our own mortality. We are aware of the basic fact that one day we will cease to exist. We are conscious of the reality of our inevitable deaths, but we don't know what it all means or what, if anything, lies beyond death.

The Spanish philosopher and writer Miguel de Unamuno wrote that our fears and anxieties around death drove us to try to figure out what would become of us when we die. Would we "die utterly" and cease to exist? That would lead us to despair. Would we live on in some way? That would lead us to become resigned to our fate. But the fact that we can never really know one way or the other leads us to an uncomfortable in-between: a "resigned despair."[1]

Unamuno refers to this "resigned despair" as "the tragic sense of life." For Unamuno, this tragic sense of life created a drive to understand the "whys and wherefores" of existence, to understand the causes, but also the purposes, of life. The terror of extinction pushes us to try to make a name for ourselves and to seek glory as the only way to "escape being nothing."[2]

There is an additional consequence to our mortality beyond this "resigned despair" and the "tragic sense of life." Our awareness of our own mortality also creates a great deal of anxiety. Because we know neither the

1. Unamuno, *Tragic Sense of Life in Men and Nations*, 38.
2. Ibid., 64.

date nor the manner of our own deaths, we are left with unknowing and uncertainty, and are plagued by angst on an existential level.

There are two basic responses to that anxiety: acceptance and resistance. We could accept the reality of death, given that the mortality rate has remained unchanged at exactly one per person regardless of our attitudes toward death or attempts to deny it. But we seem to prefer resistance. This is not surprising; we have too many millions of years of evolutionary survival programming in us to surrender to non-existence without at least putting up something of a fight, even if we cannot ultimately win that fight. And when death does come, we bury and keep our dead, as if refusing to hand them over to the indifferent ground without one last act of defiant resistance.[3]

Some psychologists maintain that practically *everything* we do is a kind of resistance in reaction to our awareness of our mortality.[4] This *terror management theory* posits that our desire for self-preservation coupled with our cognitive awareness of our inevitable deaths leads to a "terror" that can only be mitigated in two ways. First, we mitigate this terror with self-esteem—the belief that each of us is an object of primary value in a meaningful universe. Second, we mitigate our terror by placing a good deal of faith in our cultural worldview. The faith we put in a cultural worldview gives us a feeling of calm in the midst of dread. Our commitment to an understanding of the world around us makes us feel safe and secure in the face of our looming mortality.

However, when those same worldviews are threatened, so too is that feeling of calm. For that reason, we have to defend our worldviews at all cost because they protect us from facing the terror of our mortal lives.[5] Preserving our worldviews is so central to staving off our existential dread that it turns out that the more we think about death and oblivion, the more invested we become in preserving those worldviews.[6]

It seems that one of our preferred methods of defending our worldviews and fending off this core terror is the attempt to establish as many certainties as possible, to know that there is something we can be certain of. In an effort to deny our mortality and the recognition that we are not ultimately in control of our own destinies, we try to control our world and one another and we seek to cling to as many certain truths as we can along the way.

---

3. Ibid., 46.
4. Greenberg et al., "Terror Management Theory," 62.
5. Ibid., 71.
6. Ibid., 123.

We might be comfortable with uncertainties when they are restricted to trivial concerns or are unthreatening: the uncertainty of the solution to a crossword puzzle, or a sudoku, or a mystery novel are acceptable, and the resolution of those uncertainties with the solution to the puzzle or mystery brings a measure of emotional satisfaction. However, when the uncertainties involved deal with "real world" issues—whether we'll have a long and healthy life, whether our beloved will be faithful to us, whether we'll have job security, or whether we'll find or maintain happiness—we are not as comfortable. In fact, we are more inclined to anxiety.[7]

This is especially true for the anxiety we feel about any of what psychotherapist Irvin Yalom calls the "four ultimate concerns": death, freedom, existential isolation, and meaninglessness.[8] We're anxious about death. We're anxious about the choices we have to make. We're anxious about the fact that we enter and leave the world alone. And we're anxious because we fear that life has no intrinsic meaning. All of this creates in us a desire to obtain as much control and certainty as we can. We become increasingly concerned with getting "closure" and resolving our uncertainty.[9]

Even when we're not consciously looking for certainty to resolve our anxieties, we seek it out. It's not that we're even always consciously aware of our need for certainty; much of the drive to be certain is deep in our psychology. We are driven to be certain as a consequence of the fact that our thought processes are divided into two basic domains. As psychologist Daniel Kahneman argues, there is a fast-moving, automatic "system" that we're barely aware of (System 1), and a slower, effort-filled process that includes deliberative thought and complex calculation (System 2).[10] System 1 is designed for quick thinking and does not keep track of alternatives; conscious doubt is not a part of its functioning. System 2, on the other hand, embraces uncertainty and doubt, challenges assumptions, and is the source of critical thinking and the testing of hypotheses. However, System 2 requires a great deal more processing power and energy, and it can easily be derailed by distraction or competing demands on our brain power. Kahneman writes:

> System 1 is not prone to doubt. It suppresses ambiguity and spontaneously constructs stories that are as coherent as possible. . . . System 2 is capable of doubt, because it can maintain

---

7. Holmes, *Nonsense*, 9–10.

8. Yalom and Yalom, *Yalom Reader*, 172.

9. Holmes, *Nonsense*, 11.

10. Kahneman, *Thinking, Fast and Slow*, 20–21.

incompatible possibilities at the same time. However, sustaining
doubt is harder work than sliding into certainty.[11]

In short, certainty is *easier on the brain* than uncertainty is; uncertainty requires more mental effort.

Even beyond this function of the way our brains work, the human need to be certain is reinforced by the expectations of others. Experts are not paid high salaries and speaking fees to be unsure. Physicians are expected to give diagnoses that are certain even when that certainty is counterproductive to their effectiveness. Even when a little uncertainty might be life-saving in many cases—for example, ICU clinicians who were completely certain of their diagnoses in cases where the patient died were wrong 40 percent of the time—it is generally considered a weakness for clinicians and other experts to appear uncertain or unsure.[12] Thus, expectations from others often drive us to be more certain than we have cause to be.

We are creatures seeking meaning in an unpredictable world of unclear choices and random, seemingly meaningless happenstance; we crave certainty. We want to be certain about something. And so, we find that in the meaning-making areas of our lives, such as religion or politics, we are tempted to edge closer and closer to absolute certainty in doctrine, belief, and ideology.

But is such certainty even possible? Can we really know anything with certainty?

Even when we are certain that we know something, do we really *know* it or just *think* we do? Imagine I say to you, "I am certain that Lisa will say yes to our business offer." What am I certain of, really? That Lisa will, in fact, say yes or the fact that I *believe* she will say yes?

This conundrum is complicated by the fact that there is a sensation known as the *feeling of knowing* that can fool us into unmerited certainty. The *feeling of knowing* is best illustrated by that feeling of satisfaction you receive when you've figured out a crossword puzzle, suddenly understood the point your teacher was trying to make, or have had some other insight in which you finally "get" something. However, this *feeling of knowing* turns out to be just that—a feeling; it's independent of any actual knowledge. It's similar to the feeling associated with mystical states and religious experiences, which can often feel like having come to know something without actually having any specific knowledge. People who have had a mystical experience will testify to having "understanding" or "knowing" but often cannot tell you what it is they have come to know. These experiences make it

11. Ibid., 114.
12. Ibid., 263.

clear that there are instances of the experience of the *feeling of knowing* that don't involve any actual thought or knowledge. There has been no thought, no deliberation, no thought process; there is only that *feeling* you know something. Thus, the *feeling of knowing* is what cognitive psychologists refer to as a *primary mental state*—a basic emotional state like fear or anger—that is not dependent on any underlying state of knowledge.[13]

Now, the *feeling of knowing* may be an important part of how we learn—it's that boost of dopamine we get when we've learned something. Without this pleasant feeling, our drive to learn and comprehend might not be as strong. The problem is, because it is a mechanism of encouragement—it's a real confidence booster—it can drive us to rush to conclusions in our thinking, even before those thoughts have been worked out. We may be in such a rush to get that burst of good feeling that we ignore the fact that we haven't actually come to learn anything beyond our own belief. This feeling, as physician and author Dr. Robert Burton puts it, is "essential for both confirming our thoughts and for motivating those thoughts that either haven't yet or can't be proven."[14]

We human beings are often hindered in our ability to distinguish actually knowing something from the feeling of knowing something. We have a troublesome combination of a highly fallible memory and an overconfidence about our knowledge.[15] We frequently fail to understand the limits of what we can know. We often imagine that our conclusions are the result of deliberate, reasoned mental processes when the reality is that our feelings of certainty come not from rational, objective thought, but from an inner emotional state. As Burton concludes: "*Feelings of knowing, correctness, conviction*, and *certainty* aren't deliberate conclusions and conscious choices. They are mental sensations that *happen* to us."[16]

If this weren't bad enough, we're often blind to our ignorance because our brain likes covering the gaps in our knowledge. For example, you may not realize it, but you have blind spots in your visual field, which you can spot with a simple trick. If you hold your hands out with your index fingers pointing up, close your right eye and look at your right finger with your left eye, while you slowly move your left hand to the left—at a certain point the tip of your left index finger will just disappear. Keep moving your hand and the fingertip will reappear. We don't normally notice this blind spot because

13. Burton, *On Being Certain*, 23.
14. Ibid., 89, 100.
15. Pinker, *Sense of Style*, 302.
16. Burton, *On Being Certain*, 218.

our brain is really good at patching the holes in our sensory inputs and does so with our visual blind spot.

In the same way that our brain glosses over the blind spots in our visual field, it may be that we likewise cover the blind spots in our knowledge. When we are conscious and perceiving things, inconsistencies are more detrimental than inaccuracies, and so the holes in our knowledge are more troubling than the fact that the holes are filled with erroneous information.[17] As Kahneman noted above, System 1 of our mental processes is inclined to smooth over gaps in our understanding; it is a coherence-seeking machine designed for "jumping to conclusions."[18]

The reality is, then, that very often our feelings of certainty are not grounded in any reality that is certain, but simply in our belief that we have truly come to know something. Our certainty often comes merely from *feeling* that we are certain.

Perhaps this false sense of certainty is a function of our human nature. As human beings, we often find a measure of ambiguity to be a motivator toward productivity in order to resolve the ambiguity, but we are uncomfortable with prolonged uncertainty and unknowing. And perhaps our desire for certainty arises out of a deeper desire to believe that things *can*, in fact, be known.

It was Arthur Conan Doyle who said, "Any truth is better than indefinite doubt." In so doing, he articulated an attitude that has recently become an object of study. Scientific research into our reactions to ambiguity and uncertainty in the last decade has identified something known as the *need for closure*. This need for closure is a person's measurable desire to have a definite answer on some topic—"*any* answer as opposed to confusion and ambiguity." This impulse to resolve the tensions of uncertainty and ambiguity can be strong and may be what makes some people susceptible to extremism and claims of absolute certainty.[19] Even in those who are not tempted into extremism, there is nevertheless a discomfort with not knowing, with uncertainty.

It may also be the case that the desire for certainty is borne out of a feeling of powerlessness. We live in a time of increasing alienation and an increasing sense of disenfranchisement. As a result of technology and an ever more interconnected world, the world that people knew growing up is rapidly disappearing: the homogenous, ethnically privileged, culturally distinct society that many people knew is yielding to a diverse, multiethnic,

17. R. Abutarboush, personal communication.

18. Kahneman, *Thinking, Fast and Slow*, 87–88.

19. Holmes, *Nonsense*, 11–12.

multicultural society that no longer operates on the same assumptions as its predecessor. In addition, a predominantly rural way of life is yielding to a predominantly urban one. There is nothing inherently wrong with any of these changes but they can be unnerving to many. And many who find global changes terrifying feel powerless and out of control in their ability to stop them or at least to slow them to a comfortable pace. Being in command of the truth is at least being in command of *something*.

What does this all mean, then, for our quest for certainty as a way of coping with the anxieties of existence? Have we simply been going about the quest for certainty in the wrong way, relying too much on cognitive illusions and feelings instead of a more certain foundation, or should we abandon the quest for certainty altogether?

To answer that question, we will undertake a journey. We'll look at what it is we can know, whether our world is a place of certainty, and whether our language can communicate about that world with certainty. But before we can do that, we have to look at one of the great systems that we have constructed to give us meaning, to provide us with a worldview, to address our existential anxieties, and to help us find a measure of the certainty we crave: religion.

Chapter 2

Faith and Certainty

THERE COMES A POINT in our lives when we have to face the mystery of our existence: Why are we here? What is my life for? What does it all mean? Often in this encounter, we develop a sense that there is something beyond ourselves. This is the "numinous" experience—a feeling of "creatureliness," of something outside us, a consciousness of the other, the Great Mystery. Some may refer to this Great Mystery as fate, others as the universe, others as the void, and others as God.[1] All we can really be sure of as a result of this experience is that there is an ineffable *something* that lies beyond us.

Religion is one of the ways we have responded to this encounter with mystery. It, like the arts, is an effort to make sense of this mystery and to find meaning for our existence. Religion is not deterred because the questions we ask like *What is the meaning of life?* cannot readily be answered. Indeed, religion exists to ask questions that cannot be answered.[2]

That doesn't mean that religion hasn't *tried* to answer those questions. In fact, religion has very often moved from wrestling with the mystery of the ineffable to attempting to provide certainty. And far too often religion has been yet another mechanism by which people attempt to obtain certainty or to exercise a measure of control over their world and each other. This impulse toward certainty has become one of the bigger problems in religion today.

Rather than embrace mystery and wonder, wrestle with doubt, and try to discern meaning, so many people of faith simply propagate rules, declare absolutes, and close their eyes to reality when it intrudes upon the certainties they have derived from religion. Because they think that faith is about providing certainty, they find themselves trapped in a prison that

---

1. It is not an experience restricted to religious people—awe and wonder regarding the mystery of existence can be shared by all people whether they believe in a deity or not.

2. Santoni, *Religious Language*, 61.

limits their ability to think creatively and critically, that eschews mystery and doubt, and that forces them to adopt an almost willful ignorance of the world around them.

In my own work, I have seen the consequences of this understanding of religion. I have had students who struggled to admit any doubt for fear that doing so would be tantamount to admitting to a weak faith. Instead, they will often resort to projecting overconfidence about what they believe so as to prevent anyone from learning their deep, dark secret: they're unsure.

I have also seen the need for certainty act as an obstacle to those who are trying to grow in understanding their faith. Some years ago, my students and I were having a discussion on campus about the issue of full inclusion of LGBTQ+ persons in the life of the church. One student felt his heart pulling him in a different direction than that of the traditional teachings he'd been given. He knew, worked with, studied with, and had deep loving friendships with LGBTQ+ individuals. He felt that everyone should be welcomed in the church, but when it came to the question of whether these identities were intrinsically sinful, he had a harder time. When I asked him why, he said, "It's because it's in the Bible. If this verse can be reinterpreted then . . ." He trailed off. "I just need to know something is certain."

He is not alone.

There are many who fear uncertainty in their religious faith precisely because they look to their faith *for* certainty.

So, why has religion—meant to wrestle with mystery and the great questions of existence—instead become yet another purveyor of certainty? What it is about religion such that so many look to it not as a place to explore uncertainty, but as a method to banish it? To understand that, we need to look at some of the things that people assume faith and religion are for.

The Solution to Our Problems

We human beings often perceive an emptiness at the core of our selves and we long to find something to fill it that will make us whole. Our entire consumer economy and much of our culture is built around satisfying, or purporting to satisfy, this longing. Our popular music affirms the idea that some object (or some person) is the answer to that gnawing emptiness at the core of our being.[3]

Now, religion is frequently on record opposing the consumerist solution to deep existential problems. The church, for example, denounces the idea that goods, sex, money, drugs, fame, or power can ever fill that void.

3. Rollins, *Idolatry of God*, 21.

But on closer inspection, it appears that organized religion is not opposed to the idea that *something* can fill those gaps. It's just not the something that the other folks are marketing.

Peter Rollins, a religious philosopher and theologian in the "Emergent Church" movement, points out that contemporary Christianity buys right into this consumerist attitude: there is a problem you have, and the church has the solution to fix it. No, the solution is not sex, drugs, or rock 'n' roll, or the acquisition of material goods, or power and status; the solution is Jesus. And the church is here to provide you with that product.

Sometimes, I like to think of that product as God™—The Solution to *All* Your Problems$_{SM}$. This product goes beyond existential longing and is good for all manner of ills. I can almost hear the late-night infomercial:

> Is your life miserable? You need God™. Are you having trouble getting that promotion? You need God™. Do you wish you could get your life together? You need God™. And lucky for you, we have God™. God™ is like Oprah, Apple, Google, and Jason Bourne all in one. What more do you need? Oh, and if it turns out that you don't get that promotion: that's okay, it's all part of God's Plan™ (sold separately).

Rollins notes that the idea of God as the fulfillment of our desires is so all-pervasive today that most people take it for granted. Even those who don't believe in God believe that the God they don't believe in is intended to be the answer to all a person's problems.[4]

This consumer approach to faith is seen in many aspects of religion: in the prayers, in the sermons, in the marketing used to reach out to people to get new members, and even in the music. Rollins writes that contemporary Christian music is nearly identical to the music of the popular culture. Critics of this kind of music will refer to it as "Jesus is my boyfriend" music, and for good reason. The only difference between Christian music and pop music is that instead of lifting up the girl or guy or the car or the money as the object that will make you happy, Jesus is put forward as the magical cure-all to "what ails ya." The style of music is the same and the attitude is the same: you've got a problem and we've got the solution.[5] The similarity of the genres was even noted on an episode of *The Simpsons*, when Rachel Jordan, a Christian rock star played by musician Shawn Colvin, said that it was easy to make the transition from Christian rock to secular rock: "All you do is change *Jesus* to *baby*."

4. Ibid., 23.
5. Ibid., 21.

The church, and indeed much of religion in general, has become the purveyor of yet another product in a saturated market of solutions. Faith, then, becomes one more product promising fulfillment, happiness, and "unwavering bliss." In Rollins's thinking, the church takes its place in the industry of selling satisfaction and "religious hymns become little more than advertising jingles, and the clergy come to resemble slick salespeople presenting their god-product to the potential customer."[6]

But herein lies the problem and the great difficulty of this approach: the product doesn't work as advertised. Believers are not happier, more satisfied, or more successful than the general population. All of one's problems do not disappear once faith is claimed. In fact, sometimes the problems get worse. There is a long history of martyrs and saints who suffered for their faith, and, lest we forget, the founder of Christianity was *crucified* for his.

But when you've thought of religion as a product designed to solve all your problems, doubt and uncertainty will not do. Both the believer and the salesman have to be convinced of the product's efficacy. Both have to be certain. (Well, the salesman has to at least *appear* certain.) The consumerist view of religion requires certainty to work.

Resolver of Questions

Looking at religion as the solution to one's problems is not the only reason someone might associate religion with certainty. People frequently view religion as providing certainty because they look to it to answer all their questions.

If you type the words "Bible answers" into Google, the first result that comes up is a website called *Bible Questions Answered*. The site boasts that it has answered 446,916 questions at the time of this writing. The top 20 most frequently asked questions on the site are:

1. Women pastors/preachers? What does the Bible say about women in ministry?

2. What does the Bible say about homosexuality? Is it a sin?

3. What does the Bible say about tattoos/body piercings?

4. Once saved always saved? / Is eternal security biblical? / Can a Christian lose salvation?

5. Masturbation—is it a sin according to the Bible?

6. Ibid., 22.

6. What does the Bible say about interracial marriage?

7. Who was Cain's wife?

8. What is the Christian view of suicide? What does the Bible say about suicide? What about a believer who commits suicide?

9. Do pets/animals go to Heaven? Do pets/animals have souls?

10. What happens after death?

11. What does the Bible say about Christian tithing? Should a Christian tithe?

12. What is the gift of speaking in tongues? Is it for today? What about praying in tongues?

13. What does the Bible say about dinosaurs? Are there dinosaurs in the Bible?

14. What is the importance of Christian baptism?

15. What does the Bible say about drinking alcohol? Is it a sin for a Christian to drink alcohol?

16. What does the Bible say about gambling? Is gambling a sin?

17. What does the Bible teach about the Trinity?

18. What does the Bible say about sex before marriage?

19. Where was Jesus for the three days between His death and resurrection?

20. What does the Bible say about divorce and remarriage?[7]

There are some interesting things to note about this list: 25 percent of the questions are about sexuality and marriage, three of the questions are about vices, and a fifth are about eternal life and life after death. And there are a handful of questions that reflect a clash with modernity.

What fascinates me is that not a single one of the 20 most frequently asked questions has anything to do with meaning. All of these questions have to do with *doctrine*—what does Christianity *teach*? What are the rules? What am I supposed to do? At times, the questions seek to figure out how to defend traditionalist teaching in the face of scientific evidence or contemporary biblical scholarship ("What does the Bible say about dinosaurs?"; "Who was Cain's wife?"[8]). There is not one question that asks, "What is the

7. "Top 20 Most Frequently Asked Bible Questions."

8. Cain, the son of Adam and Eve, murdered his brother Abel and was forced to flee. The text notes both that he was afraid of what people were going to do to him once they found out about the murder and that he took a wife. The text is silent as to anyone else on the planet except Cain, Abel, and their parents. The question of who Cain's wife

meaning of life?" or even "How do we reconcile God's omnipotence with the presence of evil in the world?"

Perhaps it was just a function of the ranking of the questions and the deeper, more existential questions would be revealed by looking further into the site. But not even that yielded any questions on meaning. Rather, the questions being asked were more of the same, and frequently about topics even more arcane and particular: *What does the Bible say about voyeurism? What is Binitarianism? What does the Holy Spirit do? What does the Bible say about false accusations? How big is heaven? Who was Zacchaeus in the Bible? Why does it matter that Jesus rose from the dead? If God hates abortion, why does He allow miscarriages? Why do men have nipples? What is a levirate marriage? What is listening prayer? What is a cowboy church? Should a Christian pay into Social Security and/or accept Social Security payments? What is the Peshitta?*

Again, the most striking thing about these questions is how few of these questions—if any—are related to meaning and purpose. The one that comes closest is "Why does it matter that Jesus rose from the dead?," which is at least a question of *eschatology*, that part of theology concerned with the end times and the ultimate purposes of God. But that question is outnumbered by questions like "Why do men have nipples?" and "What is a séance?" So many of these questions seek to have answers to so many particulars, to make sure to get all the details right. And the website is certainly prepared to give the *right* answer to answer your question definitively.

This is not the time-honored practice of "religious questioning" so much as "getting all the answers." It is not wrestling with the questions, it's simply seeking concrete information. There is no ambiguity or mystery sought; only resolution.

Perhaps there is a reason why the questions answered here are not of the grander, existential kind. Unlike the answer to the question *What is the Peshitta?*, the answer to *Why did my loved one die so young?* does not have a definite answer. Nor does a question like *What is the purpose of my life?* Those questions have far more indeterminate answers and resist simple solutions. When you're looking to religion to be a source of certainty, it had better be able to answer your questions with certainty. For those who are seeking the answers, much like those who seek solutions to their problems, religion *has* to be certain, else it cannot do what we ask of it.

---

was is one of those intriguing clues that suggests the narrative is not attempting to be a literal account of the species' origins. The website, in order to answer this question, must itself go beyond the literal meaning of the text and conclude that Cain married a previously unmentioned sister, niece, or great-niece.

Banisher of Doubt

I have a pamphlet in my office entitled, "How to Know for Sure You Are Going to Heaven." The pamphlet is broken into a few sections with titles such as "Know What You Know," "Knowing Makes a Big Difference," and "Do You Have Certainty about Eternity? Do You Know for Sure?" The basic thrust of the pamphlet is that you can know your salvation with absolute certainty. It begins:

> We're learning more and more about everything and yet we seem to know less and less for sure. However, one of the characteristics of the first followers of Jesus was their certainty. They didn't guess . . . or hope . . . or wish. They knew for certain. They were even willing to die for that certainty! [9]

Later the author relates a story in which he asked another pastor, "When you die, do you know for certain that you will go to heaven?" and "Are you aware that it is possible to know that?" The pamphlet concludes with a final question for the reader: "Do you know that you have eternal life? You can, you know."

It is clear what this tract is about: you have a problem because you do not know what your eternal fate is. We can tell you how you can have absolute certainty about that. That certainty seems to be the entire *point* of this outreach. Do you have doubts? Are you unsure? Christianity can make you sure and resolve your doubts. You can know *for certain*. Faith is frequently painted in this light—a sure knowledge and certainty free of all doubt.

The author's opening statement gives away the appeal of this approach: "We're learning more and more about everything and yet we seem to know less and less for sure." The uncertainty in our world that our science reveals to us, the ever-expanding boundaries of human knowledge along with the ever-expanding regions of what we do not know, and our existential uncertainty about our lives all conspire to compel us to seek after certainty. And along comes a brand of religion that says, "We've got something you can be *sure* of. Really *sure*."

I suppose this is the most explicit of the attitudes we've looked at thus far in the chapter. There is certainty required for those who see religion as the provider of solutions or answers, but here certainty is marketed for its own sake. *You want certainty? We've got it! Here, take some! You can know these things for certain.*

9. Kennedy, "How to Know."

Certainty of Belief

Perhaps the greatest motivation for seeking certainty in religion is the desire to be certain of what one believes. Belief is an important element of religion, as seen by the presence of creeds and statements of faith:

> I believe in Jesus Christ, God's only Son, Our Lord,
> who was conceived by the Holy Spirit,
> born of the Virgin Mary,
> suffered under Pontius Pilate,
> was crucified, died, and was buried;
> he descended into hell.
> On the third day he rose again . . .
>
> —*The Apostles' Creed* (c. 4th century CE)

> There is no god but God; Muhammad is his prophet.
>
> —*Shahada, The Islamic Confession of Faith* (7th century CE)

> I believe with perfect faith that the Creator, Blessed be His Name, is the Creator and Guide of everything that has been created; He alone has made, does make, and will make all things.
>
> —*Maimonides' Thirteen Principles* (12th century CE)

All of these creeds contain specific assertions, either of fact, theology, or practice, and all point toward faith as a *belief system*, an affirmation of these ideas and understandings. In fact, the word *creed* comes from the Latin *credo*, meaning "I believe." Given the prevalence of creeds in religion, it is easy to see how belief becomes a central element of faith, even if it's not exactly clear *what* we're being asked to believe in.

In matters of religion, people will frequently be asked questions like "Do you believe in God?" or "Do you believe in Jesus?," but the question is somewhat ambiguous: does *believe* here mean "be convinced of the existence of" or "give credence to the claims of"? That particular ambiguity was exploited by Mark Twain when he was once asked, "Do you believe in infant baptism?" Twain famously, and brilliantly, replied, "Believe it? Hell! I've actually seen it done!"[10]

The question "Do you believe in God?" sometimes comes across like "Do you believe in Santa Claus?" or "Do you believe in ghosts?"—it's a

---

10. Quirk, *Mark Twain and Human Nature*, 5.

question that determines whether you believe in the existence of God. But "Do you believe in Jesus Christ?" is a little different. With rare exception, most people accept that Jesus of Nazareth was a historic person who actually lived and died. In this case, it appears that the question is designed to find out whether you believe that he was who the church, or perhaps even this individual questioner, says he was. That is, *belief in* in this context points to more than affirmation of something's existence, like believing in Santa Claus, Sasquatch, or UFOs; this is about assent to doctrine. It's not so much do you believe that Jesus *exists*, but do you believe *in the right way* that he exists?

Much of the warrant for this kind of thinking in the English-speaking world comes from biblical verses like:

> Jesus did this, the first of his signs, in Cana of Galilee, and revealed his glory; and his disciples *believed in him*. (John 2:11 NRSV)

> But the scripture has imprisoned all things under the power of sin, so that what was promised through faith in Jesus Christ might be given to those who *believe*. (Gal 3:22 NRSV)

Here, *believed in him* makes no sense if we're talking about the existential sense of the word. "Do you believe in Jesus, Peter?" "Believe in him? Hell, I've seen him!" Here, the sense in verses like John 2:11 (and many others in that gospel), and the verse from Paul, seem to suggest the importance of believing *about* Jesus in some way. Salvation is given to those who believe in Jesus—that is, to those who believe in particular things about him. Whether *belief* means "belief in the existence of" or "belief in certain things about," it certainly plays an important role in much of religion—in some forms more than others.

In Christianity, Protestantism elevates belief the highest. As a result of the Reformation, Protestants had dismissed the notion that salvation was accomplished through works—the mass, the prayers, the indulgences, etc.—and insisted that salvation was "by grace through *faith*." But the understanding of *faith* quickly became associated with belief. There were, after all, a number of creeds that all begin with things like "I believe in God the Father Almighty . . ." and that discuss things that are supposed to be maintained as a matter of faith. Although such creedal statements had always been a part of faith, in Protestantism they almost came to *define* faith.

In the nineteenth century, certain segments of the church even doubled down on this idea. As new scientific understandings were emerging that challenged traditional beliefs, certain Christians published a list of five "fundamentals" that they deemed essential to Christian faith. These fundamentals were five tenets that had to be believed in order to maintain authentic Christian faith: things like biblical inerrancy, the virgin birth, and so on. This movement gave rise to the term *fundamentalist*, which initially referred to those who maintained the five fundamentals but came to signify the particular worldview that was held by those who were engaged in such theological entrenchment. But if we're honest, the emphasis on certainty in faith and on belief in particular doctrines has a much wider area of application than the fundamentalists alone. Very often in religion, of whatever stripe, we equate faith with assent to doctrine or blind acceptance of specific things as true.

For those who understand faith to be about belief, certainty is very important. If your faithfulness—and ultimately your salvation and hope for eternal life—is determined by what you believe, then you want to be absolutely certain that you believe the right things and in the right way. If religion is about belief, then uncertainty just will not do.

* * *

Every single one of these understandings of faith contributes to the desire for certainty, by affirming the importance of certainty and by offering solutions for any lingering uncertainty.

But as we're about to see, this kind of certainty is impossible, and when we consider the evidence, we can only conclude that uncertainty is unavoidable. In perhaps a fitting irony, one of the strongest indications of this inescapable uncertainty can be found in the very system that so often purports to provide us with our sought-after certainty.

PART II

The Inescapable Uncertainty

...In Our Religion

"In these matters, the only certainty is that nothing is certain."
—PLINY THE ELDER, *NATURALIS HISTORIA, VOL. VI CB*

Chapter 3

Faith and Uncertainty

"Silence is the language of god,
all else is poor translation."

—RUMI

WE HAVE SEEN HOW frequently religion is cast as a belief system in which the believer must be certain. But is that what religion is? A system of belief in which we must be absolutely sure about having the correct beliefs? Perhaps not.

If you pick up any good translation of the Bible, you'll notice that it comes with a fair number of textual footnotes that provide additional information. Sometimes they explain a pun or wordplay, or they point out that a word or phrase is missing in the Hebrew but is found in various other ancient manuscripts. Sometimes, they'll show that there are variant ways to render a text: *When God began to create* or *In the beginning God created* or *In the beginning when God created*. Sometimes the footnotes point out some radically different alternative readings.[1]

And sometimes the footnotes will make the most courageous statement of all: *meaning of Hebrew/Greek uncertain*. The footnotes reveal that after consulting ancient translations and related languages with similar words, the translators were still not sure enough about the meaning of the word to translate it without comment. Such a notation can be found for the Greek word ἐπιούσιος *epiousios*, which is usually translated as "daily" (as in *our daily bread*)—a word that occurs *nowhere else in Greek literature* outside

1. Some of these are quite divergent: *those who hate David* versus *those whom David hates* (2 Sam 4:8); or *They helped David as officers of his troops* versus *They helped David against the band of raiders* (1 Chr 12:21); or *our bread for tomorrow* versus *our daily bread* (Matt 6:11).

the Lord's Prayer. One commentator notes: "Guesses include, necessary for today, necessary for tomorrow, daily, sufficient."[2] Guesses? *Guesses*? It is surprising to discover that right in the heart of the one of the most famous prayers in the world is uncertainty.[3]

But this is only one aspect of religion that points toward uncertainty.

Indeed, if religion were concerned merely with translating ancient texts, the uncertainty would be tolerable. The reality is that the uncertainty we find in our sacred texts reflects the uncertainty that is found throughout religion. We will see that religion is a highly symbolic endeavor. Everything in religion stands in the place of something else. The rites, the liturgy, the sacraments, even the clergy.[4] We will see that all religion is an attempt to point toward the ultimate reality, not to define that reality with certainty.

Perhaps this is why it is always the novices and the converts who are the "true believers." Those who have lived long lives with religion have often come to understand its subtleties, its nuances, its uncertainties. Those who truly own a tradition are frequently the ones who feel the freest to bend that tradition, to revel in its paradoxes, and to embrace its unknowing. The newcomers, on the other hand, want to know that they've bought into the right religion. They need to be certain.

But experience with religion shows that religion does not remove our uncertainty; it simply points us in the direction to travel, uncertainty and all.

Faith and Trust

There are plenty of clues as to the nature of religious faith in the language that faith employs. Let's take a look at those two verses from the New Testament we looked at in chapter 2:

> Jesus did this, the first of his signs, in Cana of Galilee, and revealed his glory; and his disciples *believed in him*. (John 2:11 NRSV)

2. Mounce, *Analytical Lexicon*.

3. There is likewise an uncertainty with the Greek word ἀρσενοκοίται *arsenokoitai* used by Paul. The word might mean male same-sex partners, it might refer to male prostitutes, and it might refer to pederasts. Because the word occurs only in Paul's writings, we are not sure what Paul meant.

4. Indeed, one of the reasons that the Catholic Church continues to insist on male clergy is that the priest *stands in* the place of Christ. Interestingly, this practice simultaneously treats the priest as a metaphor for Christ and literalizes the metaphor of Christ himself.

> But the scripture has imprisoned all things under the power
> of sin, so that what was promised through faith in Jesus Christ
> might be given to those who *believe*. (Gal 3:22 NRSV)

In the New Testament, the same Greek word that is translated as "belief"—πίστις *pistis*—can also be translated as "faith" or "trust." The verse from John's gospel, then, could just as correctly be translated: ". . . and his disciples *had faith in him*" or ". . . and his disciples *trusted in him*." This translation might make a little more sense in context. Indeed, having seen your master perform a miracle would be as likely to produce trust in him as it would be to inspire your particular beliefs about him. In fact, one might be inspired to trust in him even if you couldn't quite make up your mind about *what* to think.

The verse from Paul's letter to the Galatians is interesting because the word *pistis* or its related verb occurs twice in the text—". . . what was promised through *pistis* in Jesus Christ might be given to those who *pisteusosin*"—but in one English translation it gets translated in two different ways: "What was promised through *faith* might be given to those *who believe*." This verse could be translated in a couple of different ways, including: ". . . given to those who have faith"—a translation that makes just as much sense.

Religion is so frequently tied up with *belief systems* that we sometimes forget that *faith*, at its core, means *trust*. To have faith in someone is to trust that person. If someone is *faithful*, they're *trustworthy*. What this means is that *faith* is not belief, or belief without proof. It is, as Quaker scholar and theologian D. Elton Trueblood put it, "trust without reservation."[5] So it is just as likely that all the verses in scripture speaking of *belief* are really speaking about *trust*: trusting in God, trusting in Christ, trusting in the good news of God's coming kingdom. *Faith* and *trust*, then, are far more central to religion than *belief* is.

So why are people more likely to equate faith with *belief* rather than with either *have faith* or *trust*?

Well, if you're craving certainty and predictability, trust is hard and assent to doctrine is easy. If you tell me that all my uncertainties will go away if I merely accept particular propositions to be true, then I'm more likely to sign up for that bargain. Telling me simply to have faith and trust in God doesn't necessarily remove any uncertainty.[6] And what I want is to be certain.

---

5. Trueblood, *Predicament of Modern Man*, 53.

6. We'll explore this more fully in ch. 17, "On the Necessity of Doubt."

Faith and Uncertainty

All of the understandings of religion that we looked at in the previous chapter—the solution to all our problems, the resolver of questions, the defeater of all our doubts, the confirmation of our beliefs—all are grounded in the same desire: the desire to be certain.

But as we're about to see, those who look to religion to provide certainty will ultimately be disappointed. Religion is full of inspiration, guidance, assurance, and hope. It speaks in beautiful and poetic language, making use of marvelous imagery and profound parable. It grapples with some of the deepest, most meaningful questions there are.

But at its heart is *faith*. And with faith, as we shall see, comes uncertainty.

Chapter 4

Faith and Metaphor

וַיֹּאמֶר אֱלֹהִים יְהִי אוֹר וַיְהִי אוֹר

—GENESIS 1:3

Ἐν ἀρχῃ ἠν ὁ λογος . . . πάντα δι᾽αὐτοῦ ἐγένετο,
καὶ χωρὶς αὐτοῦ ἐγένετο οὐδὲ ἕν.

—JOHN 1:1, 3

إِذَا قَضَى أَمْرًا فَإِنَّمَا يَقُولُ لَهُ كُنْ فَيَكُونُ

—QUR'AN 2:117

RELIGION IS FULL OF words.

Law, literature, science, philosophy—these, too, are full of words and yet it seems that the words they use are different both in character and in purpose from the words of religion. So much so that many scholars and philosophers talk about "religious language" as a topic of philosophical study in and of itself.[1] There is something about the ways religion both treats and uses language that strikes many as special.

One way in which religion uses language in a special way is in the way it tends to see words as a source of power and creativity. The Abrahamic faiths all proclaim a God who creates through the spoken word. The three verses that begin this chapter from the Torah, the New Testament, and the Qur'an are all instances of words representing the divine creative power: "And God said, 'Let there be light,' and there was light"; "In the

---

1. Santoni, *Religious Language*, 7.

27

beginning was the Word . . . all things came into being through the Word, and without the Word not one thing came into being"; and "If [God] wills something to be, he says to it, 'Be!' and it will be." God speaks but a word and things come into being.

Words do not represent God's creative power alone. In religion, *word* frequently represents divine revelation. The Jewish and Christian scriptures are full of references to the *word of God* or the *word of the Lord/Yhwh*, such as "After these things the *word of Yhwh*[2] came to Abram in a vision . . ." (Gen 15:1) and ". . . and they were all filled with the Holy Spirit and spoke the *word of God* with boldness" (Acts 4:31). With rare exception, the more than three hundred verses in which the terms occur are not making references to scripture. Instead, the phrase *word of God* or *word of Yhwh* is making reference to God's revelation. That revelation might come to individuals or communities, but it most frequently comes to prophets. The phrase *the word of Yhwh came to . . .* appears 110 times in the Old Testament with the overwhelming majority of verses occurring in the prophetic books, where it represents a revelation to the prophet.

In these contexts, *word* frequently represents not only a revelation, but also power that enables the prophet to do his work. This word is looked for and hoped for and occasionally even feared, but it is always understood to be a revelation. Ultimately, the *word of God* is less about the *words* that are communicated than the reality of the encounter with the divine.

Some contexts even assume that the ultimate reality is associated with the *word*. John's gospel declares that the *Word of God* that was in the beginning with God and through whom all things were made "became flesh and set up a tent among us" in the person of Jesus. *Word of God* is used as an epithet for Jesus in the book of Revelation and throughout later Christian tradition. Jesus is presented as a revelation of God in the flesh: the "Word made flesh."[3]

Clearly, the concept of the *word* occupies an important place in religion. But how are we to understand this *word of God*, this revelation of the divine? Does God's word function like ordinary human words?

* * *

There is an old story told of St. Augustine as he walked along the seashore, contemplating the teaching of the Holy Trinity and struggling to understand it. He observed a young boy digging a small hole in the beach and filling it with water from the sea. Augustine asked the young boy what he was

2. See p. xv in the preface about the use of *Yhwh* for the name of God.
3. See ch. 5, "The Metaphors of Faith Explored."

doing, and the boy responded that he was emptying the sea into the hole he had dug. Incredulous, Augustine asked him how he could expect to contain such a vast body of water in such a small hole. The boy responded that he would sooner finish his task than would Augustine be able to comprehend the mystery of the Trinity and contain the vast mystery of God in the mere words of a book.[4]

Augustine understood the boy to have been an angel sent by God to remind him to have a little humility. For us, the story serves as parable of the futility in trying to comprehend divine mystery with human intellect. And it serves as a reminder that divine mystery cannot be fully contained in human words. Nevertheless, we keep trying to do exactly that.

Religions are full of words: scriptures, hagiographies, liturgies, hymns, devotions, sermons, meditations, doctrines, dogmas, canon laws, articles of faith, confessions, creeds, catechisms, edicts, bulls, fatwas, responsa, rabbinic rulings, talmuds, aphorisms, koans, commentaries, encyclicals, resolutions, theological statements, and press releases. The advice of the boy-angel to Augustine notwithstanding, we have very often tried to capture the divine reality in human words even as our religious traditions have warned us of the futility of doing so.

For example, in the Islamic tradition, there are 99 names of God, 99 epithets and titles used to describe the one true God. Among the 99 names are: *ar-Rahman* (the Compassionate), *ar-Rahim* (the Merciful), *al-Malik* (the King), *al-Quddus* (the Holy), *as-Salaam* (the Peace), *al-Mu'min* (the Granter of Security), *al-Muhaymin* (the Controller), *al-'Aziz* (the Almighty), *al-Jabbar* (the Irresistible), *al-Mutakabbir* (the Majestic), *al-Khaliq* (the Creator), *al-Hakam* (the Judge), *ash-Shahid* (the Witness), *al-Matin* (the Steadfast), *al-Wali* (the Friend), *an-Nur* (the Light), *al-Hadi* (the Way), *al-Warith* (the Heir), and *ar-Rashid* (the Right Guide). The highest name is *al-Lah*, literally meaning "the God."

The Islamic tradition doesn't necessarily agree as to which names constitute the 99, and both the Qur'an and the *hadith* (the tales of Muhammad and the early Islamic community) contain many more than 99 names. But the claim that there are 99 names of God is less a statement about the definitive descriptors for God than it is an admission that it takes at least that many names to get even a sense of who this God is. Having 99 names for God is a statement that no one word, or even list of words, is sufficient to define the divine reality.

The Muslim mystic philosopher Ibn al-'Arabi maintained that God (whom he called *al-Haqq* [the Real] or *al-Dhat* [the Essence]) was absolutely

4. McGrath, *Christian Theology*, 235.

unknowable because God transcended all the descriptions that human beings were able to conceive. Therefore, the names of God themselves were
signifiers of mystical relationships between the Essence and the universe.[5]
That is, the terms do not define God, they connect God to the universe.
Even in a tradition that uses a great number of words to describe God, those
words are understood to be inadequate.

This kind of thinking is not limited to religious language about God.
Many religious thinkers extend this idea to language about many other topics. Twentieth-century Jewish theologian Martin Buber argued that even the
language used to describe an authentic religious experience was inadequate.
He argued that every religious utterance was a "vain attempt" and that it was
futile to attempt to describe such an experience in human language.[6]

That hasn't stopped us. In spite of the difficulties in describing God or
religious experience, religion has continued to employ language to convey
the experience of faith. Religion has continued to employ words. But what
kind of words?

There is a special quality to the words that religion uses. Entire trea-
tises have been written on the nature of "religious language" or "religious
discourse." Philosophers have analyzed whether religious language was of a
different order from ordinary speech. Some theologians have even argued
that religious speech is fundamentally different in nature from ordinary
language. They will often insist, as did twentieth-century theologian Karl
Barth, that the language of the scriptures remains unintelligible to those
who have not received a special miracle of grace.[7]

But is this true? Is religious language altogether different from other
forms of language? Does it require special help from the Holy Spirit to understand it as Karl Barth insisted? Perhaps it's not the language that's different; maybe it's the *experience* that the language is trying to convey that is.

Philosopher of religion Alisdair MacIntyre argued that despite what
some theologians were arguing, there was a "large degree of resemblance
between religious language and everyday speech."[8] Religious language does
not depart from ordinary language in any significant way. It does not have
a different phonology, morphology, or syntax. It does not consist of an in-
decipherable code with a key available only to the believer. It appears to be
ordinary language, whether in Hebrew, Sanskrit, Aramaic, Greek, Arabic, or
English. Believers and non-believers can read it and make basic sense of the

5. Robinson, "Ibn Al-'Arabi, Muhyi Al-Din."

6. Buber, "Meaning and Encounter," 182.

7. MacIntyre, "Is Religious Language," 48.

8. Ibid., 50.

text. There might be nuances here or there that are lost on non-adherents, and context that might be lost on adherent and non-adherent alike, but it's not quite at the level of the man in the Monty Python skit whose name was spelled *Raymond Luxury-Yacht* but who insisted it was pronounced *Throat Warbler Mangrove.* Even in a specialized and often esoteric field like religion, *Luxury Yacht* is pronounced *Luxury Yacht.*

So religious language may not be fundamentally different from ordinary forms of speech, but it isn't without *any* difference. There clearly is something going on in religious language; there is enough of a difference to religious language such that people have made it an object of study. And when we study it, we quickly come to understand that the key difference between religious language and ordinary language is the degree to which religious language makes use of metaphor.

* * *

You are not a sheep.

Not literally anyway. You are still very much *Homo sapiens sapiens* and not *Ovis aries.* And yet, you, like perhaps billions of others before you, might have uttered the words "The Lord is my shepherd . . ." at some point in your life. When you think about it, it's an odd thing for a non-sheep to say.[9]

But no one notices how odd it is because everyone understands what they mean when they say it. Most people understand it to be a declaration of the relationship between the believer and God. The image of a shepherd—one who guards and guides—provides a comforting illustration of a strong yet nurturing deity. It's a metaphor.

Our religions are made of metaphors. Religious language is utterly dependent on metaphor. This is particularly evident in the Christian New Testament, where one of the main ways of talking about God and the kingdom of God are metaphorical stories called *parables.*

A parable is a short story that illustrates a moral or religious principle. Famous parables include *The Parable of the Good Samaritan, The Parable of the Sower, The Parable of the Talents,* and *The Prodigal Son.* The word *parable* itself comes from the Late Latin *parabola* by way of Greek παραβολή *parabolē,* meaning a "comparison."[10] The parables use metaphorical stories to paint a portrait of what God is like. They use a sower sowing seed, a rich

9. Given the limited vocal abilities of most sheep, it would also be an odd thing even for a sheep to say.

10. Interestingly, the word *parabolē* in Greek is made up of two elements, *para* ("alongside") and *ballein* ("to throw"), meaning that a parable is something "thrown alongside." Thus, the definition for a metaphorical story is itself a metaphor.

man who has entrusted his estate to his servants, and a man who has two sons to tell us something about our relationship with God by analogy. No one parable explains God or the kingdom of God fully, and even together they do not add up to a complete picture.[11] The parables are, like all metaphors, approximations.

Metaphorical stories like parables aren't the only places metaphor can be found. Metaphor can be found in virtually every passage of scripture. To see what I'm talking about, let's take a look at one of the plainer, more direct books of the New Testament, the gospel according to Mark.

Mark's writing is straightforward and direct. It lacks polish and overly florid language. And yet, for all of Mark's simplicity, his writing is rich with metaphor. Let's take a look at some of the opening verses of that gospel:

> John appeared in the wasteland, immersing and proclaiming a baptism of repentance for the forgiveness of sins. The whole region of Judea and all the Jerusalemites would go out to him and get baptized by him in the Jordan River while they would profess their sins. John was dressed in camel's hair with a leather belt around his waist, and he ate locusts and wild honey. He would proclaim: "Coming after me is someone more powerful than me—I'm not worthy of even stooping down to loose his sandals. I baptize you with water; he will baptize you with holy spirit."
>
> At that time, Jesus came from Nazareth in the Galilee and was baptized by John in the Jordan. Right away, as he came up out of the water he saw the heavens split and the Spirit coming down like a dove onto him. Then a voice came from the heavens: "You are my beloved son; I am delighted in you." (Mark 1:4–11)

It seems like a pretty prosaic account, and yet metaphor abounds.

First, there is John's ritual act of cleansing in water to symbolize a spiritual cleansing—the use of water as a physical metaphor. John's baptism is described as a "baptism of repentance," translating the Greek phrase βαπτίσμα μετανοίας *baptisma metanoias,* literally meaning, "an immersion of transformation," meaning a transformation of heart and mind. And so, we encounter the metaphor RECONCILIATION WITH GOD IS CHANGING ONE'S HEART. That metaphor is immediately followed by another one: ". . . for the forgiveness of sins." *Forgiveness* is an economic term referring to the cancellation of a debt. This language relies on the metaphor SINS ARE A DEBT. We are told that the people of Jerusalem and Judea come out to the

---

11. McFague, *Metaphorical Theology*, 43.

wilderness "confessing their sins." In addition to the metaphor of debt we find the metaphor SIN IS A CRIME, and a crime worthy of confession.

The opening section ends with John making a statement that one greater than he is coming after him and that John is not worthy of stooping down and untying his sandal. This is a metaphor of *synecdoche*, using a part of something to represent the whole. Here John uses one menial task to represent the entirety of being a servant, establishing the metaphor SERVITUDE IS UNTYING A SANDAL. He concludes, "I have baptized you with water; but he will baptize you with holy spirit," speaking of the spirit with the same language used of water—*immersion*—giving us the metaphor THE SPIRIT IS A LIQUID.

The metaphorical imagery continues with Jesus' arrival. After he is baptized, he comes up out of the water, and sees the "heavens torn apart" (giving us the metaphor THE HEAVENS ARE A FABRIC),[12] hears a voice, and sees the spirit descend on him like a dove. In this short but dense verse, we find images of *word*, *water*, *spirit*, and *light*—all of which are images present in the first chapter of Genesis in which God's *spirit* hovers over the *water*, and God's *word* summons *light* into being. Here in Mark we find the metaphor BAPTISM IS CREATION.[13]

This portion of the narrative ends with God's declaration to Jesus: "You are my beloved son; I am delighted in you," giving us the metaphors GOD IS A LOVING FATHER and JESUS IS A SON.

Even in a relatively prosaic book, in a fairly straightforward narrative section describing Jesus' baptism by John at the Jordan River, we find a wealth of symbolic and metaphorical imagery. And this isn't even all of the metaphors found in the passage: there are spatial and temporal metaphors found in it as well.[14]

But Mark's gospel is not alone. We see the same phenomenon in the other gospels, especially in the gospel of John, where one of the primary sources of metaphorical language is Jesus himself: *I am the bread of life . . . I am the living bread . . . I am the light of the world . . . I am the gate for the sheep . . . I am the good shepherd . . . I am the resurrection and the life . . . I am the way, the truth, and the life . . . I am in the Father and the Father is in me . . . I am the true vine . . .*

Throughout religious language, we can even see the presence of metaphor in statements that otherwise appear to be straightforward propositions

12. This metaphor is not limited to the Bible. Phrases like *the curtain of night* and *the starry canvas* also rely on the metaphor the heavens are a fabric.

13. Jesus' emergence from waters may also invoke the metaphor baptism is birth. See the section "Jesus Is the Son of God" in chapter 5, "The Metaphors of Faith Explored."

14. We'll explore these types of metaphor in greater detail in chapter 11.

like *God created the heavens and the earth, God spoke to Jeremiah,* and *God brought the Israelites out of Egypt.*[15] These statements fall somewhere in between purely literal statements like *So Jacob got up, and put his sons and wives on the camels* and purely metaphorical ones like *The Lord is my shepherd.*

But even here, there is metaphor at work. The terms *created, spoke,* and *brought,* for example, are all descriptions of concrete, physical actions. Unless we are asserting that God has a physical mouth, vocal tract, and other speech appendages, then *God spoke to Jeremiah* must be a metaphor, attempting to describe how it was that Jeremiah came to know what God wanted of him. In the same way, the experience of being liberated from slavery in Egypt was related to the experience of having been physically carried from one place to another. Thus: *God brought the Israelites out of Egypt.*

Metaphors abound throughout scripture and throughout the traditions themselves. As contemporary American theologian Sallie McFague notes: "It could be said that religious language consists of nothing but metaphors and models and theological language is rife with them."[16]

A Brief Inventory of Metaphor

It is not in the scriptures alone that metaphors can be found. They are also in the liturgies, prayers, creedal statements, and other statements of theological belief. The creeds of early Christianity—the Nicene Creed and the Apostles' Creed—are overflowing with metaphors, especially with metaphors of relationship: *God the Father Almighty, Maker of heaven and earth . . . ; Jesus Christ . . . the only Son of God, eternally begotten of the Father . . . begotten, not made . . . of one being with the Father . . . ; the Holy Spirit, who proceeds from the Father (and the Son) . . . .*[17] The metaphorical focus is on relationships: the Father to the Son, the Son to the Father, the Father and Son to the Holy Spirit, God to the world, its creation and salvation.[18]

During the time I was writing the bulk of this book, I had occasion to visit a number of different houses of worship of different faiths and traditions.[19] Each and every setting, each and every liturgy, was rife with metaphor. Even in my brief travels, the compiled list is quite substantial.

---

15. Alston, *Divine Nature and Human Language,* 18.
16. McFague, 105.
17. *The United Methodist Hymnal,* 880.
18. McFague, *Metaphorical Theology,* 112.
19. A full list can be found in the acknowledgments.

GOD IS A KING	THE CHURCH IS A FAMILY
GOD IS A FATHER	DEATH IS A WEED
GOD IS A LORD	DEATH IS DOWN
GOD IS A CREATOR	DESIRE IS A RESTRAINT
GOD IS LOVE	ENTRY INTO FAITH IS A BIRTH
GOD IS A COMPANION	EVIL IS DOWN
GOD IS A FORGIVER	EVIL THOUGHTS ARE FILTH
GOD IS A ROCK	THE FAITHFUL ARE SERVANTS
GOD IS A JUDGE	GOD'S DOMAIN IS UP/THE SKY
GOD IS A FORTRESS/REFUGE	GOD'S DOMAIN IS A KINGDOM
GOD IS A GUARDIAN	GOOD WORK IS FRUIT
GOD IS A SHEPHERD	HOLINESS IS UP
GOD IS A POTTER	LIFE IS BREAD
GOD IS A BREATH	LOVE IS FOOD
GOD IS A SOURCE	LIFE IS UP
GOD IS COMMANDER OF AN ARMY	LIVING AND DEAD ARE A COMMUNITY
GOD IS A TREASURY	MERCY IS A SHIELD
GOD IS PEACE	PRAYER IS PETITION
JESUS IS A SON	RIGHTEOUSNESS IS A ROAD
JESUS IS GOD	SALVATION IS BEAUTY
JESUS IS A KING	SALVATION IS WATER
JESUS IS A JUDGE	SIN IS A DEBT
JESUS IS LIGHT	SIN IS BLINDNESS
JESUS IS A LAMB	SIN IS A PIT/TRAP
JESUS IS AN EAGLE	SIN IS A CRIME
THE HOLY SPIRIT IS A FLYING CREATURE	SIN IS A POWER
ANGELS ARE AN ARMY	SIN IS FILTH
THE CHURCH IS A BOND	UNITY WITH GOD IS A MEAL
THE CHURCH IS A MOTHER	

In some cases, the metaphors come right at one another's heels: "We give you thanks for your great glory, *Lord God, heavenly King, O God, almighty Father, Lord* Jesus *Christ,* Only *Begotten Son, Lord God, Lamb of God, Son of the Father,* you take away the sins of the world . . . ."

Metaphor is not found in the ritual theology of liturgy and creed alone; formal theology makes considerable use of metaphor. Frequently, such theological reflection even goes beyond simple metaphor and deals with *models,* a kind of "super-metaphor" that defines not only a single relationship but also a comprehensive interpretive structure for a concept.

The significance of all of this has to do with the nature of metaphors. Metaphors are not precise, they are not exact, and they are not definite. They are a way that we approximate an indescribable reality with describable terms. They give us something to hang on to when we have nowhere else to latch our understanding. They allow us to express an idea that is not fully formed, a way to wrangle a concept on the periphery of our understanding. They are marvelous and expressive but they cannot give certainty.

In this chapter we have seen the abundance of metaphor in religious language—more evidence that religion and certainty are not easily paired. In the next chapter, we'll explore in depth some of the more foundational metaphors in religion. We will see that metaphor is not simply a tool that is used in religious language, but frequently lays the conceptual foundation for religious thought. We will see that metaphors do more than simply provide colorful ways of expressing religious ideas, they provide the framework in which those ideas are understood and developed. And we'll see that the depth of religious metaphor only reveals further uncertainty.

Chapter 5

The Metaphors of Faith Explored

WE HAVE SEEN THAT religious language—from scripture, to liturgy, to hymns, to formal theology—is full of metaphor. But not every metaphor occupies an equal status in the tradition. Some metaphors are much more prominent and influential than others. And some metaphors even provide the conceptual framework for other metaphors. To see just how deeply influential metaphorical language is in religion, let's take a look at a few of the more prominent ones from Judaism, Christianity, Islam, and Taoism.

GOD IS A KING

This metaphor is perhaps the most commonly encountered metaphor in scripture and in hymns. In fact, it is the first metaphor we encounter in the scriptures, even though it is not explicitly stated. In the first chapter of Genesis, God begins the work of creation by speaking: "Let there be light!" And there was light. This continues throughout the creation story: God summons all things into existence merely by speaking. Even though no royal imagery is mentioned directly, the metaphorical implications become clear: God accomplishes things through divine fiat. Like a king who might demand his "pipe, bowl, and his fiddlers three," God is a king who speaks and, as a result, whose will is done.

The metaphor is further expanded in the Exodus narratives in which God's role as Israel's king is made even more explicit. God goes into battle with the Egyptian pharaoh for the liberation of the Hebrew slaves. Later in the Sinai, the people of Israel enter into covenant with God through the receiving and acceptance of the Torah in what is known as the Sinai Covenant.

Scholars have noted that the form of the Sinai Covenant is not an ordinary legal code or even a standard contract. It is a *suzerainty treaty*, a contract between a king and his people, establishing the terms of the political arrangement. The outline of the Sinai Covenant follows the formula of such suzerainty treaties from the ancient Near East: there is a *preamble* in which the suzerain gives his name and titles ("I am Yhwh, your God . . ."), a *historical prologue* in which the king summarizes past deeds (". . . who brought you out from the land of Egypt, from the house of slavery"), the *stipulations* in which obligations of loyalty and fealty are imposed ("You will have no other gods before me . . . You will not make for yourself an idol . . . You will not murder . . . you will not steal . . ."), a *deposit and public reading* whereby the treaty is filed in a temple (". . . in the ark you shall put the covenant that I shall give you"), a *list of witnesses* ("Then Joshua said to the people, 'You are witnesses against yourselves that you have chosen Yhwh, to serve him. . . . See, this stone shall be a witness against us . . .'"), and *blessings and curses* depending on how faithfully the people keep the treaty (Deut 27–28).[1] The Sinai Covenant, the centerpiece of the Old Testament Law, is built on the metaphor GOD IS A KING.

The metaphor GOD IS A KING, as with all metaphors used to describe an encounter with the divine, is not arbitrary, but comes from a powerful experience of God rooted in community experience. This can be seen in the *Avinu Malkeinu* prayer recited by Jews on the sacred holidays of Rosh HaShanah and Yom Kippur. American rabbi and philosopher Neil Gillman writes that when a Jew addresses God as *Avinu Malkeinu*, "our Father, our King," that person is invoking symbols that have a "powerful resonance" among human beings. He writes that these symbols are powerful because they are fashioned out of the community's experience of God. Through this metaphor, this symbol, the transcendent becomes a "vital center" in the life of the community.[2]

The staying power of the GOD IS A KING metaphor was born out of the powerful experience of the community's encounter with God and became the dominant model of the people's understanding precisely because it resonated with their ongoing experience. That ongoing experience can be found throughout the Torah, through the books of history, and into the prophets. When the people of Israel demand a king, it is the metaphor GOD IS A KING that the prophets use to condemn the idea:

> But this word was evil in Samuel's eyes when they said, "Give us a king to judge us," so Samuel prayed to Yhwh. And Yhwh said to Samuel, "Listen to the voice of the people in everything they say to you, for it's not you they've rejected; they've rejected me as king over them." (1 Sam 8:6–7)

1. Frick, *Journey through the Hebrew Scriptures*, 212–23.
2. Gillman, *Sacred Fragments*, 82.

The people's desire for a human king is understood as a rejection of the king they already have.

The metaphor has become such a dominant concept in the tradition that it is even meaningful in the breach, as in the scene from John's gospel in which the Roman governor Pontius Pilate presents Jesus to the religious leadership of Jerusalem asking them, "Should I crucify your king?" The high priests answer, "We have no king except Caesar." The absolute dominance of the metaphor GOD IS A KING ensures that the reader understands the irony of the priests' statement even if the priests themselves remain oblivious. Without even having to say it, John levels a damning critique of the religious leadership: they have forgotten they have a king other than Caesar.

This metaphor is so entrenched that it has risen to what McFague would refer to as a *model*, a metaphor that retains its symbolic characteristics but also "suggests a comprehensive, ordering structure with impressive interpretive potential."[3] These "super-metaphors" often bring with them a whole host of supporting metaphors. GOD IS A KING does just that and brings with itself THE ANGELS ARE AN ARMY, HEAVEN IS A ROYAL COURT, THE FAITHFUL ARE SERVANTS, and PRAYER IS PETITION.

GOD IS A FATHER

Our Father, who art in heaven, hallowed be thy name . . . So begins perhaps the most famous prayer in the world, and it begins with a striking metaphor: GOD IS A FATHER.

Christians are fond of pointing out that Jesus liked to refer to God in this way and some even claim that Jesus was the first to do so. He was not; pagan religions had used the imagery for a long time[4] and in Judaism parental imagery of God was long found throughout the Hebrew scriptures. And, as noted earlier, parental imagery continues to be found in Judaism in the *Avinu Malkeinu* ("Our Father, Our King") prayer said on the high holy days. In Jewish thought, that prayer is a symbol that "captures a mix of affection, expectation, security, and anger that quickly becomes compassion—qualities that Jews saw in God."[5]

---

3. McFague, *Metaphorical Theology*, 23.

4. The Latin *Jupiter* means "Father Jove" and is a cognate of the Greek Ζεῦ πάτερ *Zeu pater*, meaning "O Father Zeus." Both the Latin *Jove* and the Greek *Zeus* come from the Proto-Indo-European root **dyēws*, meaning "sky." Thus both ancient deities bear the name "Sky Father."

5. Gillman, *Sacred Fragments*, 82.

The prophet Hosea used the parental/paternal image to describe the pained relationship between God and the people of Israel:

> For Israel was a youth, and I loved him.
> And out of Egypt I called my son.
> The more I called them, the more they went away from me,
> They sacrificed to the Masters, and to idols burned incense. (Hos 11:1–2)

The reason for the prophet's use of this metaphor is clear: the relationship between God and the people is the relationship of a heartbroken father who has done everything for his child only to receive scorn and rejection in return.

Jesus invoked this metaphor in teaching his disciples to pray, instructing them to pray to God their father. In doing so, Jesus used the term אבא *abba*—the Aramaic for "papa" or "dad"—to refer to God. This usage built on the existing biblical metaphor for God's relationship to the people by emphasizing the intimacy of that relationship. Jesus instructed his disciples to pray to God as if God were a member of the family.

This sense of intimacy is frequently lost in English, where the *thous*, *thees*, and *thines* of Jesus' prayer often suggest formality and divine majesty. But the reality is that the pronouns *thou*, *thee*, and *thy/thine* were the second-person singular pronouns—the ones reserved for intimate relationships.[6] And it is clear that Jesus intended this metaphor as a metaphor of intimacy and caring:

> Is there any person from among you, if their child asks for bread, would give them a stone instead? Or if they ask for a fish would give them a snake? So, if you who are wicked know to give good gifts to your children, how much more will your Father in the heavens give good things to those who ask him? (Matt 7:9–11)

In spite of this relatively clear indication, the metaphor GOD IS A FATHER does not necessarily mean "loving parent" to all people. In the Greco-Roman world, the *pater familias* ("father of the family") was any Roman citizen who was the eldest living male in a Roman household. He ruled that household as a petty dictatorship with authority over questions of life and death, marriage, and property. The power of the *pater familias* was unquestioned and absolute. Thus, if the *pater familias* were the source of your understanding of *father*, then the metaphor GOD IS A FATHER might mean

---

6. They were also used for master-servant relationships in which servants were called *thou* and masters *ye/you*. It was because of the servile connotations that the terms *thou/thee* fell out of use in English.

a very different thing to you. It may be that as early Christianity moved out of its Palestinian Jewish context into the Greco-Roman one, the metaphor provided by Jesus also underwent a dramatic change in interpretation.

Much of the difference between more liberal and more conservative branches of Christianity, especially of Protestant Christianity, is not over a disagreement about using the root metaphor GOD IS A FATHER, but a disagreement about what the metaphor means. To conservatives and evangelicals, God is frequently a stern father, enforcing rules and demanding discipline from his children for their well-being. To liberals, God is a loving, caring father, eager to forgive wrongdoing and to provide for his children. Usage of the metaphor does little to eliminate uncertainty; on the contrary, it increases it!

The metaphor has become an incredibly powerful one and, like GOD IS A KING, has become more than a metaphor: it has become a model. As such, it has generated a number of associated metaphors: CHRIST IS A SON, BELIEVERS ARE FAMILY, HUMAN BEINGS ARE CHILDREN, and so on.[7]

Such metaphorical models can occasionally cause problems. Models are only one step away from becoming literalized into definitions. McFague notes that models are necessary because they give us "something to think about when we do not know what to think"—that is, when we are trying to describe some ineffable encounter with the divine, they give us a way to think about that experience. But they can often exclude other ways of thinking, especially when they become literalized into *the* one and only way of understanding something.[8]

McFague notes that the writers of the Hebrew Bible, especially of the Psalms, "piled up" metaphors for God, often mixing them: *rock, lover, fortress, midwife, fresh water, judge, helper, thunder,* and so on, in a "desperate attempt to express the richness of God's being." But unlike simple metaphors, models do not embrace such diversity. Models are jealous of their territory and when a competing model of the same type comes along—like GOD IS A MOTHER—the existing models do not allow any encroachment. The reason that models like GOD IS A MOTHER have had such a hard time gaining traction is a reflection of the power of the GOD IS A FATHER model and the tendency of such models to become literalized. As McFague writes, this process of literalization is probably the single greatest risk in using such models.[9]

---

7. McFague, *Metaphorical Theology*, 23.

8. Ibid., 24.

9. Ibid.

The metaphor GOD IS A FATHER is a powerful and hopeful metaphor, a metaphor of intimacy and relationship, designed to bring comfort and hope to those who are alienated or powerless. But it is frequently seen as something other than a metaphor; it is seen as a definition. And as a definition, it has the power to destroy theological imaginations and oppress theological creativity.

JESUS IS THE SON OF GOD

In the ancient Near East, referring to someone as the "son" of a deity was a common way of associating that individual with the attributes of that divinity. Often, terms of kinship were used to identify an individual with some characteristic or quality.[10]

When the early followers of Jesus reflected on their experience of him, they concluded that to encounter Jesus was to encounter God in some way. But what did that mean? How does one understand the relationship between the immortal, infinite God and the finite, mortal man who revealed him? The only way to even begin to capture that paradoxical understanding was through metaphor and they turned to the metaphor of sonship: JESUS IS THE SON OF GOD.

It's a metaphor that follows on the model GOD IS A FATHER and, like GOD IS A FATHER, is a metaphor of relationship. But what might have been meant by this metaphor? What aspects of the relationship were meant to be described?

The early Christians cannot have had certain aspects of father-/son-ship in mind when they employed the metaphor. That father-son relationship could not have been understood in literal terms of physical resemblance, shared DNA, shared blood type, and other basic facts of biology. The metaphor must have been attempting to invoke some other aspect of the father-son relationship: intimacy, love, inheritance. It was in these resemblances that the early Christians understood Jesus as God's son.

The manner of that sonship was not uniformly understood in early Christianity, and differences can be seen even in the gospels themselves. In the gospel of Mark, the earliest gospel written—with no birth narrative, no wise men, no shepherds, or no nativity in Bethlehem—Jesus is declared to be God's son at his baptism. Jesus is baptized and, as he comes out of

---

10. We continue to see this today in titles like "Sons of Anarchy." It is also a common feature of Arabic names like *Abu Bakr* "father of the camel foal" (because of his fondness for camels), *Abu Nidal,* meaning "father of struggle," and is even found in place names like *Abu Dhabi* ("Father of Gazelles"—a place with a lot of gazelles apparently).

the water, he hears the voice of God declare him to be God's son: "You are my beloved son; I am delighted in you" (Mark 1:11). If all we had were the gospel of Mark as our Christian scripture, we might conclude that Jesus was the son of God by adoption. Indeed, there have been many over the course of Christian history who embraced *adoptionism* as a theology, a theology that maintained that Jesus had been born a full human being and was granted sonship of God through God's favor and on account of Jesus' perfect obedience to the Father. Given the deeply human portrait of Jesus in Mark's gospel, it is easy to see how some might understand Jesus' sonship as a sonship by adoption.

In the gospels of Matthew and Luke, Jesus is conceived by the power of the Holy Spirit and born to the Virgin Mary, a woman betrothed to a human husband Joseph, but who has not yet had marital relations with him. Here the sonship of Jesus is much closer to the literal sense, though it still is fundamentally different from the kind of sons of gods that pagan traditions embraced.

But even in these gospels, Jesus' sonship is not defined by biology or the fact of his conception. His "family resemblance" to God lies in things more significant. In an emblematic passage from Luke's gospel, Joseph and Mary lose track of the boy Jesus on a pilgrimage to Jerusalem. After searching frantically for him for three days, they find him in the temple in Jerusalem talking with and questioning the teachers of the law. When his mother finds him and scolds him for making his father and her worry about him, he replies, "Why were you looking for me? Didn't you know I needed to be about my Father's business?" The father to whom Jesus is referring is clearly not the father referred to in the preceding verse, i.e., Joseph, who, with Mary, was looking for Jesus everywhere. Jesus is known as God's *son* because he is engaged in the same work as his father.

The Christian doctrine of Jesus as the Son of God is one of the least-understood doctrines outside of Christian faith (and frequently within it). In the Qur'an, for example, it is written that "God, the Eternal, Absolute . . . does not give birth, nor is he born" (Qur'an 112:3) and laments that "Christians call Christ the Son of God" (Qur'an 9:30). In his commentary to his translation of the Qur'an, Abdullah Yusuf Ali notes: "Taking men for gods or sons of God was not a new thing. All ancient mythologies have fables of that kind."[11] Ali's comment is correct, but misunderstands the nature of the Christian claim, for the claim of sonship was about something else other than claiming Christ to be a demigod. To understand what claim is actually being made, we need to look at another title ascribed to Jesus.

11. Ali, *Holy Quran*, 448.

The earliest Christian confession about Jesus is in the name *Jesus Christ*. *Christ* is not a name; it's a title. The term *Christ* is the Greek translation of the Hebrew term משיח *mashiah*, meaning "anointed one." This title refers to the fact that the ancient kings of Israel and Judah were not crowned, they were anointed as a sign of God's favor and approval. Thus, the name *Jesus Christ* is a Christian declaration of Jesus' kingship. But along with that declaration of kingship was another declaration: divine sonship.

In the ancient world, kings were often deemed to be sons of the local deity; the name *Rameses* means "son of Ra" in Egyptian and *Thutmoses* means "son of Thoth." The Israelite kings were no different. In the Psalms, the psalmist asks:

> Why do the nations rant?
> Why do the peoples rave uselessly?
> The earth's kings take their stand;
> the leaders scheme together
> against Yhwh and
> against his anointed one. (Ps 2:1–2)

The nations seek to conspire against the king in Jerusalem (probably David) and to throw off the yoke of Israelite dominance over them. As the psalmist notes, however, resisting the Israelite king is "useless." God in heaven laughs and points out that it was he who appointed the king in Jerusalem. Here the king/psalmist continues: "I will announce the Lord's decision: he said to me, 'You are my son, today I have given birth to you'" (Ps 2:7). The king is the son of Yhwh; resistance is futile.

It is a theme we see repeated in the ninth chapter of the book of the prophet Isaiah. Here, Isaiah pens a coronation hymn for King Hezekiah of Judah, announcing: "For a child is born for us, a son is given to us." Isaiah is not talking about an infant; he is talking about the king, now reigning and deemed to be a son of Yhwh.

It is no surprise, then, that the earliest Christians, who maintained that Jesus was God's chosen *anointed one* and, therefore, a king, should also use the other metaphors related to kingship, including divine sonship. Nor is it surprising that they would use the same poems to make those metaphoric associations. Both Psalm 2 and Isaiah 9 figure heavily into traditional Christian understandings of Jesus' identity and mission.[12]

---

12. It is worth noting that this is one the areas of biblical interpretation in which Jews and Christians usually disagree. Jews read these passages as having to do with the kings of Israel and Judah. Christians tend to read them as future-oriented prophetic announcements. There is no need to declare which interpretation is the "correct"

It becomes clear that the use of the term *Son of God* in reference to Jesus has a good deal more going on than simply a declaration of divine paternity. Christianity does not consider Jesus to be a demigod and explicitly rejects the idea. In fact, Jesus is more frequently described as a *revelation* of God than as God's offspring. It just so happens that the terms used to describe Jesus as a revelation are borrowed from the realm of the experience of kinship. Because Jesus himself frequently invoked the metaphor GOD IS A FATHER, it was only natural to use the metaphor JESUS IS THE SON OF GOD to describe someone who was so close to God's own heart, and who was the object of messianic claims.

The term *son* is not meant in as literal a sense as it was in Greek mythology, where sons of gods—such as Heracles, Perseus, Dionysus, and others—were born as a result of divine sexual encounter. Jesus was understood as *Son of God* long before anyone speculated about his conception and birth. Even the birth narratives found in Matthew and Luke come from a time *after* Jesus had already been understood to be Son of God (as he is even in Mark's gospel, which has no birth narrative). The stories of Jesus' conception by the power of God's holy spirit and virgin birth are not the origin of the belief in Jesus as the Son of God, but a *reflection* on it.

JESUS IS THE SON OF GOD is one of the most central metaphors in Christianity. It answers the question posed by those early Christians who knew that to encounter Jesus was *somehow* to encounter God but couldn't begin to understand *how*. It is a statement that Jesus is so close to God that he bears a "familial resemblance" to God as that of a son to his father. It is a powerful statement about Jesus' messiahship, his kingship, his proximity to God's own being, and ultimately to his being a revelation of God.

JESUS IS THE WORD OF GOD

Perhaps the most powerful metaphor invoked to describe the relationship between Jesus and God is the one we find at the beginning of the fourth gospel. That gospel, the gospel of John, does not use a birth narrative or stories of divine paternity to describe the relationship between Jesus and God. Jesus' authority and relationship to the Father come from the fact that he is the incarnate word of God. In John's gospel, JESUS IS THE WORD OF GOD made flesh. In the beginning of that gospel we read:

---

one—both can be respected and honored as metaphorical interpretations of deeply held spiritual convictions.

> In the beginning was the Word and the Word was with God and
> the Word was God. That one was in the beginning with God. All
> things came into being through the Word and without the Word
> was not a single thing that came into being. In the Word was life,
> and the life was the light of humanity. . . . And the Word became
> flesh and set up a tent among us. (John 1:1–4, 14)

Interestingly, Christians are not alone in this assertion. In the Qur'an,
Mary is told, "O Mary! God giveth thee glad tidings of a Word from Him: his
name will be Christ Jesus, the son of Mary, held in honor in this world and
the hereafter and of (the company of) those Nearest to God" (Qur'an 3:45).[13]
Elsewhere, Jesus is referred to as "Christ Jesus the son of Mary . . . an apostle
of God, *and His Word*, which He bestowed on Mary, and a spirit proceeding
from Him" (Qur'an 4:171, emphasis added).[14] Christians and Muslims may
differ on their particular understandings of *how* this worked out, but they
agree that Jesus was a revelation of God—he was God's *Word*.

The Christian formula "the word became flesh" is clearly a metaphorical construction, albeit an unusual one. Unlike most metaphors, which take
their imagery from concrete experience and apply it to the abstract (e.g.,
LOVE IS A BATTLEFIELD), here the metaphor—*word*—feels, if not quite abstract, *intangible*. A word feels anything but concrete. It is ephemeral, fleet-
ing—the written, physical version really just arbitrary symbols designed to
catch a thought expressed by vibrations in air.

So what does it mean to say that Jesus is God's Word made flesh? How
does a word become flesh? What do we even mean when we say *word* in
this context?

In the Greek translation of the Hebrew Bible and in the Greek original
of the New Testament, the word λογος *logos*, translated as "word," has a
number of different meanings: *word, saying, speech, announcement, account,
discourse, subject-matter, reckoning, plea, motive, reason*. These definitions
do not necessarily make the metaphor clearer. Thinking of Jesus as the
Discourse of God made flesh doesn't give us any additional clarity. Even
looking to the underlying Hebrew/Aramaic doesn't help; the Hebrew word
דָּבָר *davar* can mean: *speech, word, message, report, advice, counsel, request,
promise, decision, theme, story, saying, title, name, matter, affair, business,
occupation, act, deed, event, thing, cause, case, something, anything, way,
manner, reason*. That's a lot of words to define one *word*.

The term *logos* that appears in John's gospel is also a term found in
Greek Stoicism. The *logos* of Stoicism is the rational principle of the universe,

13. Ali, *Holy Quran*, 134.
14. Ibid., 234.

the divine mind that lies behind all things. It is the logic governing the universe to which the Stoics were counseled to conform their lives. The *logos* did not govern the world through chance, but through reason; happiness, for the Stoic, was found through conforming one's life to this reason.

That's clearly not what John is talking about. If that is the meaning of *logos* for John, then we have to explain why that *logos* doesn't show up anywhere else in the gospel. John's Jesus does not talk about conforming one's life to divine reason. He talks about placing trust in God and in God's love and mercy. Elsewhere, in the epistles of John, we read that "God is love"—not "God is reason."

Some scholars note that the beginning of John's gospel—*In the beginning was the Word*—shares obvious similarities with the creation account in Genesis. These scholars also draw a parallel with accounts of Divine Wisdom found in the Proverbs—verses that speak of Wisdom having been at the beginning with God at the creation. Thus, the *logos* is the "creative principle" of God. But again, this does not provide a satisfactory understanding: *Jesus is the creative principle of God made flesh.* We still have to look deeper at this word *Word*.

When we look at the entire context of the biblical tradition and explore the ways that *word* is used in that context, we learn that the word that begins creation isn't done after the creation. It continues throughout the entire salvation history of the people. That same word comes through the revelation of the Covenant at Sinai and is written down on the Tablets of the Law. That word comes to the prophets throughout history, impelling them to speak that same word to the people and to the powers and principalities of the world, as with Jeremiah:

> Then Yhwh stretched out his hand, touched my mouth, and said
> to me, "I'm putting my words in your mouth. This very day I
> appoint you over nations and empires, to dig up and pull down,
> to destroy and demolish, to build and plant." (Jer 1:9b–10)

Later, that same word comes to the people in exile and offers them a word of comfort and a call to turn back and be healed. We see that the *word* is at the heart of both God's speaking and God's doing.

The *word* becomes synonymous with both God's speech *and* God's deeds. What God says and what God does are the same thing. In fact, this is sometimes quite literal: when God creates, God creates *by speaking.* God declares Godself to be the people's God. God pronounces forgiveness and mercy. God declares a new covenant. God provides a vision. All of these things are done through speech, which means that God's words *are* God's deeds. Unlike the case with human beings, who say one thing and do another, God's speaking is God's doing. But even more to the point—God's self-revelation is who God truly is. God's communication, God's Word, *is* God.

Whereas we do not have true alignment between our self-revelation and our reality—just looking at our Facebook profiles will tell us that much—God is described in scripture as being identical to God's self-revelation. God's word is as God does. It is as God is. ". . . and the Word was God . . ." And here we begin to understand the metaphor.

The metaphor JESUS IS THE WORD OF GOD is making a statement about Jesus as one who reveals God's nature through his actions. If what God says, does, and is are the same thing, then the claim that Jesus is God's word is a statement about the nature of God. Jesus extends mercy to those who have wronged him and tells us that we should do likewise. Jesus speaks truth to power and commands us to place our loyalties not in the things of the world. Jesus heals the sick, feeds the hungry, casts out our afflictions, eats meals with the disreputable. Jesus lives out a way of living that models an alternative to the self-interested, power- and possession-seeking lives that we are inclined to live. And most of all, Jesus comes to us where we are. Or as John's gospel puts it: ". . . and the Word became flesh and set up a tent among us . . ."

The implication of the metaphor JESUS IS THE WORD OF GOD is that these deeds and teachings of Jesus are revelations of God's nature: loving, merciful, forgiving, just, righteous, healing, caring, and present. As Jesus says and does, God is, because Jesus is God's Word made flesh.

Nowhere in the scriptures do we ever encounter God's Word in its original. That is, we never encounter God's Word in the original God-ese. It comes in Hebrew, or Aramaic, or Greek, or Arabic. It comes to us in our idiom, limited though it may be. As a result, God uses a lot of metaphors when speaking in human language. Because our language can only approximate the divine reality, God makes do with the tools at hand. But this use of metaphor is not limited to language alone.

To understand JESUS IS THE WORD OF GOD is to understand Jesus as a metaphor in the flesh. To the extent a human being is capable of revealing the heart of God, the metaphor JESUS IS THE WORD OF GOD declares that that is what Jesus does. We can describe God in human words and human metaphors—*love, Lord, King, Savior, Father, Mother, Spirit, Wisdom, Mercy, Grace, Shepherd, Bakerwoman, Vintner*—and this ancient Christian metaphor is making that claim that by looking at Jesus, we encounter those other metaphors in the flesh. The Word of God made flesh. Jesus is God's self-revelation in human-ese.

New Testament scholar John Dominic Crossan points out that Jesus taught about God in parables but that the primitive church proclaimed Jesus himself as "the Parable of God." And biblical scholar Leander Keck notes that Jesus' concentration on parabolic speech was because "he himself was a parabolic event in the kingdom of God."[15]

This metaphor is one of the more difficult to communicate because, in a way, it is using a metaphor to make a metaphor. When the author of the gospel uses *word*, he is not using the literal meaning. He is using the conceptual meaning of the term discussed above—*a self-revelation through communication united with action*—in order to apply that metaphor of a metaphor to Jesus.

So, Jesus is the Word of God. It turns out that that *Word* is a metaphor.

JESUS IS A LAMB

In the synoptic gospels—Matthew, Mark, and Luke—prior to his betrayal and arrest, Jesus shares a Passover meal with his disciples on the first night of Passover.[16] He is crucified the following day, the first day of Passover, dies, and is buried in a tomb before the sabbath sets in.[17] This is the narrative that is generally understood and commemorated throughout Holy Week in the Christian churches.

The narrative in John's gospel, however, has some interesting differences. Jesus shares a final meal with his disciples, but it is not a Passover meal; indeed, we are told that this was "before the festival of the Passover." Jesus is judged, crucified, and dies on the next day, the Day of Preparation for the Passover—that is, the day *before* Passover. In the final verses, it is noted that the coming Sabbath was a day of great solemnity (literally "a great day"), meaning it was a special Sabbath because of its coincidence with the first day of Passover.

This is an interesting discrepancy between the synoptic account and John's account. Was Jesus crucified on the first day *of* Passover or the day *before* Passover? To our modernist minds, intent on finding out "what

15. McFague, *Metaphorical Theology*, 48.

16. Mark 14:12, 17: "And on the first day of the [Feast of] Unleavened Bread, when the Passover lamb was being sacrificed, his disciples said to him, "Where do you want us to go and prepare for eating the Passover?" . . . After evening had come, he came with his disciples." See also, Matt 26:17, 20; Luke 22:7–8, 13–14.

17. Mark 15:42–43: "When evening had already come, and since it was the day of preparation—that is, the day before the sabbath—Joseph of Arimathea, a respected council member, who was himself also waiting for God's kingdom, dared to approach Pilate and ask for the body of Jesus." See also, Matt 27:59–63; Luke 23:53–55.

really happened," this seems like an irreconcilable factual discrepancy. But that is only because we are missing the metaphorical poetry present in John's narrative.

A clue as to what John is up to is actually provided in the synoptic accounts. Mark 14:12 tells us that the day before Passover, the date that John provides as the date of the crucifixion, is the day "when the Passover lamb is sacrificed." Another clue is found at the very beginning of John's gospel, where Jesus is declared by John the Baptist to be the *lamb of God*, the sacrifice that will remove the guilt of sin from the entire world. In the same way that the Passover lamb is sacrificed to atone for the sins of the people of Israel and to protect them from the angel of death, so Jesus is the sacrifice that atones for the sins of the world and prevents all the faithful from eternal death.

Although it is by no means the only metaphor for Jesus that John uses in his gospel, he uses the metaphor JESUS IS THE LAMB OF GOD to great power and effect. His use of this metaphor helps us to understand the time-line discrepancy: why is Jesus crucified on the day before Passover? Because as the Lamb of God, he *has to be*. In effect, the *entire narrative* is crafted to present this metaphor.

The early Christians believed that something powerful and meaningful had occurred in the life, death, and resurrection of Jesus, but they weren't necessarily clear on what it had all meant. Over time, they came to see Jesus' life and ministry in the context of the narrative of the entire salvation history from Abraham on down and saw Jesus' death as an atoning death in line with the slaughter of the innocent and blemish-free Passover lamb. (The general timing of Jesus' crucifixion at the Passover holiday helped to make this association.)

And so, JESUS IS A LAMB is used to explain with power and familiar imagery a rich theological interpretation of what was seen as a violent and unjust death at the hands of an all-powerful empire. It is a metaphor powerful enough to transform seeming defeat into a sign of God's victory over injustice and oppression.

JESUS IS A SAVIOR

It has long been the Christian position that Jesus was a savior: saving the faithful from sin and death, from eternal damnation, from alienation from God. It was not always settled as to *how* it was that Jesus saved. This question of the *work of Christ* has long been dealt with in terms of metaphorical models. Exploring the metaphor JESUS IS A SAVIOR gives us an opportunity to explore some of the models that are used to understand this aspect of Christology.[18]

Ransom

We all understand the concept of ransom: a villain or criminal holds someone captive, promising only to release that individual if payment is made. It's a pretty straightforward arrangement—frequently the fodder of crime dramas and thrillers. In the Christian context, the role of the villain is played by Satan; the captive: all the souls of humanity. The payment to release the captive: Jesus, the Son of God, offering himself in exchange for the souls of all humanity. In ransom theology, Satan agrees and trades all of his mortal prisoners for God's Son, who, in a surprise twist ending, is resurrected from the dead so that, in the end, Satan ends up with *nothing*. It really is the perfect heist story. And it's one of the oldest models in the Christian tradition, dating back to the New Testament itself: "For the Son of Man didn't come to be served, but to serve, and to give his life as a ransom in exchange for many" (Mark 10:45). Given the Jewish people's experience of being captive in Babylon and of living under Roman occupation, the image of being ransomed would have been a powerful one. A version of this model is still at the heart of the atonement theology of the Eastern Orthodox churches.

Sacrifice

This is another model borne right out of ancient Near Eastern experience. Sacrifice to a god for purposes of atonement and reconciliation was a common practice in the ancient world. In the Jewish tradition, the sacrifice of a lamb or goat without blemish was the requirement for the sin offering, the well-being offering, the guilt offering, and the Passover offering. The early Christian church reflected on the unjust and violent death of one they considered blameless (and thus metaphorically "without blemish") and saw his death as a kind of sacrifice, only with the messiah of God in the role of the lamb without blemish (see JESUS IS A LAMB above).

---

18. These descriptions are greatly simplified, and each model has a number of nuanced variants. Our purpose in this chapter is not to review these theologies in depth, but to explore the ways that metaphor is used in them.

Redemption

Redemption is one of those terms that has become so associated with religion that its origins as a model are frequently overlooked. Indeed, I will frequently ask my undergraduate classes if they have ever engaged in redemption and usually they'll shake their heads no. Then I'll ask, "Doesn't anyone of you use coupons or Amazon gift cards?" "Ooooooohhhhh . . . ," they'll say. Redemption, like so many models and metaphors in religion, comes from the social and economic spheres of life.

In the ancient world, when you got into trouble, economically or otherwise, the person who got you out of trouble was your *redeemer*. That person might be a family member who paid a debt you owed or who paid a bond to release you from captivity. For women, a redeemer might be that member of your husband's family who takes you in as his own wife following your husband's untimely death, keeping you in a network of support and providing an heir for your husband.[19] All of these were a kind of redemption and all provide the model for the work of Christ, whom Christians see as rescuing them from their circumstances of trouble and peril and delivering them into safety with a future of hope.

Substitution

Saint Anselm believed that because of our sinful rebellion, humanity had offended the honor of God and was, therefore, in debt to God. He argued that only humanity could rightfully repay the debt to God. However, humanity lacked the means to make this repayment—we would need a substitute to pay our debt for us. Since a debt of that magnitude could only be paid by God himself, Jesus—as both God and human being—was able to substitute for humanity to make the payment and make a significant enough payment to satisfy the debt.

Anselm's model uses a metaphor of debt and repayment (SIN IS A DEBT) to understand substitution. However, later models, such as the *penal substitution* model that would become widespread throughout Western Christianity, employed metaphors of crime and punishment (SIN IS A CRIME). In this model, the condemned is swapped out for another who, though innocent, takes the punishment for the crime. Jesus is the innocent who bears the punishment for humanity, which is guilty of having violated

---

19. In the biblical book of Ruth, Boaz, the man who ultimately takes the widow Ruth as his wife, is described as her גאל *go'el*, "redeemer."

the law of God. In this metaphor, humanity goes free because Christ has climbed the gallows in its place.[20]

Moral Influence

In reaction to what was seen as an overly bloodthirsty portrayal of a God who demands a blood sacrifice to be mollified for our sin, there arose a theology that saw Jesus primarily as a role model or as a guide for right conduct (JESUS IS A RULE). In this theology, Jesus is a teacher of righteousness who teaches his disciples by example. His death is seen as the consequences of his having lived a life of righteousness in an unrighteous world and is not itself necessary for our salvation; the correctness of his teaching is vindicated by his resurrection. This model places more emphasis on human agency and the ability of human beings to conform their will to the divine will, to follow in the example of Jesus and live lives of righteousness.

Solidarity

The solidarity model understands Jesus' role as one who represents God's perpetual declaration of unity with humanity. Because healing, justice, and witness are often accomplished by those who stand in solidarity with the oppressed (SOLIDARITY IS SALVATION), this model invokes solidarity to understand the salvation of God in Christ. Jesus, as God with us, descends to the darkest depths of human suffering and alienation—death upon the cross—in order to demonstrate that God is not removed from any aspect of human life (JESUS IS OUR BROTHER) and to declare solidarity with humanity even into death. Through this act of unfathomable solidarity, humanity is saved from death and estrangement from God and is healed of the brokenness of the world.

* * *

The metaphor JESUS IS A SAVIOR is built entirely on concrete experience models—the ransoming of captives, the redeeming of those in difficulty, crime and punishment, serving as a moral exemplar, and standing in

---

20. Despite the popularity of the *penal substitution* model, it is a curious model to have been used since it is highly unlikely that such substitution has ever been permitted in the Western legal tradition. There might have been instances where others *along with* the guilty were condemned (such as the condemned's family), but it is doubtful that someone was ever allowed to step into the gallows *instead of* the condemned.

solidarity as a witness. Those models, in turn, help to provide the meta-phorical imagery that attempts to capture a fundamentally astounding claim: *somehow* in the person of Jesus of Nazareth, God was reconciling humanity to God's own self.

PROPHECY IS SEEING/THE PROPHET IS A MESSENGER

The prophets of the Jewish, Christian, and Muslim traditions are those who speak on behalf of God, usually calling the people back into a covenantal relationship with God. The English word *prophet* comes from the Greek word προφήτης *prophētēs,* which means "one who speaks before (a god)." That term, in turn, was used to translate the Hebrew term נָבִיא *navi,* which comes from a root that means to speak (or sing) by inspiration or in an ecstatic state.[21] This suggests the original manifestation of the prophets were those who appeared to have had a charismatic, ecstatic experience and who could be found in "a prophetic frenzy" (1 Sam 10:5).

In addition to exhibiting ecstatic religious behavior, prophets were ini-tially associated with "seeing," a fact recorded in the scriptures themselves:

> Before this in Israel, this is what someone would say when going
> to consult God: "Come, let's go to the seer." For today's "prophet"
> was called a "seer" before this. (1 Sam 9:9)

Long after the definition of prophet had developed into the image we are more familiar with, this older sense of prophet was preserved in the fact that the prophets were often reported as having had *visions.*[22]

Even in the developed prophetic tradition, where the prophet is seen as a witness calling the people to be faithful to God's covenant, *seeing* is a central element of prophecy. The prophet has *visions,* shares the visions, and invites the people to envision the word that he or she is bringing. In ordi-nary speech, seeing is often used as a metaphor for understanding, and the

---

21. Brown et al., *Hebrew and English Lexicon,* 611.

22. Take, for example: "The vision of Isaiah, Amoz's son, which he saw about Judah and Jerusalem in the days of Uzziah, Jotham, Ahaz, and Hezekiah, Kings of Judah" (Isa 1:1); "It happened in the thirtieth year, in the fourth month, on the first of the month: I was among the exiles along the river Chebar, when the heavens opened and I saw visions of God" (Ezek 1:1); "The vision of Obadiah: so says my Lord Yhwh to Edom . . ." (Obad 1:1); "An oracle of Nineveh. The book of the vision of Nahum the Elkoshite" (Nah 1:1); "Then Yhwh answered me, 'Write the vision, make it plain on the tablets, so that the one who reads it might run'" (Hab 2:2); and "And on that day, each of the prophets will be ashamed of their visions when they prophesy . . ." (Zech 13:4).

metaphor UNDERSTANDING IS SEEING can be seen in phrases like *Oh, I see* or *Do you see what I mean?* This means that the metaphor PROPHECY IS SEEING is related to the metaphor UNDERSTANDING IS SEEING, and the prophet, of all people, has the clearest vision.

There are other metaphors that are used to understand the work of the prophet. In the Islamic tradition, there are actually two kinds of prophets. The first kind is the ordinary prophet, referred to by the term نبي *nabī,* from the same Semitic root as that of the Hebrew and Aramaic. The second kind is a particular subset of prophets, referred to as رسول *rasūl.* The word *rasūl* comes from a root related to *sending* and is frequently rendered as *messenger.* These *messengers* are not simply the angels or others who announce God's word; they are those who are sent to a particular people to bring a divine revelation. Among those referred to as *rasūl* in the Qur'an are Noah, Abraham, Ishmael, Joseph, Moses, Elijah, Jesus, and Muhammad.

It seems an odd thing that such a meaningful profession should be described with mundane terms like *speaker for, seer,* and *messenger.* This seeming ordinariness of terminology belies the extraordinariness of the work a prophet feels called to.

The experience of being a prophet is a confounding one. In the biblical text, nearly every prophet who hears the call of God tries to evade it: Moses argues that he is of "heavy speech and heavy tongue" (Exod 4:10), Jeremiah objects that he is only a boy (Jer 1:6), and Isaiah says that he is a person of "unclean lips" who lives among a people of unclean lips (Isa 6:5). Even Muhammad, responding to the first revelation he received ("Read!"), asked what it was he should read, given that he was illiterate.

After Muhammad received the revelation that he should "Read! In the name of your Lord Who creates / Creates man from a clot" (Qur'an 96:1–5), he said that it was as if these words had been "inscribed upon his heart"—itself a metaphor. For Muhammad, as with all the prophets, no words are heard and there is no thundering voice from the heavens. What they receive is an inner conviction and experience of the divine that is transformative and life-changing.

Given the weight and the awe-inspiring nature of the prophetic experience, it is no wonder that the only terms we can invoke to describe the experience are metaphors of ordinary speaking, seeing, and carrying messages. These metaphors seek to find some grounding in ordinary experience and can only hint at the ineffable encounter with the divine that the prophet has experienced.

HOLY

Holy sounds like an odd entry for a metaphor. Everyone knows what *holy* means. Holy is, well . . . *holy*. You know, what *God* is. But even here, we're dealing with a metaphor.

Our understanding of the term comes first from the Hebrew קָדוֹשׁ *qadôsh*, which has at its root a meaning of "being set apart." This reflects an element of holiness that implies otherness, as is characterized by twentieth-century German theologian Rudolf Otto's famous statement that God is the "Holy Other and Wholly Other." This otherness is a key component in the meaning of *holy*. For example, you can talk about a *holy shrine* or a *holy temple*, but it seems odd to speak of a *holy bowling alley* or a *holy sanitation facility*. Holiness requires otherness, perhaps even strangeness.

Our understanding of holiness is not limited to the Hebrew tradition. The Western religious tradition has passed through a number of linguistic filters, including those of Greek and Latin, and for readers of this book, English. The Greek word for "holy," ἅγιος *hagios*, may come from a root that means "to give honor to" or perhaps is related to a root meaning "to stand in awe of."[23] Holiness, in the Greek understanding, requires awe.

The Latin *sanctus* also carries with it the sense of being set apart or appointed to a sacred purpose. *Sacred* is another Latin word that means "devoted (to a divinity)," even through destruction or *sacrifice*. *Sacer* is itself based on an Indo-European root **sak-*, which means "to sanctify" or "to make a treaty."

In English, the word *holy* comes from the Old English *hālig*, related to the word *hāl*, which means "whole" or "healthy" and exists as the term *hale* in modern English. Thus, *holy* has as its origin the sense of "that which brings health."

Just by looking at the rich linguistic history of this concept, we find so much that is metaphor: HOLY IS OTHER. HOLY IS SET APART. HOLY IS HEALTHY. HOLY IS DEVOTED. Holiness is clearly one of those concepts that could not be defined with literal terms, but could only be defined by metaphor or, perhaps, a number of them.

Holiness has other implications. Proximity to the sacred is one of the main gauges of authority in religious tradition. Why are popes, patriarchs, ayatollahs, sages, lamas, and prophets all vested with religious authority? Because they are all perceived to be *closer* to that which is holy.

This kind of thinking is grounded in the conceptual metaphor CLOSE-NESS IS STRENGTH OF EFFECT, and is seen in sentences like, "The president

---

23. Tsialas, "[B-Greek] Etymology of Αγια/Agia."

had a meeting with his closest advisors" and "You're one of his closest friends—*you* tell him he needs deodorant." The closer things are, the more influence they have.[24] Priests, prophets, shamans, and the like have authority because they are seen as closer to the holy and thus as having more influence with it. But God is believed to be omnipresent, so can one person be physically *closer* to God than any other? Not literally, perhaps, although plenty of trouble has been caused by people who have interpreted this proximity literally. Especially those who have thought that getting a seat in the front pew was a surefire ticket to heaven.

Speaking of which . . .

HEAVEN AND HELL

The English word *heaven*—and the Hebrew שָׁמַיִם *shamayim* and Greek οὐρανός *ouranos*, which it translates—all just mean "sky" in their respective languages. As an extension of the conceptual metaphors GOOD IS UP and HOLY IS UP, the sky became the natural dwelling place for the holy and good God. The Greeks looked to their highest mountain and claimed its summit as the dwelling place of their gods; the Babylonians and Israelites aimed even higher, placing their deities above the sky itself. Heaven had little to do with life after death or anyone's eternal fate; it was simply where God dwelled in the creation.

In the biblical period, we see *heaven* in the process of becoming something of a metaphor. *Heaven* becomes synonymous with God's realm and, in the New Testament, with God. (Matthew uses the phrase *kingdom of heaven* instead of the phrase found in the other gospels, *kingdom of God*.) This is a kind of metaphorical construction called *metonymy*, and the usage of *heaven* in the Bible is similar to referring to the executive branch of the United States government as *The White House* or the Congress as *Capitol Hill*. Here, *heaven* stands in for God and God's government.

Eventually, in later Christian thinking, *heaven* becomes associated not only with God's *present* dominion, but God's *future* dominion. It represents the fulfillment of eschatological expectation for life after death. Initially, it referred to the kingdom that would come to earth, but later, in popular understanding, it became the destination for righteous mortal souls after death. *Heaven* was not simply God's dwelling place, it was the dwelling place of all righteous spirits after death. GOOD IS UP and after death, the righteous good go up to heaven.

24. Lakoff and Johnson, *Metaphors We Live By*, 129–30.

If *heaven* reflects the conceptual metaphor HOLY IS UP, then *hell* points in the other direction. The modern concept of hell as a place of eternal psychic torment is not found in the Bible. The Old Testament describes a *sheol* (also known as *the grave*), which is the realm of the dead for both the righteous and the unrighteous. In any event, although *sheol* is not a place of fulfillment or hope, neither is it a place of punishment. The closest we get to a place of divine punishment in the scriptures is *Gehenna*, a place Jesus invokes as the destiny of the wicked.

But what is this *Gehenna* that Jesus is talking about? The term is the Greek transliteration of the Hebrew/Aramaic גֵי־הִנֹּם *Gei Hinnom*, meaning "the Valley of Hinnom," which is an actual place just outside Jerusalem. During the city's pre-Israelite, Jebusite history, it was used as a place of pagan worship and child sacrifice. Even in its Israelite history, the valley was identified as a place where idolatrous practices were still performed and where sinning Israelites would go "to burn their sons and daughters in the fire" (Jer 7:31). By Jesus' time, it had long become the valley into which Jerusalem's trash was dumped and burned. As a result, it was a place "where worms don't die and the fire never goes out" (Mark 9:48).

What becomes clear is that even though *Gehenna* is an actual physical place, Jesus is not describing such a place—he is describing the fate of the wicked: they are cast into the divine garbage dump to rot and be consumed by fire. They are refuse, discarded from the plan of eternity.

Hell, is in short, a metaphor.

FAITH IS A ROAD

This metaphor is not as visible on the surface as some of the others that we've looked at so far in this chapter. Having said that, when we look closely, we can see that religions consider faith a kind of road. The Hebrew scriptures are full of phrases like "keep the way of Yhwh" (Gen 18:19), "the way I commanded them" (Exod 32:8), "your children keep walking their way before me" (1 Kgs 2:4), "they will call it 'the Holy Way'" (Isa 35:8), and "you have turned from the way" (Mal 2:8).

The Hebrew word translated variously as *path* or *way* is the word דֶּרֶךְ *derech*, which means "way," "road," "distance," "journey," or "manner."[25] The verb often associated with this noun and which occurs in a number of the examples above is הָלַךְ *halach*, "walk." True religion and faithfulness to God and to God's covenant are represented as a road along which the faithful walk. In fact, "*walking* in the way" is not simply a biblical metaphor con-

---

25. This last meaning is clearly a metaphorical extension of the other meanings.

fined to the scriptures, it is the term used to describe the sum total of the Jewish law: the *halachah*, literally "walking."

The metaphor continues in the Christian New Testament, where the Greek word ὁδός *hodos*—"way, road"—is used in the same way to describe true faithfulness: "you teach God's *way* as it truly is" (Luke 20:21), "I am the *way* and the truth and the life" (John 14:6), "he had been taught the *way* of the Lord" (Acts 18:25), and "one who brings back a sinner from their wandering *path* saves their soul from death" (Jas 5:20). In addition to symbolizing a pattern of living, *the Way* was the earliest name for Christianity.[26]

The metaphor FAITH IS A ROAD is not limited to Judaism and Christianity. The Islamic code of law and right living is known as the شريعة *shari'ah* from the Arabic word for "path to the watering hole" and is related to the Modern Arabic word شارع *shari'a*, "street."[27] Likewise, one of the traditional teachings of Śrāvakayāna Buddhism is the Noble Eightfold Path: right view, right intention, right speech, right action, right livelihood, right effort, right mindfulness, and right concentration. In the same way, Taoism is named after its central text, the *Tao Tê Ching*, which means "The Book of the Way and Its Virtue," with the *Tao* being the Way.[28] In effect, Taoism is "Way-ism."

The real power of this metaphor is not that it gives a convenient way to refer to religious living in terms of ordinary experience. It's that it, like many of the conceptual metaphors we looked at earlier, frames the way we even conceive of religious living. You will frequently hear that different religions are different *paths to God*. We talk about lives in faith as *spiritual journeys*. A spirituality-based addiction and recovery program is known as the *Twelve-Step* program. We talk about *leading people to faith* or *leading people to Christ*. Book titles in religion and spirituality are entitled things like *The Journey Beyond Yourself, Sacred Paths of Human Transformation, My Journey Into Life's Perfection, A Journey of Self-Awareness, Along the Way, A Godward Life,* and *A Course in Miracles.*

The metaphor FAITH IS A ROAD is one that not only shapes faith, it also shapes the way we *think* about faith.

---

26. For example: "If he found anyone who was of the Way, men or women, he might take them bound to Jerusalem" (Acts 9:2), and "I declare this to you, that I was of the Way, which they call a sect" (Acts 24:14).

27. Interestingly, *shari'ah* was the term used by Arab Jewish philosophers to translate the word *Torah* in tenth century translations of the Old Testament. Arab Christians have likewise frequently used the phrase شريعة الله *Shari'at Allah* to mean "the Law of God."

28. Lao Tzu and Blakney, *Way of Life*, 9.

GOD

What does the word *God* mean? At first glance this seems like an easy question; everyone knows what *God* means. But the more we look at it, the more we realize that the meaning of that term is far less set than we might have thought at first.

The religious philosopher I. M. Crombie said that the question "Who is God?" seems like a proper question at first, but it becomes clear that it cannot be properly answered. That is, if a child were to ask, "Who is Tom?" the question could be answered by saying, "Tom is my brother," or by pointing to Tom himself. But as Crombie notes, "If a child asks 'Who is God?' the child can only be given statements (such as 'He made us') by way of answer. The child can never be brought into a situation in which it is proper to say, 'That is God.'" Crombie concludes that the term *God* is an *improper proper name*— that is, it looks like a proper name (e.g., *Tom*) but does not work like one, in that its use is not based on acquaintance with the being it denotes.[29]

Crombie continues by noting that *God* seems to have the same characteristics as terms like *point* or *Huckleberry Finn* from geometry and literature, respectively. A *point* seems to have an inherent contradiction in its meaning: it is simultaneously sizeless *and* occupies a location in space. Like the term *God* (simultaneously transcendent and immanent), *point* seems to be identified by contradictory rules—the only way it can be identified. Likewise, identifying *Huckleberry Finn* as "the best friend of Tom Sawyer" is the only way a fictional character can be identified because one cannot point to the actual individual. In these ways, *point* and *Huckleberry Finn* seem to be *improper proper names*.

Crombie points out that because God is not known to anybody, we lack perfect descriptions that would define God. Even the terms we come up with to define God (*the first cause, the supreme being*) are the kind of terms about which no one can say what it would be like for something to actually fit such a definition. For example, how do you know when you have encountered the *supreme being*? Given that, Crombie asks, how can there be a fixed object to which the word *God* refers? And if there isn't such a referent, how can *God* be considered a proper name?[30] There are even those who argue that names like *God* that do not have a proper referent should not even be considered names at all, but thought of as a kind of set of descriptions.[31] We all think we know what *God* means, but once we look

29. Crombie, "Possibility of Theological Statements," 91.

30. Ibid., 93–94.

31. Platts, *Ways of Meaning*, 138.

at the word, it becomes clear that the way we use the word *God* differs from the way we use any other name.

Consider this scenario as a case in point: Two people are talking about matters of faith and one of them says, "I am hopeful about this election; I really believe God wants a president who favors a strong military." The other replies, "Well, I'm not sure about that; *my God* favors peace and reconciliation." Now, were this a conversation between two polytheists, nothing would be amiss. One might be talking about Mars and the other about Venus. But if we assume that both are monotheists, and let's even go so far as to say both are Christians, then this conversation reveals an odd phenomenon that makes it different from any other conversation.

Such a conversation would not work, for example, if you substituted an ordinary name. You can't say, "Steve really prefers a president who favors a strong military and an aggressive foreign policy" and have that countered with, "Well, *my Steve* favors peace and reconciliation." If both individuals are talking about the same Steve, then that Steve is either a hawk or a dove. One of the people in the conversation is wrong.

But with God, such statements are common. And this can only be because, as Crombie points out, unlike other individuals for whom names are used, God cannot be fully known. The meaning of *God* is not self-evident, the way the meaning of *Steve* is. The word denotes one thing—the ultimate reality of existence—but connotes different particular understandings of what that ultimate reality is like.

Even when a number of people have gathered together and are willing to declare, "We have come here to worship God," there can be no certainty that they all have in mind the same object of that worship. The objects of the statements "We have all come here to worship that statue" and "We have all come here to worship Steve" are obvious. But there can be no absolute certainty that everyone who invokes the word *God* is referring to the same understanding of the same reality. As far as proper names go, *God* does not accomplish the same thing that ordinary proper names do.

Technically speaking, of course, *God* is not a proper name; it's a job description.[32] The same is true of الله *Allah* (literally, "the God"), אֱלֹהִים *Elohim* ("God"), and אֲדֹנָי *Adonai* ("my Lord")—none of them is a proper name.[33]

---

32. The logician Joseph Bochenski argued that "God" could not be a name given that the "great majority of believers . . . do not have any real experience of God." They pray and worship God but nothing suggests that they come to know any more about God than what is contained in their creeds. As a result, he argues, the term "God" is a description. See, Santoni, *Religious Language*, 125–26.

33. The Tetragrammaton, יהוה *Yhwh*, is in fact a name. But it is interesting to note that it is completely unused in Judaism as itself (the substitute is usually *Adonai*) and

American philosopher of religion William Alston points out that this might actually be an advantage of the ambiguity regarding *God*. If we understand the term not as a descriptor—that is, not as a word tied to a concrete reality that could be either confirmed or rejected ("Yes, that is Steve")—but as a reference to "that which we have experienced," then there are two positive implications. First, we wouldn't need fancy theological descriptions for the purpose of describing the divine like *prime mover, first cause, supreme being,* or *that thing greater than which nothing can be conceived.* Even ordinary people can use the term *God*, after all. Second, using the term *God* opens the possibility that radically different religious traditions might all be referring to and worshiping the same reality. This *improper proper name* might be essential to both the democratizing of religion and to the aspirations of those who seek greater interfaith understanding and relationship.[34]

So, *God* might not be a proper name pointing to an easily definable object in the world, but does that mean the word is *meaningless*? Surely the word must mean something or have had some specific meaning at one time.

The English word *God* comes from the Germanic side of the family through the proto-Germanic root **guthan*, which is derived from the Proto-Indo-European form **ghut-*, itself from the root **gheu(e)-*, meaning "to invoke."[35] Thus, *God* is "that which is invoked." Alternatively, some linguists trace the word to the Proto-Indo-European **ghu-to-*, "poured," from the root **gheu-*, "to pour, pour a libation." This root is found in the Greek phrase χυτη γαια *khutē gaia*, which means "poured earth," referring to a burial mound. This Greek usage suggests that the ancient Germanic form may have originally referred to the spirit present in a burial mound.[36]

Neither sense—"that which is invoked" or "that which is poured"—sounds like something concrete. They sound an awful lot like metaphor. We have talked about all the metaphors we use in describing God's relationship to us or our experiences of God, but now we have to consider the possibility that *God* itself is a metaphor.

But what kind of metaphor? In her book *Metaphor and Religious Language*, theologian Janet Martin Soskice proposes the idea that *God* is a metaphor of "causal relation." That is, it is a metaphor that stands in for an as-yet-unidentified process that effects some change in the world.

---

rarely used in any formal context in Christianity. Even then, it shows up as *Jehovah*. It is also worth noting that the name appears to be a verb form, based on a root that means "to be," and can mean either "he is" or "he causes to be." So, even this name, at its deepest level, is still a kind of job description.

34. Alston, *Divine Nature*, 115.

35. Harper, "God."

36. Ibid.

We have used metaphors like this before in other disciplines, especially in science. When the term *gene* was introduced in biology, the mechanism of acquired or inherited traits had yet to be identified and was described with metaphorical language like *bearer of information* and *medium for communications*.[37] The term *gene* came to be used to describe this *bearer* or *medium* long before what we know of as genes were discovered. The metaphor of the *gene* had a "valuable vagueness" that allowed scientists to refer to features of the natural world that they were still trying to understand without having to make definitive claims about them.[38] That is, such metaphors are provisional statements: the *gene* is the genetic information conveying mechanism, *whatever that is*. Other causal metaphors can be found in astrophysics' *dark matter* and *dark energy*, terms that serve as placeholders for some as-yet-undiscovered mechanisms affecting the universe in ways similar to ordinary matter and energy.

In Soskice's view, *God* can be understood as just such a causal metaphor. "God is that which on such and such a date seemed more real to John Henry Newman than his own hands and feet," or "God is that which Moses experienced as speaking to him on Mount Sinai . . . ," *whatever that is. God* is, in the words of Frederick Buechner, that "dim and half-baked idea of whom to thank."[39]

Now, speaking of God by way of causal metaphor does not actually attempt to *describe* God. Using such a metaphor says nothing of God, but only points towards God. Through metaphor it is possible to claim to speak of God without claiming to define God. *God*, then, is a metaphor that the believer invokes to describe an experience that cannot be described otherwise. As Soskice writes: "in our stammering after a transcendent God we must speak, for the most part, metaphorically or not at all."[40]

The idea that *God* is a stand-in for an ineffable experience of the transcendent is made even more emphatically by professor and quantum physicist Paul Davies, who wrote:

> I belong to the group of scientists who do not subscribe to a conventional religion but nevertheless deny that the universe is a purposeless accident. Through my scientific work I have come to believe more and more strongly that the physical universe is put together with an ingenuity so astonishing that I cannot accept it merely as a brute fact. There must, it seems to me, be

37. Soskice, *Metaphor and Religious Language*, 121.
38. Ibid., 134.
39. Buechner, "Christian."
40. Soskice, *Metaphor and Religious Language*, 138–40.

a deeper level of explanation. Whether one wishes to call that deeper level "God" is a matter of taste and definition.[41]

People have long had the sense that there is some "deeper level of explanation" to the universe. Some fundamental level of existence, a "ground of all being" as theologian Paul Tillich would have put it. Some sense of the ultimate. It has been the tradition of billions of people over the ages to refer to that ultimate, that seeming abstraction which we cannot comprehend, as *God*. As Joseph Campbell, the great scholar of mythology and religion, said, "God is a metaphor for that which transcends all levels of intellectual thought. It's as simple as that."[42]

Even *God*, then, is a metaphor pointing beyond itself.

* * *

Throughout this chapter we have looked at some of the foundational concepts of some of the major religions: the nature of God, the nature of Christ, the nature of salvation, the nature of prophecy, concepts of the holy, the eternal fates of the righteous and the wicked, the nature of faith, and the ultimate reality. In all of these concepts we have found metaphor upon metaphor, the presence of which only reinforces the idea that religion and certainty are not easily paired.

For what we come to realize is that the deepest, most intrinsic claims that our religions make are of necessity made through language that cannot hope to define the concept with precision, but which can only suggest a likeness. And we come to understand that it is not only the occasional line from the Psalms or a parable that reveals this uncertainty; the foundational concepts of religion are inescapably metaphorical, and thus, inescapably uncertain.

---

41. Reagan, *Hand of God*, 59.
42. "Joseph Campbell Quotes."

Chapter 6

Faith as Metaphor

IN THE PRECEDING CHAPTERS of this book, we have looked at the prevalence of metaphor in religious language and the prominent role that metaphor plays in conveying religious ideas. We have seen that the prevalence of metaphor is a sign that religious language is not a realm of certainty, but of uncertainty. In this chapter, I want to go beyond that idea to an even deeper one: religion *itself* is metaphor. Let me give you an illustration of what I mean.

In the Jewish tradition, there is a body of stories and teachings known as the *Midrash*, a term based on a Hebrew root דרש *d-r-sh*, which means "to expound" or "to explain." The stories found in the Midrash do exactly that: they explain some piece of the tradition that was left unexplained or unclear by the scriptures. For example, a midrash might explain why it was that God chose Abraham, or explain where Isaac disappeared to after his near sacrifice by Abraham, and so on. A Christian midrash might be the legends that provide names to the wise men or that describe them as having traveled to Bethlehem on camels. All of these stories seek to expand on existing understanding by filling in the blanks and fleshing out some of the ideas. Nowhere in the scriptures does it say why Abraham was chosen by God, where Isaac went, the names of the magi, or how they traveled.[1] All of this is *midrash*, an interpretation in a tradition of a biblical text, whether formally stated (as in Judaism) or informally (as in Christianity).[2]

---

1. The fact that we think otherwise is the result of Christian midrash, riffing on the passages of Isaiah 60 that describe the coming of the Lord's glory: "A multitude of camels will cover [the land], young camels of Midian and Ephah; All of them will come from Sheba, gold and frankincense they will carry, and they will bear tidings of praises to Yhwh" (Isa 60:6). Christians saw the mention of "gold and frankincense" in Isaiah and used the imagery from this passage to fill in the blanks in Matthew's account of the nativity.

2. There are some who would claim that films like *The Ten Commandments* and *The Prince of Egypt* are a kind of *midrash* on the biblical text as they fill in the "missing

This is what makes a statement by Jewish theologian and philosopher Abraham Joshua Heschel so striking. "As a report about revelation," Heschel noted, "the Bible itself is a *midrash*." Although *midrash* is usually understood as a development or interpretation within the traditions, Heschel claims that the *traditions themselves* are midrash. They represent an expansion on a more primal revelation beyond human comprehension.[3] That is, even our sacred stories are an attempt to understand a more primal experience of the divine that cannot be adequately described.

Heschel understood that our religions were not intended to be understood with a literal bent, and he thought it was a grievous error to be literal-minded or to presume that our theological concepts were literally true or objectively adequate. Our religions were not to be understood as providing literal or even adequate descriptions of God—they were "intimations of His presence" in human language.[4] For Heschel, no human characterization of God or God's activity could be understood as objectively true; all such characterizations had to be understood as metaphorical attempts to capture what was beyond ordinary human experience.[5]

Things "beyond ordinary human experience" are the staples of religion. When we look at religious language, it's hard not to conclude that the subject matter of religion is far outside the realm of normal experience. Religious subject matter is frequently concerned with ineffable realities and paradoxes (e.g., God is transcendent and immanent, Christ is "truly God" and "truly human"). By embracing these paradoxes, religion reveals itself to be concerned with things that are far outside any conceivable version of our normal, everyday experiences.[6]

In order to deal with these extraordinary experiences and paradoxes, religion relies on metaphor. It really has no other option. Our religions are entire systems designed to try to mediate a human experience with the ineffable. They most frequently do this with words, as we have seen, but they also do it with ritual, pageantry, visuals, and social structures.[7]

Now, it is the case that not everything in the religious traditions is a metaphor. There are, of course, concrete things that religion addresses and

---

years" of Moses' youth and posit a rivalry (via chariot races) between Moses the man who would become Pharaoh, Moses' antagonist later in the narrative.

3. Gillman, *Sacred Fragments*, 24.

4. Ibid.

5. Ibid., 25.

6. Crombie, Possibility of Theological Statements," 85–86.

7. One of the greatest examples of a metaphorical social structure is the church's self-understanding as "the body of Christ" in the world—a metaphor of its own existence.

when we read a passage that says, "So Jacob got up, and put his sons and wives on the camels" or "Jesus returned to the synagogue," we needn't concern ourselves too much with trying to figure out what that might mean. Sometimes a camel is just a camel. But when religion moves beyond the narrative details of a story to the ultimate subjects of faith, those subjects are rendered in metaphorical language because there is no other option.

Let's take an example of something that can only be described through metaphor: love. Love is a fairly common concept, but difficult to define in ordinary language. You could describe it, I suppose, by talking about elevated heart rates, dilated pupils, and various neurochemical and physiological responses, but everyone knows that's not what we mean when we talk about *love*. What we do mean is frequently expressed through poetry, and usually talked about using a number of overlapping metaphorical constructs:

- LOVE IS A JOURNEY ("Look *how far we've come.*" "We're at a *crossroads.*" "I don't think this relationship *is going anywhere.*")

- LOVE IS A PHYSICAL FORCE ("I could feel the *electricity* between us." "There were *sparks.*" "They are uncontrollably *attracted* to each other.")

- LOVE IS A PATIENT ("This is a *sick* relationship." "They have a *strong, healthy* marriage.")

- LOVE IS MADNESS ("I'm *crazy* about her." "He constantly *raves* about her." "I'm just *wild* about Harry.")

- LOVE IS MAGIC ("She *cast her spell* over me." "The *magic* is gone." "I was *spellbound.*")

- LOVE IS WAR ("He is known for his many rapid *conquests.*" "She *fought for* him, but his mistress *won out.*" "He *won* her hand in marriage.")[8]

There are some concepts, like love, that rely on an abundance of metaphorical constructs because the concepts themselves resist any concrete definition. The concept LOVE is structured by the metaphors LOVE IS A JOURNEY, LOVE IS A PATIENT, LOVE IS A PHYSICAL FORCE, LOVE IS MADNESS, and so on. This use of metaphor and metaphorical framework is how emotional concepts are understood. Emotional experiences and states are not usually defined in a direct manner. The primary way we understand them is indirectly, through metaphor.[9]

There are those concepts, then, for which there is no language other than the metaphorical. It's not to say that you can't have a grounded

8. Lakoff and Johnson, *Metaphors We Live By*, 44, 49.

9. Ibid., 85.

experience of love—we all have experienced the feeling at some point in our lives—but when it comes to describing it in concrete terms, we come up short. As American photographer Duane Michals noted, "Even in the deepest love relationship—when lovers say 'I love you' to each other—we don't really know what we're saying, because language isn't equal to the complexity of human emotions."[10]

Our inability to express something in direct, concrete terms is not just a problem when we're talking about the nature of the divine or are attempting to describe the mechanism of eternal salvation. Even when we're just talking about love, we have no recourse but to metaphors. There are just some concepts, no matter how foundational, no matter how powerfully experienced, that defy concrete description and require us to approximate through metaphor. When dealing with such intangibles, metaphor gives us something to hold on to. As noted linguist Steven Pinker says, "Metaphor provides us with a way to eff the ineffable."[11]

And so it is with religion. Religion deals with concepts and experiences that defy concrete description, a point made by German theologian Rudolf Otto in his highly influential book *The Idea of the Holy*. Otto noted that Christianity was a religion full of words—hymns, sermons, theologies, scriptures—but which, at its core, was something that *could not* be put into words. He wrote that communicating the ineffable was actually "least of all possible by mere verbal phrase or external symbol."[12] Ordinary words were simply insufficient to describe the religious experience.

Otto even went so far as to coin a new term to describe the quality of religious experience: *numinous*. He derived his term from the Latin *numen*, which referred to the household spirits and divine presences that inhabited the world,[13] and to the "awesome sense of the religious" that the Roman Stoic philosopher Seneca had written could be experienced when beholding the powers of nature.[14] It was this "awesome sense of the religious" that Otto invoked to coin the term *numinous*.

In order to explain what cannot be said in words, we use words to talk about—or to remind others of—feelings that approximate the "numinous" mystical feeling.[15] Otto himself explored a number of such words: *mysterium*

---

10. McKenna, "ART: Picture Imperfect."

11. Pinker, *Stuff of Thought*, 277.

12. Otto, *Idea of the Holy*, 62.

13. The Latin term is linked to *nuō+men*, meaning "a nodding of the head," referring to the conferring of divine will or divine approval. And yes, that's another metaphor.

14. Reid, *Readings in Western Religious Thought*, 171.

15. McPherson, "Positivism and Religion," 59.

tremendum, awe (and *awe-ful*), *dread, mystery, stupor, wonder, fascination,* and so on, and explored the feeling of mystery that lay behind the experience of each.[16] In the end, he determined, the experience of the divine could not be expressed perfectly with words, but could only be talked around.

Of course, the words of religion are not the only source of metaphor. The rites and rituals of the religions themselves are metaphors. As linguist George Lakoff notes, religious rituals involve *metonymy*—real-world objects standing in for divine realities. The ritual serves as metaphor for the divine reality the religion is attempting to understand.[17]

Rudolf Otto agreed. He had argued that words were insufficient to capture religious reality and noted that "more of the [religious] experience lives in reverent attitude and gesture, in tone and voice and demeanour, expressing its momentousness, and in the solemn devotional assembly of a congregation at prayer" than in all the language we have come up with to define or describe it.[18] Some of the most powerful metaphors employed by religion are the rites and rituals with which religion orders its life and expression. We can see these metaphors in all manner of rite and ritual:

- The *Eucharist* is a metaphor for the fellowship with Christ in God's kingdom.

- *Studying the Torah* is a metaphor for participation in the creation of the world.

- *Jewish marriage* is a metaphor for the reparation of the world.

- The *posture of Muslim prayer* and *kneeling during the prayer of confession* in a Christian church are metaphors for submission to God.

- *Ablution* before Muslim prayer is a metaphor for the cleansing of the soul that takes place in spiritual communion with God.

- The *posture of standing* in a Russian Orthodox church is a metaphor for the resurrection.

- The *waters of baptism* are a metaphor for the cleansing power of God's love and mercy.

When we look deeply into the religious traditions, we see that the religions not only use metaphor in their sacred scripture, in their creeds, and in their theologies; they use metaphor in *everything*. Word, sacrament, symbol, sign, rite, office, ritual—all are vested with metaphor. Every aspect

---

16. Otto, *Idea of the Holy*, 12–24.

17. Lakoff and Johnson, *Metaphors We Live By*, 234.

18. Otto, *Idea of the Holy*, 62.

of religion invokes metaphor, to the point where the religions can be seen as grand metaphors themselves.

But does this use of metaphor demonstrate that God cannot be *perfectly* described only or does it mean that God cannot be described *at all*? Some theologians, like Paul Tillich, claimed that God, or *Being-itself* as he would say, was beyond *all* comprehension. But if God were completely unknowable, as Tillich claimed, then the words we used to describe God—including *Being-itself*—might as well be arbitrary, since anything said about God would be meaningless. The philosopher Paul Edwards argued that if God were as unknowable as Tillich claimed, then God could just as easily be called "a soprano, a slave, a street-cleaner, a daughter, or even a fascist and a hater" as a father, a lord, or a king.[19] Declaring God to be completely unknowable renders all language of God meaningless.

But that is clearly not how religions behave. They do not behave as if all their talk about God, the ultimate, and the divine is meaningless or arbitrary. That is because all religions believe in some measure of revelation and accommodation: the communication of the divine into the realm of the finite. Whether that revelation is the Torah, the Qur'an, or Jesus himself, that revelation is understood as communicating *something* of the divine. The danger—and perhaps the motivation behind those who argue that nothing can be known—is in religion's tendency to stray into the literal, to declare that its descriptions are, in fact, definitions; to lay claim on God as an object to be mastered rather than the subject.

Now, if I were to say, "God is just," I would be making a literal claim about God's nature, the kind of claim that many philosophers of religion object to. According to such philosophers, one cannot say anything literally about what God is. Thomas Aquinas argued as much, saying that "it seems that no name can be applied to God substantially."[20]

And this is where metaphor comes in. Understanding religion both as something full of metaphors and as a metaphor itself helps us to stake out a middle ground between the claim that God is totally unknowable and the behavior of those who act as if they have God all figured out. A metaphor can be *expressed* literally, but it is not making a *literal claim* about God.

When someone says, "God is King," all that is really being said is that "God is, literally, *significantly like a king in some way or other*."[21] Thus, the real meaning of the statement is not "God is a king," but "God is significantly like a king in some way or other." The true meaning is not in the specific words

---

19. Edwards, "Being-Itself and Irreducible Metaphors," 155.
20. Floyd, "Aquinas: Philosophical Theology."
21. Alston, *Divine Nature*, 31.

of the metaphor, but in the idea being expressed by it. The statement made is not a claim in and of itself, but is a model designed to use analogy to help the listener or reader grow in understanding.

* * *

Heschel claims that all scripture is *midrash*. The Sufi mystics of the Islamic tradition maintain that all religions can only claim to *point* humanity to God.[22] Aquinas and Otto speak of the inadequacy of language to define the ultimate with perfection. All of these reflect the highly metaphorical nature of religion and help us to see that although religion declares God or the ultimate reality to be unknowable, that reality is knowable enough to claim that it is *like* this, *in some way or other*.

The point made in this chapter and throughout this book is not that *nothing* can be known, but that what can be known is imperfect and imprecise. This is not a new idea. In his first letter to the Christian community at Corinth, St. Paul reminded his congregation that knowledge in the present life was "partial" and incomplete. To illustrate this, he used a metaphor: "For now we see with a mirror, obscured; then we will see face to face." The Greek words that I've translated as *obscured* (traditionally, *dimly*) are ἐν αἴνιγματι *en ainigmati*, from which the word *enigma* comes. Our knowledge in this life is like looking into a mystery; it is imperfect and partial. It is uncertain.

The use of metaphor doesn't make our knowledge imperfect. It is the *need* to take recourse in metaphor that demonstrates that our knowledge is already imperfect.

22. Aslan, *No God but God*, 206.

Chapter 7

The Poetry of Faith

RELIGION IS POETRY.

The great abuse of religion is that so many should treat it like prose.

If the ubiquity of metaphor in religion were not enough to convince us of the poetic nature of religion, the sheer volume of poetry in the religious traditions should. Poetry abounds in religious texts. Entire books of the Bible are poems—Song of Songs/Song of Solomon, Psalms, Lamentations—as are the oracles found throughout the writings of the prophets. The recitations of the prophet Muhammad that make up the Qur'an, while not strictly following the dictates of Arabic poetry, have a poetic feel and are frequently presented as such—in verse—in layout and translation. But poetry in religious texts goes beyond those passages that are obviously constructed using poetic conventions; poetry is at the heart of all religious expression.

In spite of the abundance of metaphor and poetry in religious texts and religious writing, most people continue to see religion as a kind of prose. It seems that most people fall into one of two camps when it comes to interpreting religion: the literalists or the spiritualists—neither of whom embrace metaphor.[1]

The literalists comprise the fundamentalists, some traditionalists and dogmatists, and, curiously, most atheists. For the literalists, the text means what it means. If the text says that God is a Father, then God is a father, with all the associations of the ordinary human word applicable to God. But not all literalists engage with religious tradition in the same way. The fundamentalists accept a religious claim as true and defend its literal meaning. The dogmatists promulgate doctrine to explain *how* these things should be true. The atheists take religious claims literally but reject them as false.

In contrast to the literalists, the spiritualists do not take the meaning of the claims literally. Instead, they tend to spiritualize away *any* literal association with the words used and prefer to see the words as arbitrary signs only.

1. McFague, *Metaphorical Theology*, 6.

Let's take a case in point. In the gospels of Matthew, Mark, and Luke, Jesus transforms the Passover meal he shares with his disciples into the feast of remembrance that Christians know as the *Lord's Supper* or the *Eucharist*. As Jesus gives to his disciples the bread and the wine of their shared meal, he makes two statements: "This is my body," he says of the bread, and of the wine, "This is my blood."

Let's imagine a panel of four experts we have invited to critique the claims made in this passage: three literalists (a fundamentalist, a dogmatist, and an atheist) and a spiritualist. How might this panel react to such a passage?

> FUNDAMENTALIST: The bread and the wine are literally the body and blood of Christ.

> DOGMATIST: The doctrine of transubstantiation explains how it is that the substance of the bread and wine change into the body and blood of Christ while the outward, observable "accidents" remain unchanged.

> ATHEIST: The bread and wine are not anything other than bread and wine. This story is untrue.

> SPIRITUALIST: The bread and wine are mere symbols and a re-membrance of what Jesus did at this meal; this could just as well have been done with orange juice and pizza and made reference to Jesus' "strength" and "life."

Sallie McFague argues that the better approach to a claim like this is not the path of either the literalist or the spiritualist, but an approach that seeks to inhabit the both/and in between. It is an approach that sees the bread and wine both as symbols of Christ's body and blood *and* as participating in that reality. It is a *metaphorical* approach that sees the poetry inherent in religion.[2]

Poetry and metaphor offer us a compelling dynamic middle ground between the literal and the spiritualized interpretations. Although metaphors are symbols for the reality they represent and not that reality itself, they are not *arbitrary* symbols; they have *something* to do with the reality they point toward. Poetry embodies this understanding: it uses language that is not the same as the object it points toward but participates in that reality at the same time. Religious language is poetic because it does exactly that.

2. Ibid., 13, 15.

For some reason, however, people do not respond to the poetic nature of religious language the way they would with any other poem. So many continue to treat religious language as a straightforward, prosaic account, something that would not happen with language we understood to be poetic:

O CAPTAIN! My Captain! Our fearful trip is done;

FUNDAMENTALIST: Lincoln was the captain of a ship.

DOGMATIST: As Commander-in-Chief, Lincoln could claim any military rank he chose, thus it is not unreasonable to refer to him as a captain.

ATHEIST: Lincoln was never a captain in the navy or of any vessel. This story is untrue.

SPIRITUALIST: Whitman uses the term captain here because it was meaningful to him, but any title of leadership would suffice. The important thing to remember is Lincoln's sacrifice for the Union.

All the world's a stage / And all the men and women merely players;

FUNDAMENTALIST: All men and women are players on a cosmic stage and are observed by some unseen audience.

DOGMATIST: Human beings are performing a script to which they are fated with lines and choices predetermined in a grand cosmic drama.

ATHEIST: Human beings are not actors and the world is not a stage; no one is watching. This story is untrue.

SPIRITUALIST: Shakespeare was an actor and playwright so dramatic imagery came naturally to him. Any illustration could be used here to talk about diversity of role and experience.

Of course, anyone with an understanding of poetry understands the use of metaphor. Whitman's Lincoln is a captain who steered his nation through perilous waters on to victory, only to die at the conclusion. Shakespeare's human being enters and exits the world performing a number of roles before the play is done. It's not hard; this is a high school English class level of literary analysis. Even students at that level know better than to take a poem literally.

If nothing else, this exercise shows the absurdity of taking poems, and the metaphors in them, as if they were literal claims of fact. And yet, we continue to do this with the grand poetry that is our religious tradition.

The Poetry of Scripture

Earlier I wrote that far more than just the poems found in scripture were poetry; all scripture is a kind of poetry. To understand the poetic nature of scripture, let's take a closer look at it. For a case in point, we'll start at the very beginning, with the creation narratives in the book of Genesis.

There are two creation narratives in the book of Genesis: the *Priestly Account* found at Genesis 1:1–2:4a and the *Yahwist Account* at Genesis 2:4b–25.[3] Each of these creation accounts is distinctive and each has an important message to convey. And each of them reveals sublime and powerful poetry.

The Priestly Account

> In the beginning of God's creating the heavens and the earth—
> the earth was formless and void and darkness was upon the face
> of the Deep—and a wind of God hovered over the face of the
> waters.

In this account, God's creation begins over formless, limitless, boundless waters—a watery abyss that was understood in the ancient Near East to represent the forces of chaos.

> And God said, "Let there be light"—and there was light. And
> God saw the light, that it was good. And God separated the light
> from the darkness.

God creates light by simple declaration. God is sovereign, king, master of all. By merely uttering the divine Word, God brings light into being. Unlike other deities in other creation narratives, who rely on violence to subdue

---

3. The *Priestly Account* is so called because it traces its origins to the priestly tradition of Israel and was likely developed during the Babylonian Exile by Jewish priests. It tends to focus on God's transcendence and sovereign power. The *Yahwist Account* is so called because its author uses the name *Yahweh* for God. This account appears to be the older of the two and is much more folkloric in nature. As this tradition was first identified by German scholars, who spelled God's name *Jahweh*, this tradition is sometimes called the *J* tradition or source.

the primeval chaos,[4] in the Israelite story God subdues chaos not through violence but through God's own sovereign, creative power and through the power of the Word.

> And God said, "Let there be an expanse between the waters, and
> let it divide the waters from the waters.

On the second day of creation, God creates a רָקִיעַ *raqîyaʿ*, an *expanse* (traditionally, *firmament*)—an extended surface or something beaten out. God creates this hammered out dome to divide the waters above from the waters below. This dome becomes the sky.

On the third day of creation, God gathers the waters under the sky into one place to create seas and allows dry land to appear. Vegetation and plants are also brought into being on the third day.

On the fourth day, God creates *lamps* to hang inside the dome of sky: a greater lamp to rule the day, a lesser lamp to rule the night, and the stars. The lamps are not identified by their more obvious names, *sun* and *moon*, likely because the names שֶׁמֶשׁ *shemesh* ("sun") and יָרֵחַ *yoreah* ("moon") were also the names of Canaanite deities and objects of idolatrous worship. The Hebrew creation story puts them in their rightful place: they're not gods—they're lamps to light the day and night, and for marking time and seasons.

The creation of the sun, moon, and stars on the fourth day might seem strange in light of the fact that there has been light since the first day. Yet again, the creation of these heavenly bodies after the light is an intentional choice for the text: it is not the sun, moon, and stars that are the source of the light; the source of the light is God.

On the fifth day, birds, fish, and sea monsters are created, followed by the creation on the sixth day of animals, insects, and human beings. As the narrative progresses, we read that God creates humanity in God's *image*:

> And God created Humanity in his image,
> In the image of God he created humanity,
> Male and female he created them. (Gen 1:27)

The creation of humanity in the Priestly Account is plural. Males and females are made at the same time, and both are made in the image of God.[5]

---

4. In the *Enuma Elish*, the creation myth of nearby Babylon, the god Marduk also creates the world by subduing the watery chaos, by slaying his mother, the sea serpent Tiamat. Scholars have long suspected a linguistic link between *Tiamat* and the Hebrew תְּהוֹם *tehôm*, "the Deep." Even if the terms turn out not to be related, the concepts definitely are: in order to create the world, the watery chaos had to be subdued.

5. Sometimes, because the second clause of the verse is traditionally translated as "in the image of God he created him," the text can give the impression that there was only one human being created. But the text is referring to *ha-adam*, to "man" as in

The text goes on to state that God blessed them and told them to be fruitful and multiply.

The Priestly Account finishes with the establishment of the Sabbath and concludes: "These are the generations of the heavens and the earth in their creation" (Gen 2:4a).

In the text, there are a number of distinct features we find: the description of the deity as *God* (Hebrew אֱלֹהִים *Elohim*), the repetition of motifs ("and it was evening and it was morning: Day ___"), and the highly liturgical nature of the chapter (appropriate for a priestly work). Perhaps the most important feature is the beautiful structure—a structure that helps us understand what's happening in this text.

There are critics of religion who point out the absurdity of creating the sun, moon, and stars on the fourth day with light having been created on the first day. And then there are the apologists for religion who argue that the order of creation—plants, fish, birds, animals, human beings—mirrors the generally accepted evolutionary process. But both approaches are missing the basic point of this narrative. It does not endeavor to be a scientific account and that fact becomes clear when we look closely at what's occurring in the structure:

Day 1	→	**Day 4**
Light		Sun, moon, stars
Day 2	→	**Day 5**
Dome of sky, seas		Birds, fish
Day 3	→	**Day 6**
Land, plants		Animals, insects, human beings
	Day 7	
	Sabbath	

We see that there is a parallel between the first three days of creation—the creation of the light and the domains of the sky, seas, and land—and the second three days of creation—the instruments of light and the creatures that inhabit the air, the seas, and the land. The pinnacle of the creation is the Sabbath, the sacred day of rest that becomes the coda to the entire narrative.

This is not a simple cataloguing of events or developments; it is a highly structured, ordered account full of parallelism, refrain, and rhythm.

"humanity" or "humankind"—not to "a man." The concluding portion of the verse and the subsequent verses make that clear. On the sixth day, human beings—*plural*—were created.

It is, in short, a poem. A beautiful, masterfully constructed poem of great theological depth and power.

All of this comes into even starker relief when we continue into the second chapter.

The Yahwist Account

Beginning in the middle of the fourth verse of the second chapter of Genesis, we encounter another creation narrative markedly different from that in the first chapter. The first thing we notice is that God is called by a different name:

> In the day Yhwh God made the land and sky . . . (Gen 2:4b)

In the Hebrew text, God is now referred to as יהוה אֱלֹהִים *Yhwh Elohim*, usually translated as "the LORD God" in most English Bibles. Unlike the case in the previous chapter, in which the deity is referred to simply as *Elohim* ("God"), here in Genesis 2 (and throughout a good portion of the material in Genesis) God is referred to by the name *Yhwh*.[6] The use of a different term for God is a clue that we're dealing with a different tradition, which scholars call the *Yahwist Tradition* on account of the name.

The next thing we notice is the time frame: the "day" of creation. Now, *day* here can mean "time period" as when we say, *Back in my grandfather's day* . . . , and is no more tied to a twenty-four-hour period than the days of the Priestly Account are. But there is no seven-day period here: creation is not an event that takes place in stages, but all at once.

It might seem at first glance that chapter 2 is simply an expansion of the sixth day from the previous chapter, but the location of the creation and the chronology make that unlikely:

> —all the plants of the field did not exist yet on the land and all the grasses of the field had not yet sprung up since Yhwh God had not caused it to rain on the land and there was no human being to work the earth . . . —Yhwh God formed the human from the dust of the earth and breathed into its lungs the breath of life. (Gen 2:5, 7)

The location of the creation is in a barren, trackless waste—a desert. It is not at all like the limitless watery abyss described in the Priestly Account.

6. Scholars generally assume the pronunciation to be "Yahweh." The traditional Hebrew text provides no vowels for this name, including instead the vowels of *Adonai* ("My Lord") as a reminder to the reader to substitute that euphemism. I likewise prefer to render it without vowels so as to preserve the mystery. See p. xiii in the preface.

Furthermore, the plants, birds, fish, and animals that should already exist by this time are nowhere to be found. Instead, nothing exists, we are told, because it hasn't rained yet and there is no one to till the soil. To remedy this problem, the human being is made to till the earth. In the Yahwist Account, the human being is the first thing made.

God's method of creation is also noteworthy. In the Priestly Account, God summons humanity (and everything else) into existence by speech; in this account, Yhwh God forms the human being from the dust of the earth. The verb used here meaning "to form"—יָצַר *yatzar*—is the same verb used to describe the work of pottery making and is at the root of the word for "potter": יוֹצֵר *yotzer*. This account is a far more intimate, hands-on account of the creation of humanity. The transcendent God of chapter 1 is here replaced with an immanent and intimate God.

There is some wordplay going on in this account, too. The human being—הָאָדָם *ha-adam*—is made out of the earth: הָאֲדָמָה *ha-adamah*. The *human being* is made from the *humus*, or better still, the *earthling* is made from the *earth*.[7] The language makes explicit that humanity is profoundly connected to the soil: we are made out of the earth.

Created next are the plants, placed in the garden of Eden, where the human being is then put in order to till and keep it. At this point, Yhwh God notes that it is not right for the human being to be alone: a "helper as counterpart" is needed. And so Yhwh God forms the animals out of the earth in exactly the same way that the human being had been formed. Each animal and bird is brought to the human being to see if it's a good helper and counterpart. None of them is, and so Yhwh God causes a deep sleep to come upon the human being and out of the human's side Yhwh God forms a woman to be the helper and counterpart.[8]

What we have encountered in this second chapter cannot be a simple expansion of the sixth day of the Priestly Account; it is just far too different:

The Priestly Account (Gen 1:1–2:4a)	The Yahwist Account (Gen 2:4b–25)
Term for God	
Elohim אֱלֹהִים ("God")	*Yhwh Elohim* יהוה אֱלֹהִים ("Yahweh God" or "Lord God")

---

7. *Earthling* is definitely my favorite term for *ha-adam*; it would be perfect but for it being hampered by 1950s B-movie sci-fi associations.

8. There are some who argue that prior to this point the human being was undifferentiated, neither male nor female, until God separated the two.

The Priestly Account (Gen 1:1–2:4a)	The Yahwist Account (Gen 2:4b–25)

Primordial State

Formless, watery abyss; waters of chaos	Arid, trackless waste; desert

Order of Creation

Light	Human (male or undifferentiated)
Sky, waters	Plants
Land, plants	Birds, animals
Sun, moon, stars	Another human being (female)
Fish, birds	
Animals, insects, human beings (m/f)	
Sabbath	

Time Frame

Seven "days" of creation	The "day" of creation

Manner of God's Creating

By divine decree and fiat; through speech	Hands on, by "forming" humans and animals from the earth

Nature of Humanity

Made in the image of God	Made from the dust of the earth in kinship with the animals

We are not the first to notice these distinctions. Saint Augustine noticed them 1600 years ago and concluded that the creation accounts might be allegorical. Given this, it would be strange to assume that the compilers of scripture failed to notice that they had two creation accounts that did not agree on major details and yet somehow put them together despite that. So, it appears that we have two different creation stories placed side by side, and their inclusion in spite of their differences is intentional.

How do we reconcile these two accounts? If one is accurate, the other must be inaccurate; or vice versa. Or perhaps both are inaccurate. But we only need to make such a determination if we view these accounts as an attempt to be a play-by-play account of the actual mechanics of the world's origins, if we think we're dealing with a science book. If, however, we are looking at poetry, then *both* accounts are true. Both accounts become poems—in different genres, different styles—that provide us with a beautiful theological reflection on the origins of the world in light of the God the authors had experienced. The tensions and differences between the two poetic accounts do not diminish either. In fact, those tensions help to make the poetic point all the more beautifully.

These two poems tell us something powerful: God is sovereign and transcendent *and* God is intimate and hands on with the creation. The creation is good, not the product of violence and destruction. Humanity is made in the image of God *and* is made out of the dust of the earth in kinship with all living things. By placing these accounts side by side, the biblical authors may also be reminding us that what we are inclined to see as separate—immanence and transcendence, our being made in the image of God and our being made of soil—find unity and wholeness in God. In God, immanence and transcendence are understood to be one and the same point.[9]

These narratives were given to us with contradictory and difficult-to-reconcile details so that we would understand that the stories were about more than the details. These stories are a kind of poetry, and truth in poetry is not found in its details, but in its metaphors. And when some Christians resist teachings of science because those teachings disagree with the details of these narratives, they miss the point of the narratives altogether. Because the details of the narratives, which so many people get hung up on, are there to frame the metaphors that make up the theological claims of the text: GOD IS A KING, CHAOS IS AN OCEAN, ORDER IS NIGHT AND DAY, GOD IS LIGHT, THE SUN AND MOON ARE LAMPS, HUMANITY IS DIVINE VICE-REGENT, GOD IS A POTTER, HUMANITY IS CLAY, LIFE IS A GARDEN, and WOMAN IS A SIDE OF MAN (or WOMAN AND MAN ARE TWO SIDES OF THE SAME THING). It is these metaphors—not the words or the details used to construct them—that convey the truth claims of the text.

The poetic nature of these accounts is what allows believing people of faith to believe in the biblical accounts of the creation *and* accept the findings of science regarding human evolution and the cosmos. The Bible is not trying to present a definitive accounting of human origins in terms of biology or of the earth in terms of geology. It is attempting to provide metaphors that point the way toward a deeper reality.

The creation stories in Genesis are wonderful and powerful and they contain truths that religious people can continue to assert as true. But their truths do not lie in whether they contradict the fossil record or whether they contradict the age of the universe observed through astronomical data. Their truths instead speak to the profound meaning that undergirds all existence, a truth so deep that only the language of poetry and metaphor will suffice to describe it.

9. Rollins, *How (Not) to Speak of God*, 26.

Faith as Poetry

The poetic nature of scripture has been apparent to many who agree that it goes beyond the obvious poetry of the Psalms or even the poetic constructions of passages like the ones we just explored. McFague describes a "poetic text" as any text made up of "novel, tensive metaphors" that presents new, alternative descriptions of reality.[10] A number of different scholars and translators share this insight. In his book *The Four Witnesses*, an examination of the four different gospel accounts of Jesus, biblical scholar Robin Griffith-Jones notes that the gospel writers resort to poetry to try to do justice to truths for which "no words are really adequate."[11]

Poet and translator Willis Barnstone has produced a book of translations of Jesus' teachings in poetic form entitled, not surprisingly, *The Poems of Jesus Christ*. In this fascinating approach, the poetry of religious faith becomes clear in the very structure of Barnstone's translation:

DILEMMAS OF THE HEART

Why argue in your heart?

What is easier to say to the paralytic,
"Your wrongs are forgiven," or to say,
"Stand, pick up your bed, and walk"?

To know that the earthly son has the power
To forgive wrongs on earth,
I say, "Stand, pick up your bed, and go into your house." (Mark 2:8–11)[12]

It is not only scriptures that can be seen as poetry—faith itself can be seen as a kind of poetry. If that is the case, then any authentic expression of faith would itself have to be a poem. Sometimes that point is made explicitly, as it is in the case of St. Ephrem the Syrian.

Saint Ephrem was a fourth-century deacon and teacher. Ephrem was a writer in the Syriac dialect of Aramaic—the language of Jesus and primitive Christianity. As a writer, Ephrem was prolific in writing polemical works and commentaries as well as *rhythmic prose* and *verse homilies*: sermons in 7+7–syllable couplets. He also wrote a substantial number of *madrashe*,

---

10. McFague, *Metaphorical Theology*, 59.

11. Griffith-Jones, *Four Witnesses*, ix.

12. Barnstone, *Poems of Jesus Christ*, 4.

stanza poems in different syllabic patterns that served as hymns. In short, Ephrem was a poet.[13]

Ephrem's status as a poet comes not only from his poetry, but also from the poetic way in which he regards his own tradition. He opposed the school of thought that sought to provide firm theological definitions, which were called ὅροι *horoi* in Greek, meaning "boundaries." Ephrem found this practice dangerous and potentially blasphemous because such "boundaries" could have a deadening and fossilizing effect on people's conception of the human experience of God.[14]

Ephrem's approach to theology rejected the Greek practice of trying to define everything, which he saw as an attempt to contain the Uncontainable and limit the Limitless. Instead, he preferred a more Semitic approach that used paradox and symbolism, a method for which poetry was far better suited than prose:

> Your mother [O Christ] is a cause for wonder: the Lord entered her
> and became a servant; He who is the Word entered
> —and became silent within her; thunder entered her
> —and made no sound; there entered the Shepherd of all,
> and in her He became the Lamb, bleating as He came forth.
>
> Your mother's womb has reversed the roles;
> the Establisher of all entered in His richness,
> but came forth poor; the Exalted One entered her,
> but came forth meek; the Splendorous One entered her,
> but came forth having put on a lowly hue.
>
> The Mighty One entered, and put on insecurity
> from her womb; the Provisioner of all entered
> —and experienced hunger; He who gives drink to all entered
> —and experienced thirst: naked and stripped
> there came forth from her He who clothes all.
>
> —*Nativity* 11:6–8[15]

In addition to providing expression for the paradoxes and symbols of faith, Ephrem made use of his poetry to push our understanding of God beyond the standard Greek philosophical categories and even to invoke the sacred feminine:

13. Brock, *Luminous Eye*, 17.
14. Ibid., 23.
15. Ibid., 24–25.

> The Word[16] of the Father came from His womb,
> and put on a body in another womb:
> the Word proceeded from one womb to another—
> and chaste wombs are now filled with the Word:
> blessed is He who has resided in us.

and:

> The Divinity is attentive to us, just as a wetnurse is to a baby,
> keeping back for the right time things that will benefit it,
> for she knows the right time for weaning,
> and when the child should be nourished with milk,
> and when it should be fed with solid food (lit. bread),
> weighing out and providing what is beneficial to it
> in accordance with the measure of its growing up.[17]

Ephrem's poetry is simultaneously able to convey profound theological meaning and do so in a way that is fresh and evocative. He has been described as the greatest poet of the patristic age and "perhaps the only theologian-poet to rank beside Dante."[18] But as we have seen, the poetry Ephrem used was not simply word and verse; his religion itself was poetry.

Poets and religion go hand in hand, and poets have always played a role in religious expression—Philo, John of Damascus, Symeon the New Theologian, Hildegard of Bingen, Daniel ben Judah, Dante Alighieri, Catherine of Siena, Omar Khayyam, Rumi, John Donne, Emily Bronte, John Milton, T.S. Eliot, Kahlil Gibran, Thomas Merton—and so many others. And poetry was frequently an important part of religious expression, as it was in medieval Celtic Christian spirituality.[19] But not every poet in religion is self-consciously so. Sometimes the poetry is revealed even in prose.

Father James Brockman compiled and translated a number sayings and teachings of martyred El Salvadoran archbishop Oscar Romero. The words and imagery of Archbishop Romero are striking and haunting, and so too is the way that Father Brockman presents them:

> Let us not tire of preaching love;
>   it is the force that will overcome the world.
> Let us not tire of preaching love.

16. In Syriac, the word that translates the Greek λόγος *Logos* ("word") is ܡܠܬܐ *melta*, which is treated grammatically as feminine and uses feminine pronouns. Likewise, Holy Spirit, ܪܘܚܐ ܕܩܘܕܫܐ *ruḥa d'qudsha*, is another feminine construction.

17. Brock, *Luminous Eye*, 171.

18. Ibid., 173.

19. Davies and Bowie, *Celtic Christian Spirituality*, 30.

Though we see that waves of violence
succeed in drowning the fire of Christian love,
   love must win out; it is the only thing that can.

—*September 25, 1977*

When Christ appeared in those lands,
   curing the sick,
   raising the dead,
   preaching to the poor,
   bringing hope to the peoples,
something began on earth like when a stone is cast
   into a quiet lake and starts ripples
that finally reach the farthest shores.
Christ appeared in Zebulun and Naphtali
   with signs of liberation:
   shaking off oppressive yokes,
   bringing joy to hearts,
   sowing hope.
And this is what God is doing now in history.

—*January 22, 1978*[20]

Romero isn't just a priest or even just an archbishop; he is a poet. And as a
poet, he is in the business of using metaphor:

To know Christ is to know God.
Christ is the homily
that keeps explaining to us continually
   that God is love,
   that God is power,
   that the Spirit of the Lord is upon Jesus Christ,
   that he is the divine Word,
God's presence among us.

Jesus Christ and the gospel are not two separate things.
The gospel is not a biography of Christ;
for St. Paul, the gospel is the living power of God.
Reading the gospel is not like reading an ordinary book.

20. Romero and Brockman, *Violence of Love*, 7, 31–32.

You have to fill yourself with faith
and stress the living Jesus Christ,
    the revelation of the Father.
You must feel, though it be in silence,
    without anyone's speaking,
    with deep faith in your heart,
that Christ is God's homily preaching to you
while you try to fill yourself with the divine power
that has come in Christ Jesus.

—*January 27, 1980*[21]

Romero sees the gospel as a kind of poem that reveals Christ, not as prose that merely describes details of his life. His relentless use of metaphor—CHRIST IS A HOMILY, CHRIST IS THE WORD, CHRIST IS THE GOSPEL, CHRIST IS A REVELATION—only serves to underscore that point.

* * *

None of this is to say that there is no history or other straightforward information in scripture. There is a grounding *in* history, and that grounding is an important element of the Abrahamic tradition. Jews, Christians, and Muslims all believe in a God who acts in history, not who performed great deeds in some lost age before history.[22] There is history and fact to be found in the narratives of religion.

But even those tellings of history and fact are in service of communicating the deeper mystery that the scripture is trying to unveil. As a former pastor of mine used to say, "There's truth in the Bible and there are facts in the Bible, and the two things ought not be confused." The history and facts in the scriptures *serve* the poetry in its task of conveying truth and meaning. The poetry does not serve the history.

Religion is poetry; the great abuse of religion is that so many should treat it like prose.

21. Ibid., 182–83.

22. The scriptures are full of historical references: the Exodus takes place after "a new king arose over Egypt," the prophets announced their missions in the reigns of particular kings of Israel and Judah or under the reign of the Persian King Cyrus, and one gospel begins its narrative during the reign of the Emperor Tiberius. All of these references serve the notion that God is active in ordinary history.

Chapter 8

Pointing Beyond the Metaphor

METAPHORS ARE EXTREMELY USEFUL in giving us the tools to talk about things outside of ordinary experience, things about which we are uncertain. But therein lies the danger: our reluctance to embrace uncertainty drives us to change a metaphor from its uncertain, poetic nature into something more certain, more definite. Metaphors are always at risk of being literalized—and killed. When that happens, we find ourselves fixed upon the metaphor rather than the reality it points toward. What was at first so useful in pointing us in the direction of the idea has now become the endpoint of the journey. This happens whenever we are grappling with ideas that are difficult to understand, whether in the sciences or in religion.

Imagery, metaphor, and model help us to understand ideas when our knowledge about the world outpaces our ability to conceptualize those ideas. Such imagery has frequently been used to state scientific theories and the analogies we have come up with have remained helpful in explaining them. For example, scientists have used analogies such as *heat is like a fluid, evolution is like selective breeding, the atom is like a solar system*, and *genes are like coded messages*.[1]

As useful as such analogies are in explaining scientific theory, there is always a danger of getting hung up on the image, metaphor, or model used. We sometimes confuse the effectiveness of a metaphorical *description* of something with a *definition* of that thing. The physicist Niels Bohr warned of the dangers in taking these images for scientific concepts too literally when he remarked, "When it comes to atoms, language can be used only as in poetry."[2]

The same holds true for theology. When we speak of Jesus as the *Son of God* we are making a statement that the relationship between God and Jesus is like the relationship between a father and son. In any other circumstance,

1. Pinker, *Stuff of Thought*, 254.
2. Sheppard, "Problematics of European Modernism," 28.

we would leave it at that and would not try to push the metaphor too far. For example, saying that the atom is like a solar system is helpful in picturing the electrons orbiting the nucleus as planets orbit the sun. But no one would seriously claim that the electrons themselves had moons or were subject to plate tectonics or might bear life the way that a planet in a solar system would. We all understand that to be pushing the analogy too far.

But for some reason, when it comes to the metaphors of faith, we are more inclined to do exactly that. Jesus speaks of God as *Father* and people look beyond the metaphor of relationship and conclude that God must be male. The prophets use the imagery of God as a *king* and people conclude that our wrongdoing offends God's royal honor. Other images of God describe God as a *judge* and people conclude that our wrongdoings are *crimes* against God.

We frequently get trapped in our own language about God. Language that was intended as a model, to help our understanding by analogy, becomes a prison in which our theological imagination and creativity become confined.

* * *

Perhaps the slide from metaphor to literalism is just a consequence of what happens in language over time, especially with symbolic language. Because religion has no other recourse but to use symbolic language, it risks those symbols being taken literally by those who use them, who forget that the truth being grasped is not the same as the language that reveals it.

The theologian Paul Tillich believed that any language that was applied to God, no matter how apparently straightforward, was actually metaphorical language. Even the words *God exists* could not be taken literally but could only be seen as a kind of poem.[3] Tillich maintained that in matters of religion we have no other recourse but to use symbolic language: "Man's ultimate concern must be expressed symbolically, because symbolic language alone is able to express the ultimate."[4]

When Tillich talked about *symbol*, he meant something that points beyond itself to a reality and *participates* in that reality. Only symbols such as these can be used in matters of faith because "the true ultimate transcends the realm of finite reality infinitely." As a result, no finite language can ever hope to encompass or express the infinite ultimate. The language of faith is the language of symbols.[5]

3. Buechner, *Now and Then*, 14
4. Tillich, "Symbols of Faith," 136.
5. Ibid., 138–39.

When we look at the characteristics that Tillich identifies as necessary for such symbols, we see that each and every one of them applies to metaphor. Metaphors are symbols that point to a reality beyond themselves, and they participate in the reality of what they point to. The metaphor simultaneously creates distance from its object—by pointing away from itself and to the object—and makes connection, by participating in the reality of what it's pointing toward. A symbol, a metaphor, simultaneously *is* and *is not* the object it's pointing to.

And so, even though a symbol is a pointer, the symbol is not arbitrary—it has something to do with what it symbolizes. For example, Romeo says, "What light through yonder window breaks? It is the east and Juliet is the sun." He does not say, "It is the east and Juliet is the star Sirius." However bright the apparent magnitude of Sirius might be, such a metaphor fails because, unlike *sun*, Sirius has none of the associations that make the original image powerful: beginning of a new day, life, light, warmth. *Sun* is an appropriate metaphor for Juliet because it is not only pointing toward her but also participates in her reality. In order for the symbol to work, it must participate in the reality of its object and cannot be entirely arbitrary. This fact about metaphors is often noticed only in the breach. A lot of humor can be generated from examples of metaphors and analogies that seem completely arbitrary, such as Douglas Adams's famously brilliant description of Vogon spaceships in *The Hitchhiker's Guide to the Galaxy*: "The ships hung in the sky in much the same way that bricks don't."[6]

A metaphor's simultaneous ability to have distance from and to identify with the reality it points to makes a metaphor useful for confronting difficult realities and painful truths, the kind of truths often confronted by the prophets of religious tradition. Biblical scholar Walter Brueggemann argues that the prophet's task is "to *bring to public expression those very fears and terrors* that have been denied so long and suppressed so deeply that we do not know they are there." To do that, the prophet has to use meaningful symbols and metaphors so that different people can engage with the prophet's message in many ways.[7] For the prophet, who needs to help the people confront a painful reality without coercion, the distance between the metaphor and what it represents becomes a valuable and indispensable tool, precisely because it *points* rather than defines. It is indirect, sufficiently far away from its reality to be safely engaged, but effective in getting you toward that reality once you've engaged it. The only kind of language that can adequately function as the kind of symbols necessary to point toward the pain-

6. Adams, *Hitchhiker's Guide to the Galaxy*, 34.
7. Brueggemann, *Prophetic Imagination*, 50.

ful prophetic reality are metaphors, because pointing is what metaphors are good at. We're just not always good at recognizing that fact.

* * *

A good friend of mine used to have a long-haired miniature dachshund named Samson. Samson was one of the sweetest dogs I've ever known. Loyal and friendly, affectionate and playful—we loved him. However, Samson never got the knack of pointing. I had grown up with a cocker spaniel who would occasionally point at birds in the yard—the purpose for which her breed had been bred, after all—and so I assumed, wrongly, that all dogs understood the concept. In fact, every time I tried pointing at something for Samson, he watched my hand instead. He was incapable of understanding that the hand was indicating something beyond it. I'd hear myself saying, "No—over *there!*" as if the dog, who could not even understand gesture, would somehow understand English. But poor Samson would only look at my hand, perhaps wondering if all the fuss I was making meant that there was a treat in it for him.

I sometimes feel that those of us who are religious folk are like Samson, focusing on the hand doing the pointing rather than on the item being pointed at. In fact, that is exactly what we do when we literalize a metaphor—we fail to see past it. The curious thing is that aside from clichés and idioms or fossilized metaphors whose meaning we no longer see, we do not have this problem with ordinary metaphor. For example, if I were to describe someone as a *prince among men*, most people would understand that I was pointing to specific qualities of nobility, integrity, and leadership. Anyone who failed to see beyond the metaphor and who thought that I was claiming the person to be royalty would generally be viewed as foolish.

And yet, if I were to say that God is a father, there are great numbers of people who would take that metaphor not as pointing beyond itself to the loving and relational nature of God, but as a declaration that God is a male parent. Rather than seeing it as a powerful metaphor for the intimacy with which God enters into relationship (as a father), so many see it as a categorical descriptor. People of faith get into fights with one another about whether God is male, whether it's appropriate to describe God as "mother," and so on, all the while missing the point entirely. Like little Samson, when it comes to matters of religion, we keep looking at the hand, rather than what it's pointing at.

One consequence of the failure to look beyond the metaphor is that our words can become idols. A notable example of this are the fundamentalists who treat their scriptures in ways that border on the idolatrous, revering the text as a perfect revelation of God. But this kind of idolatry is not limited to the fundamentalists; it can be found any time we fail to look *through* the metaphors and stop only at the words. As Sallie McFague notes, "without a sense of awe, wonder, and mystery, we forget the *inevitable distance* between our words and the divine reality,"[8] an "inevitable distance" that is obvious to those who understand religious language as metaphor.

Another way of understanding metaphor is as two active thoughts that remain in a permanent tension or interaction with each other.[9] This means two concepts that do not naturally go together become bound up in a metaphorical relationship that simultaneously highlights both the interaction and the tension between the two, something McFague refers to as "the *is* and the *is not*." A metaphor like LIFE IS A HIGHWAY, for example, requires us to confront the ways in which life *is* a highway (a journey with turns, perhaps obstacles, and stops along the way), while simultaneously recognizing that, no, life *is not* a slab of asphalt on which vehicles move.

Key to a metaphor's power is this simultaneous discontinuity and continuity. When Pat Benetar sings the metaphor LOVE IS A BATTLEFIELD two things happen simultaneously: we are jarred by the equation of love with destructive violence, and we are forced to reflect on all the ways that love is frequently painful and devastating. The best metaphors remain in this dynamic tension between the *is* and the *is not*.

But this dynamic power does not last forever; there is a life cycle to our use of metaphors:

1. The metaphor is coined: it often seems inappropriate or unconventional and may even be rejected;

2. The metaphor becomes a living metaphor: it has a dual meaning—the literal and the metaphorical—and is insightful; and

3. The metaphor becomes commonplace, dead, and/or literalized.[10]

The more frequently a metaphor is used, the more it becomes simply a stock saying, the more likely we are to be blind to its metaphorical imagery and to begin to see it as a literal reality. At this stage in the process, the tension between the *is* and the *is not* is lost; the similarity between the two concepts has become identity.

We see this process of becoming ordinary and unremarkable all the time in religious contexts. In the New Testament, for example, there are

8. McFague, *Metaphorical Theology*, 2.

9. Ibid., 37.

10. Ibid., 41.

instances of Jesus telling his disciples to "eat his flesh" and "drink his blood," after which his listeners are confused, and the disciples respond by saying, "This message is tough. Who can hear it?" (John 6:60). And yet, today in Christian churches, people line up for the Communion after being told, "This is the body of Christ broken for you; and the blood of Christ shed for you," without so much as batting an eye at this oddly cannibalistic rite. What was once shocking has become commonplace and unremarkable.

This can be true for both metaphors and metaphorical stories like Jesus' parables. Some parables—such as the parable of the day laborers, in which an owner hires day laborers at different times of the day (some as late as the last hour of the day) but in the end pays them all the same amount for a whole day's work—do retain their shock value because of the perceived injustice in them. But most parables, like many of our religious metaphors, have become so commonplace that they have become dead.

An example of a metaphorical story that has frequently lost its shocking power is the parable of the Good Samaritan. The parable is Jesus' response to the question *Who is my neighbor?*—that is, the person you're supposed to love "as you love yourself." It tells the story of a man who is robbed, beaten, and left for dead alongside the Jericho Road. A priest and a Levite (a temple official) both pass him by. Then a Samaritan comes by, takes the man, treats him, brings him to an inn, and leaves money to provide for his care, promising to pay the balance on any expenses when he returns. Jesus uses the parable to demonstrate that of the three, it was the Samaritan who was the man's *neighbor*.

This parable has become so familiar that its metaphor YOUR NEIGHBOR IS A SAMARITAN has been completely robbed of its power. "Good Samaritan" has even become something of a cliché in our language, meaning something like "a really helpful person in a time of need." This is a meaning that can be seen in the name of CVS/Pharmacy's free emergency highway service vehicle (the *CVS Samaritan*) and the name for laws that compel passersby to assist those in need ("Good Samaritan laws"). A Good Samaritan is a helpful person in a time of trouble. We all know what it means.

But here, familiarity has obscured just how shocking the story is supposed to be. The Samaritans were (and are—there are still about 500 of them left) a people who were descended from the former inhabitants of the Northern Kingdom of Israel (the "Lost Tribes") and the populations that were imported into that kingdom after the Assyrians destroyed it in 721 BCE. The inhabitants of the Southern Kingdom of Judah never saw this mixed population as authentically Israelite, and over the centuries, a fair amount of hostility developed between the Jews of Judah and the Samaritans of Samaria, a level of hostility that was keenly felt in Jesus' day. Some have argued that to understand the significance of the context of this story, you would have to imagine a modern context and substitute the word *Palestinian* for *Samaritan*.

But Jesus does more than make a simple, if unusual, substitution—he violates an established pattern. He knows that the traditional division of the Jewish people is *Kohen, Levi, Yisrael*, "priest, Levite, and Israelite," and he substitutes a new pattern: priest, Levite, *Samaritan*. It'd be like telling a story about a Fourth of July party and saying that you'll have "baseball, hot dogs, and borscht." Jesus' violation of the pattern is jarring and disruptive to the listeners' expectations: the hero of the story doesn't turn out to be an Israelite, as the pattern would have suggested. It's a Samaritan. The Other.

The trajectory of this parable illustrates what happens so frequently with our religious metaphors: they go from shocking to safe and harmless. What had started out as a paradox and contradiction (My neighbor is a *Samaritan?!?*) became the rote definition (Of course my neighbor is a Good Samaritan). What was meant to be held in tension, pointing us beyond itself, has become the end point of the journey.

This process of literalization is particularly true of models—those dominant metaphors like GOD IS A FATHER that we've looked at before. Models are particularly susceptible to being literalized and robbed of their metaphorical power. Models can become so dominant and familiar that we can fail to see them as models.

In other contexts, failing to see a model as a model would be an obvious error. In the movie *Zoolander*, vapid male fashion model Derek Zoolander is presented with an architectural model of a school he hopes to fund, the "Derek Zoolander Center for Children Who Can't Read Good and Wanna Learn to Do Other Stuff Good Too." The presenters are stunned when, rather than being pleased with the model, Zoolander is enraged:

> Zoolander: What is this? A center for ants? How can we be
> expected to teach children to learn how to read . . .
> if they can't even fit inside the building?
>
> Mugatu: Derek, this is just a small . . .
>
> Zoolander: I don't wanna hear your excuses! The building has
> to be at least . . . three times bigger than this![11]

The absurdity of mistaking a model building for the real thing works as a gag in a movie, but when the same mistake is made in our theology, it's not nearly so amusing. And it happens all the time.

11. IMDb, "Zoolander (2001) – Quotes."

Christian *soteriology*—or the doctrine of salvation—is an area of religious thought where models are frequently mistaken for the real thing. The question of *how* it was that God accomplished salvation through Jesus Christ has been a source of major theological reflection throughout Christian history. Among the many reflections on salvation that have emerged is a model based on crime and punishment: sin is an offense against God and we stand guilty of having committed a crime, the penalty being death. In this model, in order to satisfy the demands of justice, God provided Jesus who took our punishment for himself, sparing us and allowing God's justice to be satisfied. This model is one of many ways that Christians have developed to understand how it was that Jesus had worked this reconciliation between God and humanity.[12] But for many Christians, this is not a model that seeks to help people understand, it has become literalized into a *definition* of God and of the system of salvation.

Such literalization has consequences for theology. As emergent church theologian Doug Pagitt notes, the literalization of this judicial model "hamstrings God" because in a legal system it is the *law* that is central, not the judge, who, like the prosecutor, the defendant, and the jury, is bound by the law:

> In the judicial model, God must judge us according to the law. But God is allowed to show us mercy as long as the punishment for our wrongdoing is carried out. So God, who is evidently powerless to do otherwise, must offer Jesus as a blood sacrifice in our place. Yes, it breaks God's heart to have to do it, but what choice does God have? The law is the law.[13]

As Pagitt rightly points out, when this model is taken as a definition, it limits one's understanding of God. God is no longer at the center of the story—the law is—and God becomes helpless: "love, grace, mercy, compassion, and even God become minor players that must be subject to the law."[14] God becomes as small as Derek Zoolander's school and as powerless to effect any meaningful change in anyone's life.

Other models have suffered the same fate. Many of the early christological models—those exploring the nature of Christ—were rooted in Judaism's understanding of mystery and metaphor. However, such mystery and metaphor would often be lost in translation from this earliest Jewish core to

---

12. These models are discussed in greater detail in chapter 5.

13. Pagitt, *Christianity Worth Believing*, 154.

14. Ibid., 155.

the later developed, and more literal-minded Greco-Roman culture of the Roman Empire.[15]

Reflections on Jesus' nature, expressed through metaphors like *Son of God, Son of Man, Word of God, Fullness of God,* and so on, had been freely used as placeholders for mystery. But these placeholders became an issue once the metaphors they'd employed had become dead and needed to be explained. Some of the largest, and most violent, church disagreements took place over issues raised by these metaphors.[16] For example, the model JESUS IS A SON, having lost its metaphorical power over time, now had to be explained *literally.* To meet this need, creeds and doctrines were developed, which had to make extensive use of metaphor themselves (*only begotten, light from light,* etc.), a fact that is either ironic, poetic, or perhaps both.

Our inability to recognize metaphor and symbol is not limited to transcendent religious symbols alone. Even those aspects of faith that seem straightforward doctrinal claims may not have started out with the literalism that we ascribe to them. As religious philosopher Thomas Martland writes, the ancient Christian creeds were not formulated as descriptive accounts of a divine order "once and for all," but were meant to be "protective walls" against all the inconsistent and vague theology that had existed previously. Their function was more to direct religious thought within certain confines than it was to check or limit that thought.[17] Even the creeds are not attempting comprehensive definition. They are pointers, pointing in a direction framed by a wider tradition, but they do not attempt to define anything conclusively.

* * *

One of the major consequences of taking claims about God literally is that doing so exposes a number of contradictions about God: the contradiction between God's *goodness* and the existence of evil (*If God is good, why is there evil?*); God's *personality* and God's *infinity* (*How can God be infinite and transcendent and still be intimate and close?*), and God's *unchangeableness* and God's *activity* (*How can God be unchanging and still interact with the world?*).[18] These contradictions are not lost on two groups in particular: religious fundamentalists and militant atheists.

15. Ibid., 200.

16. Rubenstein, *When Jesus Became God,* 6.

17. Martland, *Religion as Art,* 119.

18. Kellenberger, *Everlasting and the Eternal,* 168, citing Stace, *Time and Eternity,* 153–54.

Indeed, the two groups that spend the most time dealing with these tensions and contradictions are the fundamentalists—who have explanations, usually unconvincing ones, for why these are only *apparent* contradictions—and atheists, who point to these contradictions as evidence that God cannot exist. In this way, both fundamentalists and atheists share the assumption that claims about God are straightforward descriptive claims meant to be taken literally. Curiously, these two groups seen as polar opposites actually have the same understanding of religion. This was an observation not lost on Joseph Campbell, who noted:

> As a result we have people who consider themselves believers because they accept metaphors as facts, and we have others who classify themselves as atheists because they think religious metaphors are lies.[19]

In neither case does anyone accept the metaphors *as metaphors*. To see how this works out, we'll take some examples from social media and other sites. First, let's look at the fundamentalists:

- One of the driest places on earth [the Sahara] once ran with water. Or Maybe it was due to a flood? #truth

- From the Bible we can already know the big bang idea is wrong: the Word of God in Genesis 1 says the earth was created before the stars. (answersingenesis.org)

- Either you believe the earth is 6000 years old or you're an atheist.

- Pat @700Club why do u strongly oppose #Creationism? #Bible clearly says Universe, earth & all in it created in 6 days (rested 7th).[20]

- Scientists discover an ocean 400 miles beneath our feet | http://ow.ly/3xAI7s | #Genesis 7:11 #Noah #flood #Bible

- Scientific Proof #God Did The #Miracle Of Parting The Red Sea (MUST SEE!) #ccot #Bible #Israel #truth #faith #belief

And now the atheists:

- My step-mother insists I shld read the #Bible before I become an #atheist. I tried. 1st page said world made in 6 days. Why wld rest be tru?

---

19. Campbell and Kennedy, *Thou Art That*, ch. 1.

20. This tweet is referring to the fact that even Pat Robertson has come out and said that the earth is older than the biblical account. It's rare that Pat Robertson and I ever agree on anything, but, hey, credit where credit is due.

- There are 400K species of beetles. How the hell did they fit on Noah's ark?? #atheism #atheist

- It's 90 degrees in the shade in Jerusalem . . . so where did Noah get two penguins and two polar bears from? #atheism

- Never seen evidence that any human can or ever did walk on water. #atheism

- NEWS FLASH: No one can walk on freaking water! Silly Christians! #atheism

- So remind me. Why did your omnipotent god need to impregnate that poor girl in order to walk the earth? Miracle she wasn't stoned. #Atheism

- SO THE #POPE ACCEPTS THE #BIBLE SPEAKS LIES! TILL DATE THEIR GOD HAD CREATED WORLD IN 6 DAYS! LOL! POPEY DEAR!

It's clear that the fundamentalists/literalists in the first group are treating the Bible in the exact same way that the atheists in the second group are: the Bible is a record of events, of factual assertions about the creation of the world or about particular events in history, including a world-spanning flood and the parting of a sea. One group accepts the claims, the other rejects them. But both groups find the text to be the same thing: a *literal*, not metaphorical, account.

Now, I understand that looking to the Internet for thoughtful reflection is not necessarily the best option. But even very educated, well-respected people who should know better make the same mistake, including a neurosurgeon:

> It says in the beginning God created the heaven and earth. It doesn't say when he created them, except for in the beginning. So the earth could have been here for a long time before he started creating things on it. But when he did start doing that, he made it very specifically clear to us the evening and the morning were the next day because he knew that people would come along and try to say that, "Oh, it was millions and millions of years." And then what else did he say in the very first chapter? That each thing brought forth after its own kind. Because he knew that people would come along and say, you know, this changed into that and this changed into that and this changed into that. So at the very beginning of the Bible, he puts that to rest.[21]

---

21. Corn, "Ben Carson."

And an evolutionary biologist:

> Let children learn about different faiths, let them notice their incompatibility, and let them draw their own conclusions about the consequences of that incompatibility. As for whether they are 'valid,' let them make up their own minds when they are old enough to do so . . .[22]

> [The religious fundamentalist believes that] the book is true, and if evidence seems to contradict it, it is the evidence that must be thrown out not the book.[23]

These quotes—of both literalist and atheist alike—share the presumption that religion is in the business of making verifiable truth claims of the same kind that, say, science does. The "incompatibility" referred to in the second of these three quotes is the incompatibility of the details among religions, as if those details were the truth claims of the various religions. In the third quote—a description of the reaction of the fundamentalist who defends scripture at all costs—the same presumption is embedded: the scripture is making falsifiable truth claims of the kind that science can easily disprove. The folly of the fundamentalist, in this view, is in adhering to the falsified claims of the text in the face of contradictory external evidence. Both of these perspectives fail to appreciate what the biblical text, or even the enterprise of religion, is really about.

A similar failing is found in this quote from late journalist and author Christopher Hitchens, who said, "Literature, not scripture, sustains the mind and—since there is no other metaphor—also the soul."[24] Hitchens is able to employ *soul* as a metaphor, but does not seem to imagine that there might be other metaphors in religion. It's not that Hitchens sees the poetry of religion as prose. It's that he doesn't even see it as any kind of literature. Perhaps he sees it as some kind of technical manual. He would not be the first, among believers and non-believers alike.

The failure to see the language of religion as poetic, metaphoric language not only causes the fundamentalist and the atheist to see religion as a system of straightforward truth claims, it frequently causes them to conflate religion with the reality it points toward. That is, they both can mistake *religion* for *God*.

Throughout his book *god Is Not Great: How Religion Poisons Everything*, Hitchens levels a number of devastating critiques against religion:

22. Dawkins, *God Delusion*, 340.
23. Ibid., 282.
24. Hitchens, *god Is Not Great*, 5.

believers have acted with violence, religion has been the enemy of reason, religion has often used fear and hate, religion has been used to reinforce cultural prejudices, and religion is clearly man-made.[25] I agree with every single one of those points: believers have acted with violence, they have often opposed innovations in science when it conflicted with their worldviews, they have used religion as a tool to maintain an unjust status quo, and yes, they constructed the religions themselves.

But so what? All of those things can be true without affecting the reality of God at all. God's existence is entirely independent of what any of us might *think* about God's existence one way or the other. Key to this line of thinking is a serious error: the conflation of religion with God. Hitchens's attack on God's existence only makes sense if the religion he disparages and the God he doesn't believe in are the same thing. He betrays his fallacy when he assumes that because he finds a given metaphor for God to be faulty, so too must be the object it points to. Because he finds the language describing God to be absurd, he concludes there cannot be a God at all. But all of this only makes sense if the religion or the religious language for God and God are the same thing.

This conflation of religion and God is not a phenomenon limited to non-believers; believers, too, frequently confuse their religion for the God the religion points toward. Religions are man-made; they are the metaphors that *people* have constructed to try to identify the divine mystery they believe lies at the heart of reality. But so very often, people seem to forget that the religion is *pointing* at that reality; it is not that reality itself.

In late 2015, a professor at Wheaton College, an evangelical Christian college, was suspended because, in a statement in which she pledged to wear a headscarf throughout Advent as a declaration of solidarity with Muslims, she said that Christians and Muslims "worship the same God." Although her superiors did not object to the declaration of solidarity or to the wearing of the headscarf, they strongly objected to the notion that Muslims and Christians worshiped the same God, and for that reason suspended her.[26]

Now, to be fair, from the college's point of view, the only proper understanding of God is the Christian, Trinitarian theology that affirms that Jesus is God, the Son of God, the Second Person of the Trinity, through whose sacrifice on the cross the salvation of humanity is made possible. Since Islam rejects the divinity of Christ (although it affirms his messiahship and prophethood) it cannot be said to be worshiping the same God, or so the thinking goes.

25. Ibid., 1–13.

26. An, "Do Muslims and Christians."

But note what has happened: such a position—and it is not the only one of its kind; there are many analogs in many different religious expressions—confuses a tradition's *understanding* of God with *God*. Such an equivalence between understanding and reality can only be made when one's understanding of the subject is perfect—and our understanding of God is not. Yes, Islam and Christianity (and Judaism, Bahá'í, Zoroastrianism, etc.) have very different conceptions of God. They all use different metaphors to describe the unknowable God, the Eternal One. But no one is in a position to say that all those metaphors are not pointing in the same direction. To claim that different religions worship different gods because they have different conceptions of God is like claiming that different stargazers are looking at different skies because each is focusing on a different constellation. Each may have a different understanding of what the sky looks like, but the same sky looms above them all. And yet, we continue to fail to distinguish between our religions and the divine reality to which they point. We continue to fail to see a distinction between the journey and the destination.

For believer and non-believer alike, religion is often seen as the *end* in the journey rather than the signpost pointing you along the road. Believers all too often see that signpost and imagine that they have reached their destination; the non-believer sees the shoddy condition of the signpost and concludes that the destination does not exist.

What is it about religious language such that people keep taking it for something other than metaphor and poetry?

Martin Buber claimed that because God was not "comprehensible," lacking in form or image, human beings were often driven to provide symbols, images, and ideas of God out of ordinary human experience to have something to hold on to. Buber believed that all of the images we came up with were "untrue" but were tolerated by God as a way for us to encounter God on human terms. But then, Buber said, the symbols "always quickly desire to be more than they are," more than signs and pointers. When this happens, they are no longer pointers, they become *obstacles*.[27]

Buber claims that this process in which the signs and pointers are confused for the presence they point to is what leads philosophers and critical thinkers to reject both the image and the God it symbolizes. That is, the philosopher-atheist realizes that the literal claims of the symbols are ridiculous and rejects both them and the metaphysical reality they supposedly embody. In this way, the fundamentalist/literalist and the atheist have once again claimed the same version of religion, neither one seeing through the symbols to the mystery that stands behind them. In response,

27. Buber, "Meaning and Encounter," 184–85.

Martin Buber argues that people of faith are called not only to reject the symbols that have become literalized (just as the philosophers and atheists have done), but also to move beyond them to the reality those symbols were first invoked to describe.[28]

So why does this happen? Why are people reluctant to see metaphors as metaphors, models as models, symbols as symbols? Why are so many inclined to take metaphors literally and see models as the things themselves?

Much of the resistance to seeing metaphors as metaphors comes from the consequences of doing so. Tillich argues that there is something in us that resists the attempt to interpret symbols as symbols, something that is not comfortable admitting that religion employs metaphor. Something that fears that doing so makes religion less true, less convincing, less certain. Symbols and metaphors—as pointers beyond themselves—admit the uncertainty of a religious claim. If we were to be comfortable with symbol and metaphor, we'd have to be comfortable with uncertainty. And so, in order to maximize certainty and retreat from the uncertainty of symbols, many people retreat into literalism, taking all the metaphors at face value.

However, according to Tillich, doing so is fraught with theological consequence. Literalism, for Tillich, deprives God of God's majesty. Further, he believed literalism was a kind of idolatry. It was "calling something ultimate which is less than ultimate" and denying the honor which is due to God.[29] Those who take religious metaphors literally and at face value reduce God to the level of the symbol. In an effort to be certain in matters of faith, people stray away from faith into the certainty of an idol. That idol may have the same name as the God who is meant to be worshiped, but in the end the symbol is no longer pointing at the object of worship; it has become the object of worship.

Neil Gillman points out that the metaphors we use to describe God "straddle two worlds"—the world of concrete, familiar experience and the world that lies beyond nature and history. Because these worlds are in tension and invariably work against each other, the impulse toward "concreteness"—or certainty—leads us into idolatry. As Gillman says, "We have molded a conceptual golden calf."[30]

Peter Rollins agrees, noting that when we fail to recognize that the term *God* always falls short of that toward which the word is supposed to point, "we will end up bowing down before our own conceptual creations forged from the raw materials of our self-image." For this reason, Rollins

28. Ibid., 185.

29. Tillich, *Symbols of Faith*, 143.

30. Gillman, *Sacred Fragments*, 105.

notes, Meister Eckhart famously prayed, "God rid me of God"—a prayer acknowledging that the God we are in relationship with is bigger than, better than, and different from our understanding of that God.[31]

For Buber, Tillich, Gillman, and Rollins, the literalist assertion that our human definitions and human language can actually *describe* God is a kind of *conceptual* idolatry—only instead of an idol of wood or stone, it's an idol of thought. As Rollins points out, it's not idolatrous to use language that we claim is somehow connected to God, but it is idolatrous to the claim that we somehow *understand* God.[32]

Understanding literalism as a kind of idolatry helps us to understand the inclination to take metaphors literally and to see models as the objects being modeled themselves. Doing so satisfies the same needs that idolatry does. The holes in our lives, the sense that we're incomplete in some way, the vacuum that we feel in our souls—the same one that is exploited by the consumption-industrial complex and Madison Avenue—drives us to seek a way to abolish the void. We long to find something concrete to hold on to, something certain that we can ground ourselves in. That craving for certainty upon which consumerism, demagoguery, fundamentalism, and idolatry all depend leads us toward literalism.[33]

Uncertainty is unnerving—and we are not delivered from our uncertainty by metaphors that merely point the way. And so, rather than accept the reality of metaphor and admit our inability to know, we, like an insecure man who seeks to possess the woman he "loves" out of fear of losing her, seek to box God in and control God out of fear of losing our certainty in God. Our desire to define God is a reflection of our desire for certainty. If we can just be *sure*, if we can define God to our satisfaction, then perhaps we can find the certainty that we seek.

* * *

There is a Zen Buddhist saying: "Do not mistake the finger pointing at the moon for the moon." It comes from a story of the Buddha, as told by Thích Nhất Hạnh in his book *Old Path, White Clouds*:

> [The Buddha said,] I must state clearly that my teaching is a method to experience reality and not reality itself, just as a finger pointing at the moon is not the moon itself. A thinking person makes use of the finger to see the moon. A person who

31. Rollins, *How (Not) to Speak of God*, 19.

32. Ibid., 18.

33. Rollins, *Idolatry of God*, 14–15.

only looks at the finger and mistakes it for the moon will never see the real moon.[34]

The Buddha's teaching is a *method to experience reality and not reality itself.* We craft religions as vehicles to help people to experience the reality, but religions are not themselves the reality. Religion is full of metaphor and metaphors are first and foremost *pointers.*

Earlier we noted that even the rites and rituals of faith—the Eucharist, Torah study, Muslim prayer, ablution, standing prayer—are a kind of metaphor. None of those rites is done for the sake of the rite itself, but rather for what the rite *represents.* The rites and traditions of the religions are themselves pointers to a deeper reality. But so often, we mistake the finger pointing at the moon for the moon and so will never see past it to the reality beyond.

The reason so many non-believers treat religious claims literally and religion as an end in itself (often a self-serving end) is because so many people of faith do exactly the same thing. Perhaps it's a function of our need for certainty; it is easier to cling to rite, rituals, doctrines, dogmas, creeds, hierarchies, structures, and institutions than it is to acknowledge that not even these things are the end points on our journey but are simply pointing the way. We want to know that we've arrived, that we've finally got it, that everything is okay, and it's all figured out. Recognizing faith as mystery and metaphor denies us that certainty, and we're not having any of it.

Honesty requires us to admit that our religious traditions are steeped in uncertainty. Far from being refuges of easy answers, free of doubt, our religions instead invite us into embracing unknowing. Through metaphor, poetry, and symbol, our religious traditions reveal not certainty, but uncertainty; not definition, but mystery; not the moon, but the finger pointing at the moon.

---

34. Nhất Hạnh, *Old Path, White Clouds,* 211.

The Inescapable Uncertainty

. . . In Our Language

Language is memory and metaphor.

—Storm Jameson

It is not in our religious traditions and religious language alone that we find uncertainty. Uncertainty is found in *all* of our language. We think in, express ourselves with, and receive information through a medium that is unavoidably uncertain.

In this part of the book we're going to explore this most human of phenomena. We're going to look at the essential role that language plays in our ability to perceive, describe, and communicate our experience of the world to one another. When we look at language in depth, we will discover that language is full of uncertainties. There are all kinds of obstacles to communication that make our ability to effectively communicate uncertain. We will see that language is built out of metaphors and poetic constructions that do not capture the truth with precision, but only point the way. We'll see that this astounding and astonishing human medium is nevertheless full of uncertainty.

Chapter 9

Mathematics and the Language of God

If there is a God, he is a great mathematician.

—PAUL DIRAC

WE HAVE SEEN THAT in matters of faith—in describing ineffable experiences and concepts of deepest meaning and ultimate reality—we have no other option but to turn to metaphor and symbol to describe and communicate that spiritual reality. Because of that need to take recourse in metaphor and symbol, our ability to capture and claim to know that ultimate spiritual reality is full of uncertainty.

But what about ordinary things that *are* perceptible with the senses, like the physical universe around us? Is there any way to capture that reality with certainty? It turns out that we have developed a pretty effective method for describing the universe: mathematics. As a system, mathematics is subject to a lot less ambiguity than religious language is. There are not competing traditions of mathematicians who argue whether 2+2=4, nor are there dissenting mathematicians who maintain that 2+2=5 and consider the rest to be hopelessly misguided heretics. Mathematics, it seems, could be a system that might actually have certainty. And if it can actually describe the world, so much the better.

Galileo observed, "Mathematics is the alphabet in which God has written the universe." Indeed, it has been demonstrated that the story of the universe is written in mathematics—the best tool for describing its many intricate processes has proven to be the language of math.[1]

Scientists and mathematicians have noted that mathematics has an uncanny ability to describe the natural world. Math proves time and time

1. Frenkel, *Love and Math*, 2.

107

again to be an astonishingly accurate predictor of natural phenomena. Concepts like *pi* and the *golden ratio* keep showing up in new and unexpected places.[2] Mathematics that were developed in one area of study are revealed as effective in others. Equations discovered by Newton that he used to describe the physics of falling objects were later used by him to describe the orbits of the planets. Mathematics that were developed as an exercise in pure theory to explore knots turn out to be applicable in understanding DNA replication and string theory.[3]

Not even mathematicians understand why this should be the case. In his renowned article "The Unreasonable Effectiveness of Mathematics," mathematician Eugene Wigner wrote, "The enormous usefulness of mathematics in the natural sciences is something bordering on the mysterious and . . . there is no explanation for it," adding that math's appropriateness for formulating the laws of physics was "a wonderful gift which we neither understand nor deserve."[4]

The fact that mathematics can describe the universe so well has even led some mathematicians to argue that the physical world *is* a "giant mathematical object."[5] So closely related are the mathematical descriptions of the universe and the universe itself, that even if the universe is not somehow mathematical in its essence, mathematics nevertheless remains as the best way to describe the universe, *whatever that is.*

It appears, then, that math might be able to describe the world with some measure of certainty. But can it *communicate* that world with certainty? Is mathematics even a language?

Math, like all human language, is built on some of the same deep-seated mental and cognitive systems that language relies on and that we use to process and interpret information about the world. But the fact remains that mathematics is not a language that anyone speaks as a native speaker.[6] Nor is it a language that embodies human experience, the way that our ordinary languages do. No one has ever had an experience of *pi* or of a five-dimensional sphere. Even were math a language, it would be a language separated from ordinary human experience.

For example, since the work of Einstein, it has been known that space-time is curved and that gravity is what causes the curvature of space-time.[7]

---

2. Livio, *Golden Ratio*, 5.

3. Livio, *Is God a Mathematician?*, 213–18.

4. Wigner, "Unreasonable Effectiveness of Mathematics," 2, 14.

5. Tegmark, *Our Mathematical Universe*, 246.

6. Livio, *Is God a Mathematician?*, 240.

7. We'll talk about this more in chapter 15.

The mathematics of physics can demonstrate this easily. But how do ordinary people understand space as *curved*? Indeed, how can emptiness be curved? The only way we can begin to understand this idea is by translating it into terms and images that we are familiar with.

As a kid, I was fascinated with a demonstration that the astrophysicist Carl Sagan used to explain this phenomenon of gravity. He dropped a heavy ball onto a stretched fabric surface marked with a grid pattern, such that the surface warped around the ball and the straight lines of the grid became curved. The distortion caused by the ball on this flat two-dimensional surface created a warp into the third dimension. When he rolled a smaller ball into this surface its path would be deflected by the warp in the fabric and the ball could even be made to orbit the larger mass for a time. As Sagan explained, "Gravity is only a pucker in the fabric of space moving objects encounter. Space is warped by mass into an additional physical dimension."[8]

It was a beautiful and effective demonstration, even if as a kid all I could think about was *Where can I get a surface like that to play with?* The demonstration took a mathematical reality and translated it into ordinary language and experience, but the fact of the matter is that in order to describe this reality, Sagan had to make something to represent nothing (the fabric of the surface for the fabric—a metaphor—of space), and he had to eliminate a whole dimension so that we could even picture it. We can picture curvature in two dimensions because we have the luxury of being able to comprehend a third dimension. But how on earth can we picture the curvature of the three dimensions in which we live into a fourth? Or worse yet, if the string theorists are right and we live in an eleven-dimensional universe, how do we even begin to comprehend that, let alone explain it in ordinary language? There always seems to be a disconnect between the mathematical reality and the ordinary language we use to communicate that reality.

Take, for example, the fact that many physicists posit that our universe is a *three-dimensional sphere*.[9] What is that? The *sphere* you're probably thinking of right now is what mathematicians call a *two-dimensional sphere*, that is, a *two-dimensional* plane that is curved into a spherical shape in the third dimension (Fig. 1). So, when scientists and mathematicians say *three-dimensional sphere*, what they mean is a three-dimensional space curved into the fourth dimension.[10]

---

8. National Geographic, "Experiment in Gravity."

9. Some, like noted physicists Alexi Starobinski and Yakov B. Zeldovich (and some noted non-physicists like Homer Simpson), have proposed a torus or doughnut-shaped universe.

10. Tegmark, *Our Mathematical Universe*, 32.

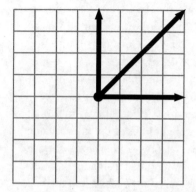 

Fig. 1. *A traveler on a finite plane departing from a specific point in any direction eventually comes to the boundary of the plane. When that plane is curved into a sphere, it remains finite in surface area, but becomes boundless. A traveler setting out from any point and traveling in a straight line will eventually return to the starting point.*

But what does a three-dimensional spherical space look like? How do we even picture such a thing so as to even describe it? This is really hard for us to imagine because we, being creatures who have evolved to make sense of three-dimensional space, can picture a two-dimensional space curved into three dimensions but we cannot envision what a three-dimensional space curved into the fourth dimension must look like. The only way we can do it is to reduce our three-dimensional universe, once again, to a two-dimensional surface or to invoke analogies using everyday objects. But when we do so, something is lost—something of that mathematical certainty is sacrificed for the ability to communicate it in everyday language.

For example, balloons are often invoked when trying to describe the expanding universe. The description of the universe as a balloon is helpful in communicating the idea, but it's imperfect because we tend to think of a balloon as a three-dimensional object rather than a two-dimensional plane curved into the third dimension. As a result, we will often misunderstand that in the balloon analogy our universe is only the *surface* of the expanding balloon. All three dimensions of our physical universe are represented by the two-dimensional surface of the balloon: just as the surface of the balloon expands and points on that surface move away from each other, so too does our three-dimensional space expand with all the constituent galaxies moving away from each other. There is no center to the universe, just as there is no center to the surface of a sphere. Everywhere is the center. And everywhere is moving away from everywhere else (Fig. 2).

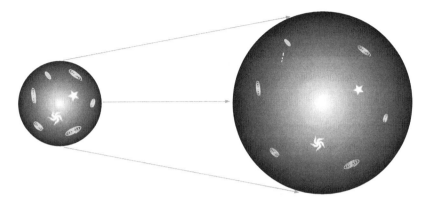

Fig. 2. *The universe is like the surface of an expanding balloon: every point recedes from every other point.*

But here's the thing, in order to make sense of the concept of an expanding universe, a number of things had to happen. First, right off the bat, a whole dimension needed to be sacrificed to accommodate the fact that we human beings cannot conceive of a fourth dimension. Then, the science had to be analogized to something in ordinary experience—the surface of an expanding balloon—that an individual could relate to. It's also worth noting that in order to illustrate it in a book, our two-dimensional sphere had to be reduced by yet another dimension to a one-dimensional sphere (the circles in Fig. 2). These reductions and analogies are unavoidable, especially if we want to communicate about these ideas in ordinary language. But ordinary language is far removed from mathematical language.

Take a look at what the expanding universe looks like in the language of mathematics:[11]

$$H^2 = \left(\frac{\dot{a}}{a}\right)^2 = \frac{8\pi G}{3}\rho - \frac{kc^2}{a^2} + \frac{\Lambda c^2}{3}$$

Even were I to render this in words, noting the Hubble parameter, Newton's gravitational constant, density, pressure, the cosmological constant, and the square of the speed of light, it would not make comprehension much easier. Mathematics, even when the symbols are turned into words, is hardly the clearest medium of communication for the average person.

11. Siegel, "Most Important Equation."

Take another example: the warping of space-time that is represented by Carl Sagan's stretchy fabric surface. Scientifically speaking, that phenomenon is understood in the following way:

> Space-time is a four-dimensional Hausdorff differential manifold on which a metric tensor is imposed that solves the Einstein field equations. That metric tensor gives rise to geodesics, and objects that are not experiencing any other force move along the geodesics described by that metric.[12]

Most people, including the author of this book, have little idea about what any of that means. There are people who can look at the above equations or read the above descriptions, understand the concepts, and know what they mean. For the rest of us, it's enough to know that the universe is like the surface of an expanding balloon and that space-time is like a stretchy fabric table with a bowling ball on it. Actually, to be fair, there are undoubtedly a great number of mathematicians and physicists who need to think of it in those ordinary ways too. We are not capable of understanding mathematical reality without recourse to symbolism and analogy.

And here's where the uncertainty creeps back in, because even mathematics is a *symbol*-based system. The variables and symbols stand in for concepts and phenomena in the real world. No one, not even the mathematician, is able to process the reality of the universe without using symbols. As a result, there are those who argue that this need to use symbols demonstrates a distance between the mathematics and the reality it describes, much as we saw earlier with the distance between the metaphor and the religious reality it sought to describe.

There are some mathematicians, noting mathematics' "unreasonable effectiveness" at describing the physical universe, who argue that mathematics has its own existence quite apart from human thought or effort. That is, they maintain that math is real, that there is a mathematical reality that pervades existence and that we are *discovering* math. Others argue that mathematics is simply a construct created by the human mind, and that we're *inventing* math.[13] But even those who understand mathematics as having a separate, real existence apart from us still have to use some human symbol like π to stand in for the ratio of a circle's diameter to its circumference. The need to appeal to symbols and representations is inescapable, whether that symbol is a Greek letter or a balloon with galaxies drawn on it.

---

12. Greene, interview with Stephen Colbert.

13. Livio, *Is God a Mathematician?*, 10–11.

Some scientists even argue that the scientific and mathematical descriptions themselves may simply be stand-ins, convenient descriptions that predict the right results but may not have anything to do with the reality they describe. This is particularly the case with quantum physics, where some scientists no longer believe there is a direct relationship between a description of a quantum phenomenon and the physical reality. The renown physicist Erwin Schrödinger said that a completely satisfactory representational model of the quantum reality was "not only practically inaccessible, but not even thinkable." He added, "To be precise, we can, of course, think it, but however we think it, it is wrong."[14] According to Schrödinger, our mathematical models may be good descriptors of the *results* of quantum mechanics, but may fail altogether to describe in reality what those mechanics are. Our mathematical models are consistent with the data we observe but may not tell us anything about the reality that yielded that data. It is as if we had an equation that predicted how fast and far you could go in a car but could only guess at what the engine was like under the hood. The ability to predict the results doesn't mean we've imagined the engine correctly—it just means we've found an equation that happens to work.

So, even if mathematics were the perfect descriptor of the universe, no matter how effective it might be in doing so, it remains a poor medium for communicating that reality to creatures whose conceptualizations are grounded in the concrete experience of a three-dimensional world. Perhaps mathematics is the language of God, capable of describing the realities of the universe. But when it comes to us, we human beings need to rely on another system. Fortunately, the same capacity of human intelligence that allowed us to come up with mathematics allowed another higher level abstract process: ordinary human language.[15]

The problem is that our ordinary, natural language is not always adequate to the task of describing the mathematical reality—because, as we will now see, our language has uncertainty written into its very fabric.

---

14. Martland, *Religion as Art*, 116.

15. Smith, *Evolution of Language*, 75.

Chapter 10

The Slipperiness of Language

The single biggest problem in communication
is the illusion that it has taken place.

— George Bernard Shaw

LANGUAGE IS A PARADOX. It possesses great power to reveal and, at the same time, to obscure the truth. In this chapter, we will explore a number of different obstacles to communication and reflect upon the ways in which meaning can get lost from one speaker to another. Sometimes meaning from one language to another is conveyed inaccurately. Sometimes we misinterpret context, or subtext, or intention. Sometimes we pick the wrong meaning when a statement is ambiguous. Sometimes we take a figurative statement literally. Sometimes our expectations about what we're hearing lead us astray, and sometimes we flat-out just hear a statement incorrectly.

In looking at all these obstacles to clear communication, we will come to see that the enterprise of language and communication is full of uncertainty. Inasmuch as language is the medium that we use to convey our experiences and understandings of the world to one another, uncertainty in our language means that we cannot avoid uncertainty in our experience of our world.

Translation

The most obvious kind of obstacle to communication is the barrier between languages. The differences between languages are not limited to the fact that different sounds (e.g., *səbaka, kalb, skylos*) and different symbols (e.g., собака, كلب, σκυλος) are used to represent the same concepts (e.g., *dog*)—though that is indeed a barrier. The bigger problem is that, in addition to different sounds and symbols used to represent concepts, the concepts do not always line up exactly from language to language.

Fig. 3. *A dog. Or* كلب. *Or* כלב. *Or* собака. *Or Hund.*
Or σκυλος. *Or chièn. Or canis. Or* ॶP. *Or* . . .

Sometimes there is a lexical gap: Language A has a term for Concept 1 that Language B does not. When this difference arises, you will often hear observations like, "It's very hard to translate this term" or "What a curious people the speakers of A must be to have a term for . . ." If the foreign term is useful, it will either be translated as a *calque* (e.g., *masterpiece* from Dutch *meesterstuk* or *gospel*[1] from Greek ἐυαγγέλιον *euangelion*) or will be brought into the language as a *borrowing* (e.g., *Schadenfreude, déjà vu,* and *perestroika*). In each case, a decision must be made either to translate the sense of the word, to simply borrow the word as is, or to coin a new term for what is perceived of as a new concept. You can almost imagine the process going something like this:

Alex: This piece of art is amazing. The Dutch would call it a
        meesterstuk.

Pat: What does that mean?

---

1. *Gospel* comes from the Anglo-Saxon *gōd spel,* meaning "good news," a calque of the Greek word *eu* + *angelion* meaning "good news."

Alex: Literally, it means a "masterpiece."

Pat: Hmmm. Masterpiece, eh?

Alex: Yeah, it really shows this artist's *Schadenfreude*.

Pat: *Schadenfreude*?

Alex: Yeah, it's a German word that means "joy in other people's troubles." It literally means "harm-joy."

Pat: Hmmm. *Schadenfreude*, eh?

In each case, a decision is made as to whether native words will suffice to communicate the idea or whether the foreign term should be adopted wholesale, adding a new nuanced concept into the target language. Generally, if there is a similar enough concept already in the language, the new concept will borrow or mimic that structure. In the above case, other terms like *masterful* and *master key* may have paved the way for a new English coinage *masterpiece*, whereas nothing remotely like *harm-joy* existed in English, so the word had to be adopted wholesale as *Schadenfreude*.

There is also the *false friend*, the word in the source language that looks like a word in the target language but has a rather different meaning. These are the bane of foreign language students everywhere who will stammer out a sentence in what they think is an accurate rendering of their thoughts, saying something like *Ich bin voll* in German for *I'm full* only to be horrified to discover that, rather than saying that they have had enough to eat, they have announced to everyone that they're pregnant. Sometimes this even happens within a language among dialects: I once brought the conversation in a room to a halt when I asked a Brit about the *suspenders* he was wearing, not realizing that *suspenders* in British English meant *garters* in American. (The British call suspenders *braces*.)

Then there is the difference in *semantic field*, the range of meanings a word can have. The most famously tragic example of this is the Japanese word *mokusatsu*, a word that may have cost hundreds of thousands of lives.

Toward the end of the Second World War, the Allied leaders issued a demand for the unconditional surrender of Japan and declared that refusal to do so would result in "prompt and utter destruction." When reporters asked the Japanese prime minister about the government's response to the ultimatum, he used the word *mokusatsu*, derived from the word meaning "silence" and may have intended it as a politician's "no comment." The range of possible meanings for the term, however, includes: "take no notice of; treat (anything) with silent contempt; ignore [by keeping silence]; remain in a wise and masterly inactivity." It was with one of these other senses—"treat with silent contempt"—that U.S. officials understood the statement, seeing it as yet more evidence of the empire's "fanatical Banzai and Kamikaze spirit."[2] The response was devastating: two atomic bombs dropped on Hiroshima and Nagasaki. Whether the fault was with the translator for not including the alternate senses, the U.S. officials for perhaps not wanting to hear that the translation was "ambiguous," or with the prime minister for choosing a purposefully vague politician's term is, at this point, irrelevant. There was misunderstanding between languages and a great many people died.

Of course, failures in communication are not limited to different language contexts. They happen with great regularity in same-language contexts too.

Mishearing

One of the most basic obstacles to communication is simply mishearing what has been said. This may be the function of a poor acoustic environment in which the statement cannot be heard perfectly, and the brain is forced to fill in the gaps. It may also be a function of the brain misparsing what has been heard. The brain's expectations of what its sensory input will be can shape what is actually perceived. A child who knows neither the words *pledge* nor *allegiance* might hear the first line of that pledge as *I led the pigeons to the flag . . .* because her brain is much more familiar with the words *led* and *pigeons* and interprets the sound input accordingly. In the same way, our brains can sometimes be primed for certain kinds of input, either in speaking or reading. For example, the college campus where I work is a very politically active campus and in our worship services there I have frequently heard my students attempt to lead the congregation in the *congressional prayer* rather than the *congregational prayer* indicated in the bulletin.

Mishearing spoken speech is often a source of humor and amusement. The party game "Telephone" is an example of this: someone whispers a phrase in the ear of their neighbor and that person turns and whispers it to the person on the other side, and on it goes. When the whispered phrase makes it back to the original person, it frequently bears little resemblance to the original.

And then there are the collections of *mondegreens*,[3] the humorous mis-hearings of a phrase such as *Gladly, the cross-eyed bear* instead

2. "Mokusatsu: One Word, Two Lessons," 95.

3. The term itself is a *mondegreen*, having been coined by American writer Sylvia Wright after mishearing a line in a poem. She wrote: "When I was a child, my mother used to read aloud to me from Percy's *Reliques*, and one of my favorite poems began,

of *Gladly the cross I'd bear; Olive, the other reindeer* instead of *all of the other reindeer*, and so on. Sometimes these mishearings result in a more subversive meaning than was originally intended, such as when members of the Rolling Stones thought that the Beatles had sung *I get high* rather than *I can't hide*. (This may have had more to do with the Rolling Stones' predilections than their hearing ability.)

From the outset, mishearings make clear that even in one's own language the communication enterprise is fraught with peril.

Meaning

What does a word *mean*? Understanding the meaning of a word is not as simple as we are led to believe by our dictionaries and vocabulary flashcards. What a word means often goes beyond those compact definitions.

Modern thinking on meaning started with the father of modern linguistics, Ferdinand de Saussure. Saussure understood the *meaning* of a word to be the "counterpart of a sound pattern"—that is, the concept or object that an arrangement of sounds points to.[4] Saussure noted that this relationship was purely arbitrary; there is no reason why the sounds [d] [ɔ] and [g] (or the letters *d-o-g*) should mean our four-legged canine companion, but they do. In English *dog* means that creature, and that creature means *dog*. And so, the *signifier* (the sound pattern) and the *signified* (the object it points to) are bound up in relationship together.

But what is the *signified* of a given *signifier*? The meaning of a word is not as fixed as dictionaries would have us believe. The task of defining a word precisely is an extremely difficult matter, involving complex properties and relationships.[5]

No dictionary can ever provide all the shades of meaning and subtleties of definition that human beings provide to a word. However, because all human beings possess an innate understanding of these subtleties, no dictionary *needs* to be perfectly precise. For example, people possess the ability to perceive that a word can have an abstract or concrete interpretation,

---

as I remember: *Ye Highlands and ye Lowlands / Oh, where hae ye been? / They hae slain the Earl o' Moray, / And Lady Mondegreen.*" The actual fourth line is "And laid him on the green." Wright explained the need for a new term: "The point about what I shall hereafter call *mondegreens,* since no one else has thought up a word for them, is that they are better than the original." Wright, "Death of Lady Mondegreen," 49.

4. Saussure and Harris, *Course in General Linguistics,* 134.

5. Chomsky, *Language and Problems of Knowledge,* 27.

sometimes both within the same sentence.[6] The following sentence illustrates this concept:

> Lisa wrote a sermon about forgiveness, which is eight pages long—sixteen if it's double-spaced.

In the first clause, *a sermon about forgiveness* is an abstraction—referring to the work or the collection of ideas, whereas in the second clause it is made concrete, describing an actual, physical printed sermon. This is a nuance that everyone understands but few would include in any definition of the word *sermon*. Even a simple word like *sermon* clearly means much more than a simple definition would suggest.

There are also those words that are hard to define because their definition seems to be, for lack of a better word, undefined. We all know what they mean, but sometimes struggle to come up with a nice, compact definition. For example, what does the word *game* mean? Did you think of board games first or sporting events? Competitions against someone else or against yourself? We all know what *game* means, but it is one of those words that isn't the easiest to pin down. After all, it's an extraordinary thing that one word could possibly encompass both a sporting contest (*baseball game*), a card puzzle (*game of solitaire*), and a training exercise for the military (*war game*). And then there are words like *obscenity*, which defy easy definition, even though everyone knows what they "mean." Supreme Court Justice Potter Stewart famously made this point when he noted that *obscenity* was difficult to define. "But," he continued, "I know it when I see it."[7]

Implied Meaning and Subtext

As I sit here writing this chapter, there is a young college student across the table. It's that time of year when colds are making their rounds and this young man is sniffling. Repeatedly. I reach into my bag and pull out one of those travel packets of tissues. "You need a Kleenex?" I ask him. "No, thanks. I'm good," he responds. He has misunderstood my statement; it wasn't a question. It was a face-saving declaration to him that he needed a Kleenex. He understood the *text* of my question but neither the *subtext* (your constant sniffling is driving me crazy) nor the *implied meaning* (please blow your nose).

This kind of miscommunication happens all the time, and the difference in the perception of a subtext between two speakers can make

6. Ibid., 29.
7. *Jacobellis v. Ohio*, 197.

the dynamics of conversation very different. Consider these two different exchanges:

1. Alex: What are you doing tonight?

   Pat: I'm going to the movies with my friend Chris.

   Alex: That sounds like fun.

2. Alex: What are you doing tonight?

   Pat: Nothing. Probably just sitting around and watching TV.

   Alex: (*Dejectedly*) Oh.

In the first example, there is little subtext other than Alex's interest in information. When the information is received, Alex feels satisfied. In the second example, Alex is disappointed with this exchange, even though, on its surface, the question is identical to the one in the first example. In theory, Alex should feel the same satisfaction felt in the first example.

However, as you've probably already figured out, the question "What are you doing tonight?" was not a request for information in the second case. It was a prompt for invitation and, unlike a neutral request for information, this question has a right answer. The question really means "Why don't we do something tonight if you're not busy?" and the exchange is expected to go like this:

Alex: What are you doing tonight?

Pat: Nothing. Why don't we go get some dinner and see a movie?

Alex: That would be great.

This is a satisfactory exchange from Alex's point of view because the implied meaning of the question has been addressed. Individuals get into trouble when they fail to perceive the hidden question behind the question, as did a former student of mine who upon being asked to "come over and see" the new apartment of a female friend, did exactly that: he went over, looked around, commented approvingly, and left. He did not, as his friend expected, hang out, stay for dinner, watch a movie, and then go home. He wound up in the doghouse for a few days—never understanding why.

Sometimes, the error lies in imagining there to be an implied meaning that *isn't* there. That too happens all the time, occasionally with dire consequences.

In the middle of the twelfth century, Thomas Becket, the archbishop of Canterbury, found himself in a feud with the reigning king of England, Henry II. After serving a brief time in exile abroad, Becket returned to England at the king's invitation. After his return, he excommunicated a bishop loyal to the king. Frustrated, Henry stalked the halls of his palace and lamented out loud. According to one tradition, he said, "Will no one rid me of this troublesome priest?"[8] Or, according to other historians, "What miserable drones and traitors have I nourished and brought up in my household, who let their lord be treated with such shameful contempt by a low-born cleric."[9] In either case, a group of knights understood the king's ranting to be giving them a command and immediately rode to Canterbury, where they brutally and very publicly murdered Becket in the cathedral. In this instance, the knights interpreted the king's statement as having an implied meaning: go kill the archbishop.

The question of subtext and implied meaning is present in another very common kind of speech: indirect speech. In an episode of *Curb Your Enthusiasm*, Larry David and his wife, Cheryl, have gone to an exclusive restaurant where the wait for a table is nearly an hour. Larry approaches the maître d':

Larry: I'm curious; about how long is the wait?

Maître d': I'm afraid it looks like forty-five minutes to an hour.

Larry: Forty-five minutes . . . no way to get in—

Maître d': No, we're very crowded this evening, sir.

Larry: Nothing else can be done?

Maître d': Nothing that *I* can think of, sir.

Larry: Things are done, right? I hear things are done.

Maître d': From time to time.

Larry: (*Surreptitiously sliding his palm across the host stand and dropping something in the maître d's hand*) Anything you can do . . .

8. Ibeji, "Becket, the Church and Henry II."
9. Caris, "10 Tiny Miscommunications."

> Maître d': Actually, I think we can accommodate you right now.
> Would you like to follow me?[10]

The entire content of this conversation is taking place on an indirect, implied level. Larry does not approach the maître d' and ask whether he can bribe him for a table. Nor does the maître d' ever directly suggest that he try.[11] The reasons for indirect speech are complex and frequently involve all manner of social implications, particularly the desire for all parties involved to save face.[12] What is clear is that there are not only utterances that depend on reading the subtext, there are also entire conversations that require careful attention to subtext and implied meaning. Misunderstanding can occur when one party or the other to a conversation is oblivious to the implied subtext or supplies subtext when none exists.

Having said that, misinterpreting statements is possible even when there is no subtext to parse.

Ambiguity

The issue raised in the *mokusatsu* incident we looked at earlier is by no means limited to foreign language translation. There is enough ambiguity in one's own language to cause trouble.

Words frequently have multiple meanings, which contribute to what is known as *lexical ambiguity*. This can happen with *homonyms*—words that look (and frequently sound) alike—and *homophones*—words that sound alike. Take the following example:

> The audition went terribly. I was in pain from having broken my
> arm the day before and, on top of that, I managed to annoy all
> the other actors. On account of the cast, I'll never get that part.

To what is *cast* referring? To the group of actors who put on a performance or the plaster that keeps an arm stiff so that it can heal from an injury? The fact that the two concepts have the same sound and spelling creates an ambiguity. Of course, that very feature of homophones is what makes them fodder for humor and puns.

Other kinds of lexical ambiguity can be created when one word has a number of different semantic properties, a number of different features

---

10. Gordon, "Affirmative Action."

11. It turns out in any event that Larry slipped the maître d' his wife's prescription for skin cream, rather than the $20 bill he had stashed in the same pocket.

12. Pinker, *Language, Cognition*, 304.

of meaning.[13] For example, the verb *to marry* means "enter into a marital union with," but it can also mean "to officiate at a wedding." I once used this ambiguity to great effect in a game of "Two Truths and Lie," in which you make three statements and the other players have to guess which one is false. So, I said, "I married my best friend from nursery school." Knowing that I was single, the other players were all set to declare that one the lie when suddenly one of them shouted, "Wait a minute! He's a *pastor!*" The jig was up.

Not all ambiguity is word-related; sometimes entire sentences are ambiguous. Take the sentence *I saw the dog with my binoculars*. Who has the binoculars—me or the dog? In general, it is far more likely that I have the binoculars than old Fido, but the sentence does not make that clear. Is the prepositional phrase *with my binoculars* modifying the verb phrase *I saw* or the noun phrase *the dog*?

This kind of ambiguity is known as *structural ambiguity* and is caused by the way our languages are structured and by the way that our brains interpret those structures. As with other kinds of ambiguity, structural ambiguity is frequently a source of humor, usually at the expense of the authors of church bulletins:

- The associate minister unveiled the church's new tithing campaign slogan last Sunday: "I Upped My Pledge—Up Yours."
- Eight new choir robes are currently needed, due to the addition of several new members and to the deterioration of some older ones.
- Wednesday, the Ladies Literary Society will meet. Mrs. Johnson will sing "Put Me in My Little Bed" accompanied by the pastor.
- The ladies of the church have cast off clothing of every kind and they may be seen in the church basement on Friday.
- For those of you who have children and don't know it, we have a nursery downstairs.
- The Rev. Merriwether spoke briefly, much to the delight of the audience.[14]

Sometimes ambiguity results not merely in humorous misinterpretation, but in genuine confusion. These "garden path" sentences (so called because they "lead you up the garden path," i.e., *mislead* you) are the result of words whose place in the structure is ambiguous. The effect is momentary

13. Fromkin and Rodman, *Introduction to Language*, 170.
14. Robinson, "Humorous Quotations."

confusion—*Wait, what did I just read?*—and a need to reread the sentence. Here are a few:

> The horse raced past the barn fell.
>
> The man who hunts ducks out on weekends.
>
> Cotton clothing is made from is grown in Egypt.
>
> Fat people eat accumulates.
>
> The prime number few.
>
> The old man the boat.[15]

Many of these ambiguities would be eliminated in speech where the rhythms and intonations of talking would make the meaning clearer ("The man who *hunts* ducks out on *weekends.*" "The *prime* number few.") However, these examples serve as a reminder that the written word, which many of us feel is somehow more stable than the spoken, can contribute just as much confusion.

It's why those who really care about the use of written language are sometimes such sticklers for punctuation, as in the common Internet joke that pits *Let's eat grandma!* against *Let's eat, grandma!*, noting: "Punctuation saves lives!" Others will point out that punctuation can only go so far; clarity in writing requires careful attention to sentence structure and an awareness of the ways that the various elements of the structure might be interpreted by a reader.

Structural ambiguity can also be resolved by a better understanding of context. Note how the meaning of an ambiguous sentence changes depending on the context:

a. (Curious to see how well my new binoculars worked, I looked up on the hillside and) I saw the dog with my binoculars.

b. (I was looking all over for my binoculars when I looked out onto the lawn and) I saw the dog with my binoculars.

It is often the case that context is not only helpful in clarifying meaning, it's essential.

Context

Consider the following statements:

15. Pinker, *Sense of Style*, 119.

I married my cousin.

I was boxing all night.

Lisa said that Phil knocked her up.

Jerry was really pissed last night.

Every once in a while I find a random goldfish in the sheets.

Did you manage to find helium for your shark?

I'm sure I can stash your wallet somewhere in my taco if need be.

Some of these might seem straightforward, others bizarre. But how does your understanding of these sentences change with some context provided?

I married my cousin.

(spoken by a pastor about a ceremony he performed)

I was boxing all night.

(said by the owner of a packaging company)

Lisa said that Phil knocked her up.

(said by a someone from Britain, where *knock up* means "to wake up by knocking on someone's door")

Jerry was really pissed last night.

(spoken by a Brit, for whom *pissed* means "drunk")[16]

Every once in a while, I find a random goldfish in the sheets.

(said by someone discussing how he liked to eat crackers in bed)

Did you manage to find helium for your shark?

(spoken to someone with an inflatable shark balloon)

I'm sure I can stash your wallet somewhere in my taco if need be.

(said by someone wearing a taco costume for Halloween to someone in a costume without pockets)

In each case, once some context was provided, the meaning of the sentence likely changed, in some cases even *gaining* meaning where before it had seemed nonsensical.

In his book *Is That a Fish in Your Ear?: Translation and the Meaning of Everything*, translator David Bellos notes that "what an utterance means to

16. These last two support George Bernard Shaw's statement that "The United States and Great Britain are two countries separated by a common language."

its utterer and to the addressee of the utterance does not depend exclusively on the meaning of the words uttered."[17] An understanding of context and the identities and relationships between speakers is essential. The linguistic meaning of the words uttered is not enough.

This is perhaps nowhere more needed than when it comes to the interpretation of biblical texts. In courses I have taught that involve biblical interpretation, I am usually repetitive to the point of obnoxious on this point: context matters. None of the texts of holy scripture arose in a vacuum or descended from the sky pre-chiseled on stone tablets. They arose in a specific place, at a specific time, in a specific historical context— a context removed from our own by at least two thousand years and thousands of miles. Yet, the tendency to read the scriptures as if they had been written by a white, English-speaking, suburban American Methodist is extremely commonplace.

It makes me wonder whether a thousand years from now interpreters will make the same attempt to understand our culture without any attempt to understand the context. Imagine for example what statements like *Dave Roberts stole home* and *Elvis is King* would mean to people who didn't understand baseball or know that the United States was a republic. And yet we routinely attempt to interpret and apply biblical texts without truly understanding what an *abomination* is, for example, or what the biblical rules of purity really are.[18]

The question to ask in interpreting biblical texts is "What did this mean to the people who wrote it and first read it?" Once there has been an appropriate inquiry into the context that helps us to answer that question, *then* we can ask, "Given that, what does it have to say to *us*?" But without understanding the original context and the meaning within that context, we will never be able to truly understand how to translate that meaning into our context and situation. Of course, the question of context goes far beyond the interpretation of ancient religious texts. It is essential to understanding much of what is spoken and written.

---

17. Bellos, *Is That a Fish*, 74.

18. Few people know that *abomination* translates the Hebrew word תּוֹעֵבָה *tō'evah*, which refers to improper worship or a detestable cultic practice and not a *moral* wrong (perhaps the sound of the English word is partially to blame). In the same way, contemporary Christians frequently misunderstand Jewish rules of ritual purity that governed access to sacred precincts to be statements of *moral* purity.

Figurative Meaning

Understanding otherwise straightforward language is not complicated only by contextual misunderstandings. A significant problem in communication is that sometimes words just simply fail to mean what they mean. Sometimes the word we encounter is being used with a figurative meaning, albeit one grounded in the concrete physical meaning of a word (for example, my use of *grounded* and *concrete* to describe the meaning of a word). We have seen that some words have multiple meanings, but sometimes a word has both a literal and a non-literal or *metaphorical* meaning. Take, for example, the sentence *Elsie is a cow*.

There are two possible interpretations here. First, I could be talking about an actual cow named Elsie, such as the mascot for the Borden Dairy Company. On the other hand, I could be saying something very disparaging about a woman named Elsie. The difference hangs on whether I am using the word *cow* in its *literal* or *metaphorical* sense. All kinds of utterances rely on words that use a *figurative meaning* beyond the literal meaning:

- Simile, a comparison using like or as: "Phil is attracted to risky behavior *like a moth to a flame.*"

- Metaphor, the use of a word in a non-literal sense to make a comparison: "To her I was an *open book*, but to me she was a *locked vault.*"

- Metonymy, a kind of metaphor where something closely related is used for the thing actually meant: "*The crown* demands loyalty of all its subjects."

- Synecdoche, the use of a part to signify the whole: "Jamilah is an important *voice* in this struggle."

- Personification, the attribution of human qualities to inanimate or non-human objects: "The mountains *rule* over the plains below."

- Apostrophe, direct address to a person or thing not literally listening: "*Time,* slow down; you move too fast."

These figurative senses are also frequently found in *idioms*, those expressions that cannot be understood using the meaning of their separate words and have a separate meaning of their own: *an eight-hundred-pound gorilla, a hot potato, an arm and a leg, hit the nail on the head, not playing with a full deck*. Bellos notes that all these various figures of speech are just evidence of the "irresistible desire of words to mean something else."[19]

---

19. Bellos, *Is That a Fish*, 88.

The ambiguity due to these figures of speech is even more complex than the lexical or structural ambiguities we've looked at. Language is a far slipperier thing than most of us realize. A lot of that slipperiness comes from these figures of speech and those words that embody that "irresistible desire" to mean something else. These figures of speech add a great deal of expressiveness to language, but they also add a fair amount of uncertainty.

Chief among these uncertainty-causing figures of speech is the metaphor and, as we're about to see, in language metaphors are *everywhere*.

Chapter 11

Language and Metaphor

ONE OF THE BEST episodes of the television series *Star Trek: The Next Generation* is an episode in which the starship *Enterprise* is sent to negotiate with an enigmatic race known as the Tamarians, with whom all prior attempts to communicate have failed. When the *Enterprise's* attempt at communication also fails, the Tamarians, in a last-ditch effort to build a relationship, transport their Captain Dathon and *Enterprise* Captain Picard to the surface of the planet below. There the two are confronted by a strange, nearly invisible beast against whom they must defend themselves. Throughout their time together, the Tamarian captain keeps saying phrases over and over, like "Darmok and Jalad at Tanagra," that Picard cannot understand. Eventually, it becomes clear to Picard that Dathon is attempting to communicate something through these odd turns of phrase. He comes to learn that in Tamarian folklore, Darmok and Jalad were two hunters who met on the island of Tanagra, where they fought and defeated a beast and became friends. Picard realizes that their situation and that of Darmok and Jalad are meant to be the same; the alien captain's intent is to build relationship through mutual struggle. The strategy takes a tragic turn when Dathon succumbs to wounds sustained fighting the beast.

Throughout the episode, both Picard and the crew of the *Enterprise* above, each trying to resolve this crisis, describe the alien mode of communication as being "through metaphor." In the end, when Captain Picard is able to communicate with the alien vessel using the phrases he has learned from Dathon, it is a triumph for him and for both species, now on friendly terms. As the alien ship is about to depart, the officer in command says, "Picard and Dathon at El-Adrel," indicating that the struggle here will live on as an example in the future. The episode is one of the most poignant and meaningful of the entire series and has long been a fan favorite.

There's just one problem: the aliens aren't communicating through metaphor. They're communicating through *allusion*. There's actually not a single metaphor spoken by the aliens throughout the entire episode. Ironically, the human speakers use them throughout:

- "Is there any *way* to *get through to* them?"
- "*Close the channel*, Mister Worf."
- I'm *betting* they're not going *to push it that far*.
- I'll *take that course* when it's the last one left.
- The *apparent* emotional dynamic *does seem to support* that assumption.
- The name *clearly carries a meaning* for them.
- We will have *tipped our hand* to the Tamarians.
- *Open a channel* to the Tamarian ship.
- They have *closed the channel*.
- Now *the door is open* between our peoples.

It is we humans who communicate through metaphor. And we do it all the time.

A metaphor is a figure of speech in which a word or phrase literally denoting one kind of object or idea is used in place of another to suggest a likeness or analogy between them.[1] The term itself is a kind of metaphor, coming from the Greek μεταφερειν *meta* + *pherein*, meaning "to carry beyond" or, as the Romans would have put it, *trans-fer*. As linguistic phenomena go, metaphors are extraordinarily common.

Metaphors abound in ordinary speech and such ordinary speech might be near impossible without them. Metaphors are drawn from a number of different arenas of ordinary experience:

Animals	That joke *flew right over his head.* That guy was *dogging* me with questions all day. I can't trust Anna; she's a real *snake*.
Parts of the body:	The *head* of our organization is a wealthy man. Have you met Alexander? He's my *right hand*. I'm a *shoulder* for you to cry on. No, he's not an *asshole*; he's just a *dick*.

---

1. Gove, ed., *Webster's Third New International Dictionary*, 1420. I was really tempted to write, "Webster's dictionary defines 'metaphor' as . . . ," but that would not have been a metaphor; that would've been a cliché.

Nautical terms:	We need to *try a different tack* with our business strategy.
	Are you *on board* with our program?
	She and I *hit some rough seas* but we're doing okay now.
	We're getting ready to *launch* our new product *line*.
People:	I'm not going to be your *whipping boy* anymore!
	She thought he was her *knight in shining armor*, but he turned out to be the *court jester*.
Objects:	This proposal is the *cornerstone* of our entire marketing plan.
	Be careful, or you'll induce a *chain reaction* that could lead to a *domino* effect.
Sports:	Wow, Javier, you really hit a *home run* with that sales *pitch*.
	It didn't go well with Mary; I was hoping to *get to first base* but I just *struck out*.
	We were all ready to begin the new initiative, but instead we just had a *false start*.
Military/war:	The abortion debate is *ground zero* of this year's election contest.
	I had to do an *about-face* when I realized I was wrong.
	Beware of Rachel; she's a real *loose cannon*.
Religion:	Have you tried this cheesecake? It's *heaven*.
	My 8:30 econ class is *hell*.
Science/nature:	You don't want to be a part of that committee, it's a *black hole* for good ideas.
	She's really become a *star* in our organization.
	You're my *sunshine*, my only *sunshine*.

Some of these metaphors have become so common as to have become clichés. But they all have the same thing in common: they are all the application of a word with a literal meaning in a figurative way.

If we say that someone's business presentation was a *home run*, we are not suggesting that somehow, as part of that presentation, the presenter took bat to ball and hit it out of a ballpark. If we say the presentation did not go well and so the team had to *take a different tack*, we are not suggesting that they were aboard a sailing ship and adjusted the sails to go in a different direction. If we were to claim that it was *hell* to sit through, no one is claiming literal eternal fiery torment. If one of the presentation reviewers suggested that the presenters had been *cherry picking*, we would not expect to see a basket of cherries on the table. Unless, of course, we were watching a Zucker, Abrahams, and Zucker movie like *Airplane!* or *The Naked Gun*, where much of the humor comes from taking such ordinary metaphors literally:[2]

2. IMDb, "Airplane! (1980) – Quotes."

> McCroskey: Johnny, what can you make out of this? *(Hands him the weather briefing)*
>
> Johnny: This? Why, I can make a hat or a brooch or a pterodactyl . . .
>
> Rex Kramer: Steve, I want every light you can get poured onto that field.
>
> McCroskey: Bein' done right now.
>
> *(On the runway, a truck dumps a full load of lamps onto the ground)*

Taking metaphors literally is also the source of the humor for the character Drax the Destroyer in the film *Guardians of the Galaxy:*[3]

> Rocket: *(About Drax)* His people are completely literal. Metaphors go over his head.
>
> Drax: *Nothing* goes over my head . . . ! My reflexes are too fast; I would catch it.

When we use a metaphor, we do not use it arbitrarily. We do not, for example, say, "I want every light you can get *dropped* onto that field" or "*stacked* onto that field." There is something about the act of shining a lot of light onto an object that evokes an image of pouring water but does not evoke an image of stacking things. In order for metaphors to be successful, they have to go beyond the literal meaning of the word without making the literal sense irrelevant. In a typical metaphorical statement, a speaker "builds on" the relevant meaning of the literal term by presenting the literal term as a model of the subject, drawing out the resemblances between the model and the subject. It is these *resemblances* that are at the heart of using a metaphor.[4] There is a resemblance between pouring water into a basin and shining copious amounts of light onto an airfield that those who use the metaphor seek to highlight.

Despite the list of common metaphors above, our ordinary metaphors don't simply take the form of clichés and turns of phrase. Our language is full of metaphorical constructions. Here are some taken from the front page of the *Washington Post* that I have in front of me today:

---

3. IMDb, "Guardian of the Galaxy (2014) – Quotes."
4. Alston, *Divine Nature*, 23.

Obama *weighing* authority on guns. In a response to the latest
mass shooting during his presidency, President Obama is seriously considering *circumventing* Congress with his executive
authority and imposing new *background* requirements for buy-
ers who purchase weapons from *high-volume* gun dealers. . . .[5]

A *vacuum* at the top for the House GOP. McCarthy *drops* bid for
Speaker. Move *stuns* caucus; contest now *wide-open*. The infa-
mously *fractious House* Republican Conference *sank deeper into
chaos* Thursday after Majority Leader Kevin McCarthy abruptly
withdrew his bid to replace John A. Boehner as speaker, a *stunning move* that *left* the *party scrambling* to find a new leader and
deeply uncertain about how to effectively manage the House . . .[6]

The *Rise and Fall* of a Nominee. "I'm not the one": How Mc-
Carthy became a bystander on his big day. . . .[7]

With *echoes* of the presidential *race*, an angry *insurgency takes
no prisoners*. Less than a year after a *sweeping* electoral *triumph*,
Republicans are on the *verge* of ceasing to function as a national
political party . . .[8]

And that's just from above the fold. Metaphors are inescapable at the level of
ordinary speech, especially when abstract ideas are concerned.

In his book *The Stuff of Thought*, renowned linguist and cognitive
scientist Steven Pinker demonstrates the ubiquity of metaphor by de-
constructing the opening sentence of the United States Declaration of
Independence. The demonstration reveals just how much of our abstract
political thought is rendered in metaphors grounded in the concrete experience of life. Here is that sentence in its entirety with all the metaphorical
constructions in italics:

When in the *Course* of human events it becomes necessary for
one people to *dissolve* the *political bands* which have *connected*
them with another and to assume among *the powers of the earth*,
the *separate* and equal *station* to which the Laws of Nature and
of Nature's God entitle them, a decent respect to the opinions

---

5. Eilperin, "Obama Weighing Authority."
6. Debonis et al., "Vacuum at the Top."
7. Debonis et al., "'I'm Not the One.'"
8. Tumulty, "With Echoes."

of mankind requires that they should *declare* the causes which *impel* them to the separation. [9]

We see right away a number of metaphors and metaphorical concepts found in that one sentence: A SEQUENCE OF EVENTS IS MOTION ALONG A PATHWAY, ALLIANCES ARE BONDS, A SOVEREIGN STATE IS A SOURCE OF PHYSICAL FORCE, UNDERSTANDING IS SEEING (*declare*, from the Latin "to make clear"), and CAUSES OF BEHAVIOR ARE FORCES.[10] Pinker's exercise makes it clear how abstract political ideas are rendered in terms borrowed from concrete, physical experience: courses, loosened bonds, and vision.

But the presence of metaphor in language goes even deeper than the turns of phrase and images we can spot easily. Beyond the metaphors that we know we're making, and the ordinary turns of phrase we're accustomed to, there are metaphors hidden in our language.

Sometimes these hidden metaphors take the form of clichés and idioms whose meaning we understand, although the memory of the original referent has been lost. Referring to a movie as a *blockbuster* is applying to the smashing success of that film the metaphor of a World War II high-yield bomb that literally busted (i.e., destroyed) city blocks. Referring to the leader of a criminal enterprise as a *kingpin* is applying to that individual the metaphor of the tallest pin in a game of ninepins bowling. To refer to a criminal informant as a *stool pigeon* is to apply to that person a metaphor of the tame birds, often tied to frames (called "stools"), that were used to lure (and thus betray) their fellow birds.[11] But not all our hidden metaphors are hidden in clichés and idioms. Some of them are hidden in plain sight.

Returning to the first line of the Declaration of Independence, Pinker helps us to find many more metaphors than first meet the eye:

> When *in* the *Course* of human *events it* becomes *necessary for* one people to *dissolve* the *political bands* which have *connected* them with another and to *assume among* the *powers of the earth*, the *separate* and equal *station* to which the *Laws of Nature* and of Nature's God *entitle* them, a *decent respect* to the opinions of *mankind requires* that they should *declare* the causes which *impel* them *to* the *separation*.[12]

The metaphors in this one sentence include: TIME IS SPACE, A SEQUENCE OF EVENTS IS MOTION ALONG A PATHWAY, A SITUATION IS A THING, NEED

9. Pinker, *Stuff of Thought*, 235–36.
10. Ibid.
11. Partridge et al., *Concise Dictionary of Slang*, 41, 437.
12. Pinker, *Stuff of Thought*, 236–37.

IS AN UNYIELDING FORCE, BENEFIT IS DIRECTION TOWARD, ALLIANCES ARE BONDS, AFFILIATION IS PROXIMITY, A SOVEREIGN STATE IS A SOURCE OF PHYSICAL FORCE, STATUS IS LOCATION, A MORAL OBLIGATION IS A RULE, ORIGIN IS MOTION AWAY FROM, APPROPRIATE IS FITTING, UNDERSTANDING IS SEEING, HUMANITY IS A FAMILY GROUP, CAUSES OF BEHAVIOR ARE FORCES, and INTENTION IS MOTION TOWARD A GOAL.[13]

Now, granted, while some of these metaphors might have occurred to us with ordinary reflection on the text (ALLIANCES ARE BONDS, for example), most of them would have remained opaque to us without the use of a good dictionary of word origins. But at the time they were coined or borrowed they were alive with metaphoric power.

Every language has to address the problem of identifying ways to refer to new concepts or objects that enter the consciousness of the language. Some languages opt for a fairly literal-descriptive approach. In the Cherokee language, for instance, there are very few nouns as we would call them. Instead, most words for things are really small mini-sentences. The word for alligator is *tsu-la-s-gi*, which literally means "It has four feet." *Tsu-la-s-gi* is also the word for an iron pot (the kettle kind with feet).

Not every language is so descriptive or attempts to deconstruct every object. Most languages resort to metaphor for new coinages, something that even a language like Cherokee does as well. In attempting to identify a new idea to a community, one might come up with a novel term altogether, but that would not necessarily convey the idea without additional illustration and example. Coining new words out of the blue isn't something we're good at, and in any event the purpose of language is to be *understood*. Rather than create a word out of thin air, it's much better to use an old word in a metaphorical way. In this way, the wordsmith evokes in the mind of the listener an idea similar to the original concept.[14] That is, in trying to describe a movie that had unbelievable success, I could coin the word *flamboolie* and then try to explain it, or I could just use the term for something really explosive—*blockbuster*—and evoke the image of explosiveness in my listener's mind. Using metaphors is generally more common, because it's generally more successful at communicating ideas than inventing entirely new words.

Without a literal description for every object, metaphor becomes the most productive method for new coinages, especially for abstract concepts that are hard to describe literally. Sometimes the metaphors invoked for this task are *too* successful, entrenching themselves so deeply in the language that we no longer even recognize them as metaphors. In English, many of

13. Ibid.
14. Ibid., 237.

those metaphors used in coinages have become fossilized: we no longer see their metaphorical roots. This process happens with native English words—for example, we have forgotten that *for* means "forward"—but is especially common with words borrowed from Latin or Greek (as with *declare*, "to make clear," and *political*, "belonging to a city"). Linguist Guy Deutscher, using a metaphor of his own, refers to these accumulated fossilized metaphors as having been "deposited, layer after layer . . . as a reef of dead metaphors."[15] Deutscher even provides a sample sentence full of such dead metaphors:

> Sarah was thrilled to discover that the assessment board had decided to make her barmy rival redundant, after she suggested that he had made sarcastic insinuations about his employers.[16]

As with the first line of the Declaration of Independence, there are many metaphors in this sentence that can only be spotted by someone with a good etymological dictionary. But careful analysis reveals just how full of metaphors even this simple sentence is:

> Sarah was *thrilled* ("pierced") to *discover* ("uncover") that the *assessment* ("sitting by") *board* ("plank") had *decided* ("cut off") to make her *barmy* ("full of froth") *rival* ("person from the river") *redundant* ("overflowing"), after she *suggested* ("carried under") that he had made *sarcastic* ("flesh-tearing") *insinuations* ("twistings") about his *employers* ("those who fold").

Each of the metaphors found in the sentence appears quite ordinary to us now and we don't think of them as metaphorical at all. But each one suggests a time when the imagery must have been ripe and powerful—"I was *pierced* to hear . . ."; "His comments were so *flesh-tearing* . . ."; "That process seems really *overflowing* . . . ."—and only became unremarkable with time and use.

This is not a phenomenon limited to English. It happens in all languages, though it may be harder to spot in English because so many of our metaphors were borrowed from French, Latin, and Greek and their metaphorical roots are less transparent. (Indeed, the only Anglo-Saxon metaphors in the above example sentence are *thrilled* and *board*.) But resorting to metaphors for abstractions is a phenomenon across languages and is frequently done in similar ways. In Latin, the verb *decidere* meant "to cut down" and was used for the concept of making decisions—the sense with which it was borrowed into English. But take a look at the list below. Other languages have made the same metaphorical leap in their words for the concept of *deciding*:

15. Deutscher, *Unfolding of Language*, 118.
16. Ibid., 124.

- German: *ent-scheiden*, from *scheiden*, "to separate"
- Ancient Greek: διαιρεω, *diaireō*, lit. "to take one from another, cleave in twain"
- Swahili: *–kata shauri*, lit. "cut matter"
- Basque: *erbaki*, lit. "to make (someone) cut"
- Indonesian: *memutuskan*, from *putus* "severed"
- Akkadian: *parāsum*, "cut"
- Biblical Hebrew: גָּזַר *gazar*, "cut"[17]

Hidden metaphors are not found only in languages like English that have borrowed all their concepts from other languages. Even in languages that are much more "home grown," metaphors, living and dead, abound. In a way, the abundance of these metaphors is evidence of how useful they have been.

When our ancestors needed to describe new, abstract thoughts, they had to turn to metaphors from the concrete, physical world. They used metaphors that would have been powerful and insightful when first coined (like *sarcastic/flesh-tearing* above), but which we hear today as simply the word for a given object or concept. Today we would have a hard time describing sarcasm without resorting to the word *sarcastic,* but at one point someone struggled to explain that particular form of harsh irony and came up with the metaphor *sarcastic/flesh-tearing,* which fit the bill nicely. So nicely, in fact, that we no longer even realize that today's fossilized metaphor had once been a living thing.

This process of fossilizing the metaphor, however, shows just how useful the metaphor was. Metaphor is the chief mechanism through which we can describe and even grasp abstraction, and frequently our *only* choice when it comes to conveying abstract ideas. If we had not been able to use a physical metaphor like *tough* to describe a conceptual idea like *tough legislation,* what other alternative would there be? As Deutscher notes, we could say that the legislation was *inflexible, strict, repressive, oppressive, firm, stern, stringent, unyielding, unbending, harsh,* and so on. But in none of these cases would we have avoided a metaphor. Every single term derives from an experience of the material world. He concludes, "The truth of the matter is that we simply have no choice but to use concrete-to-abstract metaphors."[18]

Some might argue that a word like *sarcastic* is hardly a metaphor because its literal meaning is only available to a group with specialized knowledge. To them, words like *insist* (Latin, "stand upon"), *declare* (Latin, "make clear"),

---

17. Ibid., 126.
18. Ibid., 127.

and *deduce* (Latin, "draw out") do not bear on a discussion of metaphors because they were literal terms as soon as they entered into English. However, linguist Elizabeth Closs Traugott argues that although these metaphors might appear to have been so long dead so as to be understood to be literal, they still reveal something important about the human process of conceptualization. They show that English speakers, in coming up with phrases like *put before you, point out,* and *put down,* are using the same conceptual system that the ancients used when they first came up with *present* ("to be before"), *indicate* ("point toward"), and *submit* ("put under").[19]

That is, even the dead Latin metaphors reveal a way of metaphorically interpreting the world, a scheme of conceptualization that we still see in the English metaphors we use today. Just as different languages use metaphors for *cutting* to describe "deciding," the fossilized metaphors in our language reveal a consistent attempt to use particular metaphorical frameworks and templates as ways of conveying meaning.[20]

Furthermore, that metaphors should have become fossilized does not change the fact that language as a whole is alive with metaphor; it simply demonstrates that metaphor is the raw material of linguistic creativity. Indeed, the fossilized metaphors, much like the fossilized remains of the dinosaurs, make it clear that there was once a living entity here, and one that filled a vital linguistic (or ecological) niche.

Just as plants and animals flourish in lands where the soil has been enriched by generations of plants and creatures living and dying, so too it is with language. The living metaphors that inhabit the terrain of our language today are themselves nourished by the rich soil that lies beneath, a soil made fertile by all the metaphors living and dead that have come before. Language is, and has always been, alive with metaphor. The fossil record makes that clear.

Living by Metaphor

Metaphors do far more than provide illustrative images for objects, ideas, and actions. They frame the way we conceive of these objects, ideas, and actions. In their classic work on metaphors, *Metaphors We Live By*, George Lakoff and Mark Johnson explore just how deeply our language—and our thinking—is shaped by metaphor. The metaphors they describe are not the usual surface variety (like *war is hell* and *life is a highway*), but instead are the unspoken metaphors that define entire systems of thought.

19. Traugott, "'Conventional' and 'Dead' Metaphors," 41.
20. Ibid., 18–19.

In the opening pages of their book, Lakoff and Johnson provide a compelling example of these conceptual metaphors and how those concepts can structure our understanding of an everyday activity. To illustrate this, they provide us with the concept ARGUMENT and the conceptual metaphor that defines it, ARGUMENT IS WAR:

- Your claims are *indefensible.*
- He *attacked every weak point* in my argument.
- His criticisms were *right on target.*
- I *demolished* his argument.
- I've never *won* an argument with him.
- You disagree? Okay, *shoot!*
- If you use that *strategy,* he'll *wipe you out.*
- He *shot down* all of my arguments.[21]

Lakoff and Johnson point out that metaphors aren't just a way of *talking* about arguments, they frame the way we *think about* arguments. Indeed, for English speakers, arguments are thought of as a kind of war that we can win or lose, and in which we attack positions and defend our own. They conclude: "Many of the things we *do* in arguing are partially structured by the concept of war."[22]

This conceptual metaphor becomes a "metaphor we live by" because it structures the actions we perform when we argue. Such a metaphor shapes how we prepare for, participate in, and suffer the consequences of an argument. We might assume such a way of viewing an argument to be natural, but Lakoff and Johnson encourage us to imagine a culture where arguments are not viewed through the metaphorical lens of warfare, and instead are viewed in a context in which no one wins or loses, where ground is neither gained nor lost. For example, a culture that viewed an argument through the lens of a dance, where the object were to "perform in a balanced and aesthetically pleasing way," would view arguments differently, carry them out differently, and talk about them differently.

In addition, metaphors are systematic in the way they illuminate concepts. The example of ARGUMENT IS WAR is not the only example of the way that metaphors establish a systematic way of engaging a topic. TIME IS MONEY is another:

---

21. Lakoff and Johnson, *Metaphors We Live By*, 4.
22. Ibid.

- You're *wasting* my time.

- This gadget will *save* you hours.

- I don't *have* the time to give you.

- How do you *spend* your time these days?

- That flat tire *cost* me an hour.

- I've *invested* a lot of time in her.

- I don't *have* enough time to *spare* for that.

- You're *running out of* time.

- You need to *budget* your time.

- Is that *worth* your while?

- He's living on *borrowed* time.

- I *lost* a lot of time when I got sick.

- *Thank you for* your time.[23]

The metaphor TIME IS MONEY isn't just expansive, it's productive as well. You can use almost any concept borrowed from our everyday experience with money to conceptualize time. It's hard to think of a money-related concept that you *couldn't* use with time. Thus, TIME IS MONEY is not just a metaphor, it's a metaphorical *system* that is capable of producing many different metaphors.

Metaphors are not just convenient or arbitrary illustrations of ideas and objects. They shape the very way we experience these ideas and objects. They become essential in framing not just given concepts but often entire worldviews and ideologies. As linguist and translator James Underhill puts it: "Language itself cannot escape metaphor. So how can we hope to escape it?"[24]

The Inescapable Symbols

Language is more than a collection of some obvious metaphors and a few not-so-obvious dead metaphors; language itself is metaphorical, both in content and nature. Metaphors make up a surprisingly large portion of language.

23. Ibid., 7–8.
24. Underhill, *Creating Worldviews*, 91.

Should we be surprised by this? After all, metaphors are symbols and language is an inherently symbolic enterprise, using symbols of sound to represent objects and concepts in the world.

The metaphorical nature of language has been noted by linguists who study language origins. Historically, such linguists focused on the development of individual languages or on child language acquisition. Today, many current researchers are focusing on the question of where language as a whole came from. We can imagine how early humans might have learned to associate a sound-symbol with an object ("Tree!"), but how did they develop the ability to say things like, "Look out, Grog, there appears to have been a saber-toothed tiger behind that tree!" The research suggests that the development of language itself may be due to the same mechanism that produces metaphors: analogy.

Analogy is, after all, at the root of how metaphors are made: the application of a literal term to a non-literal occurrence based on a sense of similarity. Language development also uses analogy by perceived similarity, although the similarity in such situations has less to do with similarities between any given words and more to do with a recognition of a similarity in *function*.[25] Let's explore what that means.

Let's imagine that as a language learner, I encounter the following sentences: *The girl reads a book*, *Nathan reads a book*, and *Isabella rides a bicycle*. From these sentences, I learn that a grammatical sentence can be made by the formula NOUN + (VERB + /s/) + NOUN. With this knowledge, I can produce sentences like *Nathan rides a bicycle*, *The girl rides a bicycle*, and *Isabella reads a book*. I have never heard these sentences, but by analogy with the sentences I do know, I can create them.

I can even create other sentences with new nouns and verbs as I learn them. If I learn *rock*, *throw*, *climb*, *tree*, and *Aditi*, I can create sentences like *Aditi climbs a tree* and *Isabella throws a rock* just by plugging in the new words I have learned into the places where I discovered other similar words in the formula. Using this method of analogy, I can even create sentences like *The rock reads the king*, *The bicycle climbs Nathan*, and *Isabella rides the tree*. These sentences are somewhat nonsensical, but they are *grammatical*. I have done all of this through a process of linguistic analogy, which, as the linguist Ferdinand de Saussure noted, is identical with the principle of linguistic creation in general.[26]

This linguistic creativity allows us to fashion novel expressions, but it does not always guarantee that they'll be meaningful (e.g., *The rock reads*

---

25. Hashimoto et al., "Linguistic Analogy for Creativity," 187.

26. Saussure and Harris, *Course in General Linguistics*, 194.

the king).[27] However, that same linguistic creativity used to generate the sentence gives us the ability to reinterpret the sentence as meaningful, either through the application of metaphor (*rock* refers to a reliable person, *read* refers to gauging the emotional state of someone), or by reinterpreting the sentence through invention and innovation: carving a stone statue of someone reading a book written by the king.[28] Linguistic analogy is the great wellspring for human linguistic (and artistic) creativity.

This source of creativity is significant. Historically, linguists and cognitive scientists have assumed that our ability to communicate through language was what gave humanity an adaptive edge. That is, because we could say, "Look out, Dan, there's a saber-toothed tiger over there!" or "Don't eat any of the berries the Neanderthals are selling," we had an evolutionary advantage. However, other linguists have noted that it was the *creative power* of language, not simply its ability to communicate, that gave human language the ability to be adaptive and, by extension, to help us be adaptive.[29]

Linguistic analogy makes language itself more diverse and complex. Speakers are able to form utterances that go beyond their direct experiences—that is, they can say things they have never heard before.[30] This, in turn, allows human beings to embrace more diverse and complex concepts and to envision their world in new ways. Linguists Takahashi Hashimoto, Masaya Nakatsuka, and Takeshi Konno have submitted a bold hypothesis: around fifty thousand years ago, *Homo sapiens* acquired the ability of linguistic analogy and suddenly became able to unconsciously develop linguistic knowledge. As a result, we developed linguistic creativity and grammar.[31] In effect, our entire human linguistic enterprise is the result of a process of

27. Chomsky demonstrated this principle when he came up with a sentence that is perfectly grammatical but semantically nonsensical: *Colorless green ideas sleep furiously.*

28. This creative process was used in a Stanford University competition in which participants were invited to make Chomsky's sentence meaningful (see the above footnote) using not more than one hundred words of prose or fourteen lines of verse. C. M. Street's entry illustrates the process of creative reinterpretation nicely: "It can only be the thought of verdure to come, which prompts us in the autumn to buy these dormant white lumps of vegetable matter covered by a brown papery skin, and lovingly plant them and care for them. It is a marvel to me that under this cover they are labouring unseen at such a rate within to give us the sudden awesome beauty of spring flowering bulbs. While winter reigns the earth reposes but these *colourless green ideas sleep furiously.*"

29. Hashimoto et al., "Linguistic Analogy for Creativity," 189–90.

30. This property of language has been a source of fascination and amusement for me for a while. After years of collecting them informally, my friend Steve Wanczyk and I set up a website (originalsentence.com) to allow people to submit utterances they believed had likely never been said before in the history of the language.

31. Smith, *Evolution of Language,* 190–91.

analogy, the same process that allows us to think metaphorically. It seems that metaphor and human language are inextricably bound together.

The relationship between metaphorical thought and human language development has even been observed by those studying the origins of our species. As our ancestors evolved, there was a sudden and unusual expansion of the prefrontal brain regions in the later hominids. The anthropologist Terrence Deacon observed that these regions of the brain look as if they have been "deluged with some massive new set of . . . inputs." What is that input? Language itself. The human brain's evolution did not simply produce language; its evolution was also shaped *by* language. We have a "cognitive bias" toward the "strange associative relationships of language." As journalist Christine Kenneally writes in her review of Deacon's work, "Having adapted to language, we can't not be language-creatures. *For us, everything is symbolic.*"[32] We human beings are inescapably creatures of symbol, using and adapting symbols to make sense of and communicate about our world.

In fact, it seems that metaphor is our main mechanism for dealing with *all* our symbols. The mathematics that are so good at describing our cosmos nevertheless have to be apprehended in more concrete, yet still symbolic, terms. We define time in terms of space ("I went *to* France *from* Germany. I'll be in France *from* Thursday *to* Sunday.") and define space beyond ordinary experience in terms of ordinary experience ("The *fabric* of space-time is *curved*.) This process of *metaphorical abstraction* is what allows us to extend concrete meanings to abstract concepts.[33]

The relationship between our ability to use metaphor and our ability to use language may be just the tip of the iceberg. Our ability to use metaphor may also be at the root of our cognitive development. It may have given rise to the complex mental structures that make up human intelligence. Metaphor may be at the heart of our ability not only to speak, but to *think*, and thus is at the heart of what makes us human.

But is language entirely metaphor? What lies at the root of language? Is there anything concrete at the bottom of this deep pile of metaphor? There must have been some concrete starting point upon which the whole linguistic enterprise was founded, some shipwreck beneath the reef of metaphors that make up language.

It has been noted that in hominids, language control and hand control are closely related cerebral functions. Gestures are an integral part of human speech, not just charming add-ons to our verbal process (especially for those of us with Italian heritage). Gestures seem to be connected with the

32. Kenneally, *First Word*, 252 (emphasis added).

33. Coolidge and Wynn, "Numerosity, Abstraction," 78.

very brain processes that make language possible.[34] What that means is that our likely starting point for language is literally that: *pointing*. Words for *this* and *that* were likely the first words, and from them came almost everything else. But the one thing that all subsequent words had in common was the same: they were all still *pointing*.

But how does this process work itself out? How do we get from *this* and *that* to Shakespeare? Once again, metaphors play a role. Our ability for metaphorical abstraction allowed us to begin take our most basic, physical experiences and apply them to the broader world. The "basic" domains of experience come from natural kinds of experience, such as our bodies, our interactions with our physical environment, and our interactions with other people within our culture.[35]

When we look at the most basic expressions of language we see the prominent role that these foundational domains of experience have in the way we think about reality. It can be surprising to realize just how much of our own bodies are used to build spatial and temporal metaphors:

- *ahead*: at the head of
- *aback*: toward the back of
- *in front*: at the forehead of (*front* used to mean "forehead")
- *behind*: at the hindquarters, rear
- *beside*: at the side
- *before*: at the fore
- *beneath*: at the "nether regions"[36]

We start with our bodies—with ourselves—and gesture outward, pointing to our experience of the world. Our pointers are sometimes our hands, indicating *this* or *that*, *here* or *there*, guiding others in the direction of the object of our attention. And our pointers are sometimes our words, guiding others in the direction of an idea or a feeling that cannot be captured, but whose direction we can indicate.

Some of the most basic concepts of our lives—love, time, ideas, understanding, arguments, labor, happiness, health, control, status, morality, and so on—have to be pointed at. They have to be understood by using images from even more basic domains of experience because they are not clearly

---

34. Fischer, *History of Language*, 49.
35. Lakoff and Johnson, *Metaphors We Live By*, 117.
36. Deutscher, *Unfolding of Language*, 140.

delineated enough on their own terms so as to get by without metaphor.[37] And so, once again, we point. That most primitive of gestures—there at the dawn of our language ability—remains our most effective tool as we attempt to communicate with one another our experience of the world. We point with our hands. We point with our words. We point with metaphor.

Metaphor and Certainty

The implications of all of this are important. If language is predominantly made up of metaphor and is metaphorical in its nature, then language is not so much capturing reality as *pointing* toward it. Shakespeare's observation that "a rose by any other name would smell as sweet" is a reminder that there is a distance between the object and the term we use for it. This is all the more so when the object we're describing is an abstraction, or a feeling, or an idea that cannot be touched, seen, or heard.

Metaphor gives us the ability to describe abstraction. It gives us the ability to develop language. It may have even given us the ability to think in the way that we do. But the metaphorical nature of language does not allow us to capture the truth of reality with certainty. It only lets us point in its direction.

37. Lakoff and Johnson, *Metaphors We Live By*, 118.

The Inescapable Uncertainty

. . . In Our Senses

"Everything we hear is an opinion, not a fact.
Everything we see is a perspective, not the truth."

—*Marcus Aurelius*

Chapter 12

Through a Mirror Dimly

WE HAVE JUST SEEN that the language we use to communicate information about the world is unavoidably uncertain. We can never completely eliminate uncertainty from the medium we use to describe, interpret, and explain our world.

But let's leave language out of it for a moment. What about our understanding of the world from our own observations? Can we not have certainty about what our senses are telling us? Can't we be certain that our experience of the world is accurate?

As I write this chapter, I am seated at a table. I can see the laptop in front of me and the table underneath it. I can feel the force of the chair beneath me as it resists the downward pull of gravity on my body. I can hear the clack of the keys as I type the words that appear slowly upon my screen. I can smell the aroma of my coffee as I raise the cup to my mouth and can taste it as I begin to sip. Let's leave aside the great questions of existence for a moment. Can I not know that I am, in fact, sitting at a table, writing on my computer, drinking a cup of coffee? Can't I be certain of those things, at least?

It depends on whom you ask.

The ancient philosophers understood the senses as one way of knowing something, but they considered them to be less reliable than using reason. Plato maintained that the world we lived in was a world of shadows, shadows of what is truly real—the *ideal*. When we look at a tree, for example, we are not seeing a real tree. Instead, we are seeing the "shadow" of the ideal tree, which exists in the realm of forms or ideals and is accessible only to the philosopher through the use of reason. All trees are shadows or distortions of the true, ideal tree in the realm of forms.

According to Plato, then, these ideals are what are real and certain. Those of us who imagine that we are perceiving a table, a computer, and a cup of coffee are mistaken. We are perceiving only the shadow of those things, not the thing itself. To truly know something, to truly understand something with certainty, you have to use reason.[1]

Even those thinkers who understood that information came through the senses didn't always trust their senses. Saint Augustine, the great theologian of late antiquity, believed that our senses could be subject to deception. What we perceive might be an illusion or a trick. But, he reasoned, even if that were the case, there was something that we could know, something we could be certain of: our own existence. Augustine said that the one thing we know that does not come to us through our senses is that we exist. Even if we are being deceived through our senses, we exist. As he said, "For if I am deceived, I *am*. For he who *is not*, cannot be deceived."[2]

René Descartes, the great French philosopher, came to a similar conclusion. After engaging in a thought experiment in which he chose to doubt anything that was possible to doubt—anything that could be false, an illusion, or a deception—he found himself struggling to find something to be certain of. It was then that he realized that of all the things he could discount as false, illusory, or deceptive, the one thing he couldn't doubt was that he was *thinking*. "Here I make my discovery," he wrote, "thought exists; it alone cannot be separated from me. I am; I exist—this is certain."[3]

Is that all? Is the only thing we can be certain of that we exist and are thinking? Is there nothing else? Not even Descartes was willing to go that far. He did believe that there were reasonable conclusions we could come to about our bodies and the physical world. But he admitted that the ordinary life did not always allow us the time needed to make a careful inquiry about everything. As a result, our lives are "vulnerable to errors regarding particular things, and we must acknowledge the infirmity of our nature."[4] We can be certain of our own existence. Beyond that, we may accept what our senses tell us, but always with a measure of skepticism and humility.

Descartes seems to be saying that outside of our own existence, uncertainty is unavoidable; we cannot know for sure. He is not alone in this. The Scottish philosopher David Hume argued that all we had were "perceptions" of the world around us, and our perceptions were not the same as the objects themselves. Further complicating matters, because our only source of information is our senses, we have no objective measure by which we can

1. Plato, "Knowledge and Opinion," 1–7.
2. Augustine, "Three Things True and Certain," 8–9 (emphasis added).
3. Descartes, "Meditations I and II," 19.
4. Ibid., 27.

tell if our senses are giving us accurate information. Everything we think we know is in doubt.[5]

But are our senses really that unreliable? Isn't there any way to tell if our senses are lying to us or if our perceptions are false? The seventeenth-century German philosopher Wilhelm Leibniz thought so. He even proposed a set of criteria for determining whether what we were perceiving was real or not. He said that if something were "vivid, complex, and internally coherent," it was likely that it was a real phenomenon other than something being dreamed.[6] Even so, this determination was a *provisional* yes—we could be reasonably sure that the information received from our senses was reliable. We wouldn't be wrong to rely on things that were *probably* true, but we could never be *absolutely* certain.

That's all well and good for philosophers, you may be thinking, but do I really have to go through my daily life thinking like that? Do I really have to start thinking things like, *There's a beautiful bird on the back porch; at least I think so until it can be proven otherwise*? Such a burden of proof may work well in a laboratory or a courtroom, but do I really have to live my whole life that way? Well, only if you'd rather employ esoteric thinking rather than common sense.

At least, that was the thinking of the twentieth-century British philosopher G. E. Moore, who approached the question from a common-sense perspective. Moore thought it was absurd to speak of reality in only the most skeptical way. He once began a presentation by saying, "I am at present, as you can all see, in a room and not in the open air; I am standing up, and not either lying down; I have clothes on, and am not absolutely naked." He continued:

> Suppose that now, instead of saying "I am inside a building," I were to say, "I think I'm inside a building, but perhaps I'm not: it's not certain that I am," or instead of saying "I have got some clothes on," I were to say "I think I've got some clothes on, but it's just possible that I haven't." Would it not sound rather ridiculous for me now, under these circumstances, to say "I think I've got some clothes on" or even to say "I not only think I have, I know that it is very likely indeed that I have, but I can't be quite sure"?[7]

It's precisely this kind of level-headed thinking that takes all the fun out of philosophy and theology. And indeed, the simple fact is that however much we might doubt our certainties, our day-to-day practical philosophy

5. Hume, "Of the Academical or Sceptical," 35–36.
6. Leibniz, "On the Method of Distinguishing," 30.
7. Moore, "Certainty," 59.

is exactly as Moore describes. Whatever the philosophers might argue about whether we can trust our perceptions and our senses, the reality is that the ability to function in the world requires us to trust them. We might conclude that the pile of laundry in front of us is an illusion created by our minds, but on the off chance that it might be real, we have to act like it is and do the laundry anyway.

But even so, it may turn out that the philosophers' speculation about the trustworthiness of our senses might not be entirely baseless. Perhaps we ought to be a little more skeptical about what we can learn through our senses. Our experience has shown that to be true.

* * *

On February 26, 2015, the Internet broke.

A woman posted a photograph of a dress on social media. She asked people to say what color the dress was because she and her friends were unable to agree and were "freaking out."

This kind of disagreement happens all the time. I had a years-long argument with a friend of mine about whether a particular shirt I owned was blue or green. I saw it as green. She saw it as blue. I have the same argument now with a different friend about the color of my couch. But as blue and green are on the same spectrum and the shirt could arguably have been said to have been blue-green (or was it green-blue?), that argument was simply about where an individual drew the line between the two colors. The dress was different.

People saw the dress either as blue with black stripes or as white with gold stripes. That is not a difference between two people who simply draw the border between two neighboring colors in different places. This was a fundamental difference in the perceived nature of the dress.

And that difference caused a crisis around the globe as people took to shouting at each other that the dress was one version or another. It upset a lot of people who could not understand how it was that other people could possibly see such divergent versions of the same reality.

Fig. 4. *The Dress.*

Of course, the neuroscientists explained that the problem was not in our eyes—it was in our brains. We do not see with our eyes; we see with our brains. Our brain interprets visual signals received in the retina and tries to make sense of them. In this case, the difference in the colors you saw all seemed to depend on whether you perceived the dress as being in low light (as a result of which your brain interpreted the darker colors as being in shadow and saw the dress as white and gold) or whether you perceived the dress as being in bright light (as a result of which your brain interpreted the darker colors as being the true colors of the dress). The brain frequently "normalizes" signals from the retina that do not correspond with what the brain expects to see. These expectations are based on the brain's general experience of the world, especially stored memories and habits.[8]

This normalization of sensory input is not limited to sight alone. A well-documented phenomenon known as the McGurk Effect demonstrates

8. Deutscher, *Through the Language Glass*, 248.

the way that the brain's interpretation of visual signals overrides the interpretation of an auditory signal.[9] In documenting the effect, researchers ask
subjects to watch a video of someone repeating a syllable a number of times.
Those who watch the video will report the speaker as saying *da da da da
da* or even *ga ga ga ga ga*. When the video is replayed and subjects are only
able to listen to the audio, they clearly hear *ba ba ba ba ba*. The audio has
remained unchanged. What is different is the lack of visual interference. Because the speaker's lips are not coming together, the viewer's brain interprets
the sound being made as anything other than a /b/ sound. Once again, the
brain's expectation of the event is key in determining how that event will be
perceived, whatever the objective reality is. Our *cognitive paradigms*—the
mental patterns and expectations that our brains have—influence the interpretation of the data that our brains receive.

It is jarring to so many people to discover that our brains should
interpret the physical world in such starkly different ways. How is any
claim on objective reality ever to be trusted? If one listener can hear *da da
da* and another *ba ba ba*, or if one rational person could look at a dress and
see it as white and gold and another equally rational person could see it
as blue and black, then how could we know at any given moment whether
our eyes and ears were truly relaying objective reality? Could our senses
really be unreliable?

In 2008, advocates for bicycle safety produced a video they entitled
"An Awareness Test." In the video, two teams of four—one team in white,
the other in black—run around passing a basketball back and forth among
teammates. The voiceover asks, "How many passes does the team in white
make?" The teams begin to run in and among one another, passing their
ball to their team members wearing the same color shirt. If you're atten-
tive, you'll count thirteen times that the white team passed the ball. The
voiceover confirms this: "The answer is thirteen." And then continues,
somewhat jarringly: "But did you see the moonwalking bear?" The *what?*
Sure enough, the video rewinds and as you watch again, no longer focusing
on the moving, weaving, ball-passing basketball players, you see a man in
a bear costume walk nonchalantly to the very *center* of the screen and start
moonwalking. The advertisement concludes with the statement, "It's easy to
miss something you're not looking for. Look out for cyclists."[10]

It's an attention-getting advertisement, but at the same time it's jarring because when you watch the rewind of the video, you can't believe that
you ever *didn't* see that guy moonwalking in a ridiculous bear costume. It

9. Rosenblum, "McGurk Effect."
10. "Test Your Awareness."

makes you think that perhaps the question asked by Chico Marx in the Marx Brothers movie *Duck Soup*—"Who are you going to believe: me or your own eyes?"—isn't so absurd after all. Perhaps our senses aren't as trustworthy as we like to think.

Of course, that's nothing new. Magicians and illusionists have been using these little defects in our senses for centuries, taking advantage of misdirection and what psychologists refer to as "inattentional blindness."[11] Another popular Internet video shows a man performing a card trick in which he asks a woman to pick a card. At the end of the trick, he reveals that the backs of all the other cards have changed color from blue to red. It seems like a nice little trick, but nothing terribly remarkable until you realize the entire video is misdirection. Because what you didn't notice while the trick was taking place was that the color of the man's shirt, the woman's shirt, the background, and even the table covering had all changed over the course of the short trick.[12] With our attention focused on trying to keep track of the card and looking for any trickery by the magician, our brains simply failed to pay attention to any other detail. When the video rewinds and shows the trick from a wide angle, you're astounded at how much is going on that you never noticed the first time.

Can we ever trust our senses to give us accurate information about the world we live in? On balance, of course we can. Our species would hardly have survived this long were we not able to rely on the information our senses provide us. But that does not mean that we can rely on that information with absolute certainty. Uncertainty is built into the way we perceive the world.

11. Burton, *On Being Certain*, 155.

12. Wiseman, "Color Changing Card Trick."

The Inescapable Uncertainty

. . . In Our Science

Chapter 13

Science to the Rescue! Or Not.

THUS FAR WE HAVE seen that our religious traditions are full of uncertainty. The language we use to communicate about the world to one another is likewise full of metaphor and contains uncertainty. Even our senses have the potential to convey inaccurate perceptions about the world around us.

Perhaps the ancient philosophers were right and the only way to access truth is through reason and the application of philosophy. Would that work for us? Can our science find us the certainty we seek? Can science help us be rid of uncertainty?

To be sure, there are entire branches of science that deal with uncertainty. There is *chaos theory*, for one, which seeks to understand how small changes in circumstances can have widely different effects in the end, such as the way a butterfly flapping its wings can change the course of a hurricane weeks later.[1] Such sciences are devoted to uncertainty. But surely, even if science acknowledges the uncertainties in the world, science itself is interested in producing certainties, things we *can* rely on, right?

To find out, let's take a look at science to see what science does, how it does it, and what it claims to know. We'll find that in addressing the uncertainties of the world, science may not be the solution we've been looking for. We'll see that not even the "hard sciences" are refuges for those who crave certainty.

Part of the reason that we look to science as having all the answers is that we don't always have the proper understanding of science in our media and popular culture. If there is one thing that science and religion have in common, it's that the media do not understand either. The news is often full of reports about the pope having issued some new doctrine, when in reality he was merely clarifying a position the church had long held. And there are frequently articles about science having revealed some fantastic new understanding when it has done nothing of the sort. In both cases,

1. Smith, *Chaos*, ch. 1.

the misrepresentations are probably due to the fact that the media do not understand the language of either science or religion and assume them to be saying things they are not. We see this all the time: a scientist states that the universe might be a multidimensional *holographic projection* of a two-dimensional mathematical reality, and the media reports that scientists believe we're living in a hologram. Another scientist will discuss a scientific *theory* and the media will treat it as something like guesswork.

One of the main ways that science is popularly misunderstood is when it comes to science's findings. In the popular imagination, science is about finding answers, and this is reflected in our popular culture. Whether it's in the forensic laboratories of *CSI*, the mathematical equations used in *Numb3rs* to solve crimes, or Spock's computer on *Star Trek*, science is there to solve the riddle, find the criminal, or rescue the *Enterprise* from imminent destruction. But science doesn't really work like that.

Scientists are concerned with solving problems, but rarely do they ever produce anything like definitive solutions. Instead, their experiments are designed to collect and analyze data about the phenomenon they seek to explore and to draw some preliminary conclusions. Contrary to what we might wish, this process is not designed to eliminate uncertainty altogether. In fact, the entire scientific method is full of uncertainty.

So let's see how the scientific process works by considering a hypothetical investigation. We'll go through it step by step looking at the way science is done and the questions it must ask as it proceeds. As we go through this investigation, we'll follow the scientific method closely and explore together the uncertainties that arise in the work of science itself.

The Hypothesis

For our hypothetical research, we will examine a hypothetical product: Product X. Product X is an oxygen-carrying solution that could potentially deliver oxygen to oxygen-deprived tissues after a stroke or a heart attack. As such, it has great life-saving and therapeutic potential by reducing brain damage. However, it has been suggested after some use that Product X causes constriction in the blood vessels of the brain in human beings, which could have serious health implications and could offset any reduction in brain damage the product might otherwise have. A scientist interested in testing the benefit of Product X as a post-stroke treatment will attempt to find out whether it does indeed cause this constriction.

Now, in the popular imagination, and especially in the way it is presented in the media, science seems to be a fairly straightforward business:

inject the subject with the substance to be tested and see what happens. However, the scientific method isn't just about proving that X causes Y. It is as much involved in *disproving* that there is *no* link as it is in *proving* that there *is* one.

The proposition that there is no link between two phenomena (in our case, between Product X and blood vessel constriction) is known as the *null hypothesis*. Its opposite, the proposition that there is a link between two phenomena, is known as the *alternative hypothesis*. In our case the null hypothesis would be "Product X does not cause blood vessel constriction in the brain" and the alternative hypothesis would be "Product X causes blood vessel constriction in the brain." Science is interested in rejecting the null hypothesis as much as it is in affirming the alternative hypothesis. In fact, one cannot truly affirm the alternative hypothesis until one has rejected the null hypothesis.

Because the scientist cannot simply administer Product X to patients and see what happens, she will have to set up a slate of experiments using research animals in laboratory conditions. The benefit of a laboratory experiment is that the researcher can try to eliminate as many variables as possible by creating conditions such that the only variable is the one being studied. If the researcher can ensure that all the laboratory animals are of the same approximate body mass, are maintained under the same conditions, are receiving the same amount of Product X, are observed for the same time, are breathing the same mix of air, and are observed in the same way, then some of the uncertainties can be eliminated. But even so, a researcher can only account for the variables that she knows about—if there is some effect that science is yet unaware of, she obviously cannot eliminate the variables involved in that effect.

Statistics are essential in science and scientists use statistical methods to determine which effects are caused by random chance and which ones are caused by the phenomenon that is being examined. These statistical models are used to describe a world in which random chance is responsible for the effect being tested. In our hypothetical, these statistics will determine a model in which random chance alone is responsible for variation in the diameter of blood vessels in the brain. This statistical model is known as the *distribution under the null hypothesis*—that is, the results we should expect to see if Product X has no effect whatsoever. This model of probability will show that there are some blood vessels that will be constricted, some that will be dilated, and some that remain unchanged, and it will describe predicted ranges for each. It is not a definitive, certain understanding, but it is a workable one, rooted in statistical probabilities.

The Sample

Uncertainty is not limited to the statistics used in an experiment. Another uncertainty that arises is over the *sample size*: how many animals should our scientist examine in order to conclude that there is, in fact, an effect caused by Product X? To answer this question, scientists rely on a *power analysis*, another statistical model by which statisticians can calculate the minimum sample size needed for an experiment in order to determine whether there is a demonstrable effect. This statistical inquiry is based not on absolute certainties, but on probabilities determined by the mathematics of statistical analysis.

This aspect of an investigation is more important than most people realize. The size and the nature of the sample go right to what is known as the *statistical power* of a given study. The relationship between the statistical power of a study and the reliability of its findings has been underappreciated in the lay and scientific communities alike.[2] For example, if Product X is only tested on five laboratory rats, the data our scientist would receive wouldn't be inaccurate, but it might not be able to tell us much. The larger the sample, the more likely that data obtained from the sample are predictive of the broader population.

The sample also needs to be sufficiently representative of the population being studied. This fact has come increasingly into focus in analyses of political polls, where traditional methods of telephone-based polling have not yielded samples that reflect the changing reality of the electorate. Such polls can't reach many of the younger members of the population because they don't possess landline telephones. In such a case, the population reachable by landline telephones skews older and is less representative of the electorate at large.[3] A scientist wants to make sure that her sample population reflects the larger population just as much as any political pollster does. To do otherwise leads to bad information.

Sometimes the size of the sample cannot be helped. For example, a study of the effects of traumatic brain injury in those injured by a blast in combat is limited to those service personnel who have been exposed to blast injury. Of that small population (relative to the entire U.S. population) not all injured members received the same treatment for that injury, and thus, the population of injured service members who have received the same (or substantially similar) treatments is even smaller.

2. Button et al., "Power Failure," 365.
3. Zukin, "What's the Matter with Polling?"

But let's return to our hypothetical. What constitutes a good sample size: the number of blood vessels that are examined or the number of animals in which such blood vessels are examined? If on a given animal we are able to examine an average of ten distinct blood vessels, and we are examining ten animals, does that give us ten data points or one hundred? Is each blood vessel "independent" such that it can be counted separately as a data point for our study? In such a case, what appears to be a sizable data sample can conceal a problem known as *pseudoreplication*, where different observations from the same animal are sometimes seen as independent pieces of information rather than one. Pseudoreplication can lead to results that are less predictive than would be initially assumed.[4]

For the purposes of our hypothetical, our scientist is able to procure a large sample of laboratory animals that her statistical models assure her will give her study appropriate *statistical power*. Now she must collect the data.

The Data

The collection of the data may be the most objective part of the entire process. The scientist's aim here is to ensure that her methods eliminate as many extraneous variables as possible and that they capture data that will help determine whether she can reject the null hypothesis.

First, she measures the blood vessels in the brains of laboratory rats without Product X. She places the rat in a harness and measures the size of the brain's surface blood vessels over time, taking measurements, say, every 15 minutes for a few hours. Then after she has collected data from a number of these *control animals*, she begins a course on animals with Product X. She measures each animal's blood vessels, administers Product X, and then makes her observations every 15 minutes, noting the width of the blood vessels over time.

The Analysis

After a good-sized sample of such animals, our scientist has a fair amount of data to analyze. She notes that the blood vessels in rats that received Product X were on average 25 percent narrower after the two hours of the experiment than those who were not given Product X.

Has she demonstrated anything? Mathematically speaking, she must first demonstrate that she has been able to reject the *null hypothesis*. This

---

4. Lazic, "Problem of Psuedoreplication," 2.

statistical analysis will analyze the results compared to the *distribution under the null hypothesis* and determine within a certain probability whether she can draw any conclusions from the data.

To a lay person, a 25–percent change suggests an effect, but not so to the scientist. She understands that a statistical analysis is necessary to determine the *probability* that the data she has gathered actually rejects the null hypothesis. The application of statistical analysis will determine whether a difference in measurements of 100μm and 75μm is *statistically significant*. If, for example, the distribution under the null hypothesis accounts for such wide-ranging diameters of blood vessels in the brain, then finding them in the data might not be significant. For example, such an analysis might conclude that finding a 25–percent variance in blood vessel diameter is only 20–percent likely to demonstrate that the null hypothesis can be rejected and therefore that Product X has an effect. In that case, a 25–percent change wouldn't necessarily be a sign that Product X had done anything. It's four times more likely that such a variation is just the usual range of difference.

But for the purposes of our hypothetical, let's imagine that the statistical analysis has concluded that there is a 90–percent chance that this 25–percent difference does indeed lead to rejection of the null hypothesis. Our scientist hasn't proved that Product X is definitively causing constriction, but statistically speaking *something* is going on. But even here we are dealing with *probabilities*, with the likelihood that our scientist has been able to demonstrate some effect.

More uncertainty comes in. Twenty-five percent may be statistically significant, but is it *actually biologically* significant? That is, does a 25–percent reduction in the size of a blood vessel *do* anything? Is this actually "constriction"? How do you define "constriction"? At what point is a vessel "constricted"? Ten percent? Twenty-five? Fifty? You have data, but in order to craft a *finding*, a measure of subjective interpretation enters into the process.

But let's say that the scientific community generally agrees that 25 percent reduction in vessel diameter constitutes a "constriction." So now that all the data is in, can our scientist say with certainty that Product X causes constriction of blood vessels in the human brain? No. All she can say is that in the dozen or so animals that she studied, on average, blood vessel diameter of brain surface vessels was reduced by 25 percent when the animals were administered Product X. That's it. In order to conclude that it will happen in human beings, the data has to be replicated in larger animal models and eventually in people, and reasonable conclusions drawn. The findings of our scientist's study might be enough to bring Product X under more scrutiny by the Food and Drug Administration and perhaps convince it to require more preclinical studies before allowing the product to progress to human clinical trials, but it is not an absolute declaration that Product X *is* dangerous. All we have at this point is one study.

The Ever-Present Uncertainty

But let's imagine further that other scientists have been able to replicate our scientist's study and have obtained the same or similar results. After a while a consensus has emerged that, yes, Product X does indeed cause constriction and is likely to do so in human beings.

But note what this is not: it is still not an absolute declaration of certainty. The declaration that Product X is likely to cause constriction in the blood vessels of the brain in human beings is a generalization from animals to people. Even were such an effect to be recorded in one human being, that doesn't guarantee that it will necessarily occur in another human being. Even after we have addressed all the uncertainties of probabilistic statistical models, sample size, data analysis, and data implications, we still are not able to make a declaration of absolute certainty.

* * *

In the end, that's okay. Such declarations of certainty are not what the scientific enterprise is about. Scientific conclusions are always interim conclusions because a future experiment or observation may overturn the conclusions drawn from any given experiment. Scientists rarely proclaim an absolute truth or absolute certainty. Such an absolute truth or certainty would be hard to come by in science. As one commentator notes, "Uncertainty is inevitable at the frontiers of knowledge."[5] This provisional nature of scientific results can be seen in a number of different ways.

Newtonian physics is probably the first true "scientific" understanding of the universe developed using the scientific method of hypothesis, empirical observation, experimentation, and replicability. Newton's theory of gravity helped to explain the orbit of the planets much more effectively than earlier models. And for a long time, Newtonian (or "classical") physics was the primary model for explaining the universe. It didn't explain *everything*, but it explained things far more effectively than any other system up to that point.

And so, when Einstein proposed his theory of relativity, not only did it represent a significant change in the way we conceived of the universe, it dramatically improved our ability to model it. One thing it did not do,

---

5. Achenbach, "Age of Disbelief."

however, was *replace* classical physics. Apples still fell to earth at $9m/sec^2$, force still equaled mass times acceleration, and velocity still equaled distance divided by time. Einsteinian physics *supplemented* classical physics' description of the universe. And Einsteinian physics was itself supplemented by quantum physics, which may be supplemented by string theory or some other theory in the future.

In the same way, scientific understandings in biology continue to be revised and reworked. In the early nineteenth century, French naturalist and scientist Jean-Baptiste Lamarck published his own theory of evolution in which he maintained that an individual's acquired traits could be passed down from generation to generation. A creature's adaptation to its environment could become an inheritable trait in that creature's offspring. The idea existed side by side with Darwin's theory of natural selection until later scientific understandings (involving sex cells and, later, DNA) put that theory to rest in favor of Darwin's. However, even that determination remains provisional; recent studies in the field of *epigenetics* seek to explore how environmental factors, such as malnutrition and exercise, can actually create traits that can be passed on to succeeding generations.[6]

Likewise, early theories about the nature of the neural network of the brain were divided among those like Italian physician Camillo Golgi, who argued that neural information was passed along via networks of connected cells, and those like Spanish neuroscientist Santiago Ramón y Cajal, who argued that the cells responsible for the communication of neural information were discrete units separated by gaps, or *synapses*. Somewhat ironically, Ramón y Cajal used Golgi's own staining method to show that neurons were, in fact, discrete units communicating through the release of chemical neurotransmitters across a synaptic gap. However, even this victory of the *neuron doctrine* over the *reticular theory* is provisional: subsequent research has discovered *gap junctions* where neurons are indeed physically coupled together and where information is passed along through this physical mechanism.[7] Science, it seems, rarely settles a question definitively. Nor do scientists claim to have done so.

Ordinary people don't always understand why scientists are reluctant to make such definitive claims. We usually assume that science is in the business of identifying certainties, and so we interpret scientific reluctance to proclaim the discovery of particular facts and truths as evidence that scientists are just guessing. Part of this may be simply a function of our psychology and human nature: those who are certain will always take their

6. R. Abutarboush, personal communication.
7. Ibid.

opponents' admission of uncertainty as tantamount to evidence that their opponents are wrong. And part of the confusion is due no doubt to the popular understanding of the words *fact* and *theory*, which sound, respectively, more and less certain to lay people than their scientific understandings warrant. As evolutionary theorist Stephen Jay Gould noted:

> Moreover, "fact" does not mean "absolute certainty." . . . In science, "fact" can only mean "confirmed to such a degree that it would be perverse to withhold provisional assent." I suppose that apples might start to rise tomorrow [rather than fall according to the theory of gravity], but the possibility does not merit equal time in physics classrooms.[8]

The purpose of the scientific method is not to declare certainties. It is to identify theories and models that are consistent with the data and more likely than not to be true. But let's be clear about this: the reluctance of science to declare absolute certainties does not mean that its conclusions yield to any other belief system merely because that other system's adherents are more certain. A scientific model of planetary formation or of evolutionary biology might ultimately prove to be wrong, but it's still the best model out there. Someone's certainty in the cosmology presented by an ancient text does not trump scientific explanations. Science may admit uncertainty; that is not the same thing as saying that science is unreliable.

As reliable as science may be, for many lay people, science can frequently be uncomfortably non-committal. Ordinary people want resolution and quick and easy answers, but science cannot always provide those. In fact, too much certainty—in the form of bias or unquestioned presumptions—can interfere with science's ultimate task: to seek greater understanding through observation and experimentation, a task for which uncertainty, not certainty, is essential.

Embracing uncertainty is a fundamental aspect of science. The philosopher Karl Popper defined intellectual honesty in science as trying to *refute* a theory of the world rather than to prove it. That is, true scientific rigor is not in defending the scientific status quo, it is in challenging it—undermining the certainties of the established point of view. Another philosopher of science, Thomas Kuhn, believed that science advanced when increasing numbers of contradictions forced rethinking and abandoning a prevailing theory. Recognizing uncertainty is not a problem in the sciences. It becomes a driving factor for a deeper, more comprehensive understanding.[9]

8. National Research Council et al., *Role of Theory*, 28.

9. Holmes, 177.

The enterprise of science has proven itself to be extraordinarily effective. Science is effective primarily because it challenges accepted conventions, subjects theories to rigorous questioning, and is willing to embrace the uncertainty inherent in the system itself. In the end, science does not resolve our uncertainties; it revels in them.

The Inescapable Uncertainty

... In Our World

There are more things in heaven and earth, Horatio,
Than are dreamt of in your philosophy.

—WILLIAM SHAKESPEARE, HAMLET, ACT I, SCENE IV

We have seen that the metaphorical nature of our religious tradition is a clue that religion is, ultimately, not a source of certainty, but uncertainty. We have seen that the metaphorical nature of language does not allow us to capture the truth of reality with any certainty; it only lets us point in its direction.

We have seen that our senses do not always convey an objective view of the world around us. Further, we have seen that the great enterprise of science and its application of reason does not eliminate our uncertainty about our ability to understand reality.

But surely there is a reality to point to, no? Even if we cannot describe it with certainty, or can't be sure we're perceiving it correctly, the world we're attempting to describe must have a stable, certain core, even if we struggle to define what that is.

Well, our understanding of the world has changed a great deal over the centuries. As that understanding has grown, so too has our awareness that the world is not quite as simple and manageable as we had once believed. In fact, the more we have come to learn about our world, the more we have come to understand that reality is stranger and less comprehensible than we'd ever imagined. For those seekers of certainty who long to find a certain and easily comprehended world, the universe proves to be a disappointment.

In the chapters that follow, we're going to take a look at our evolving understanding of the universe and see what it has to say about our longing for certainty. We'll discover a cosmos that in our understanding went from a nice, compact, manageable world to a world of unbelievable complexity that defies descriptions in absolute terms and resists our wishes for a simple, cut-and-dry universe. In so doing, we'll find a world of wondrous and marvelous beauty. But we won't find a world of certainty.

Chapter 14

The World Knocked Off Its Foundations

THE WORLD USED TO be a simple place: just a nice flat disk covered by a dome of sky, surrounded by water on all sides. Simple. Manageable. Well, okay, the world was never really like that, but we once believed that it was.

Such interesting views of the world—or *cosmologies*—can be traced back to some of the earliest civilizations. The cosmology of ancient Babylon, for example, consisted of a seven-tiered pyramidal *E-kur* (earth) separated by the four seas from an inverse seven-tiered pyramid, *Lower E-kur* (the underworld), all of which was surrounded by a three-tiered heaven containing eight heavenly spheres corresponding to the planets, sun, and moon (Fig. 5).[1]

---

1. Warren, "Babylonian and Pre-Babylonian Cosmology," 139.

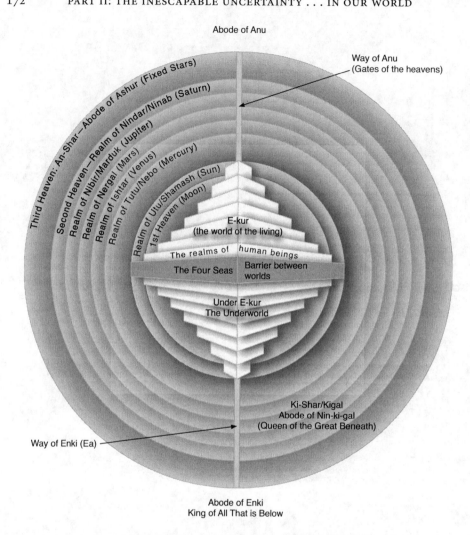

Abode of Anu

Way of Anu
(Gates of the heavens)

Third Heaven: An-Shar–Abode of Ashur (Fixed Stars)

Second Heaven–Realm of Nindar/Ninab (Saturn)

Realm of Nibir/Marduk (Jupiter)

Realm of Nergal (Mars)

Realm of Ishtar (Venus)

Realm of Tutu/Nebo (Mercury)

Realm of Utu/Shamash (Sun)

1st Heaven (Moon)

E-kur
(the world of the living)

The realms of   human beings

The Four Seas   Barrier between
worlds

Under E-kur
The Underworld

Ki-Shar/Kigal
Abode of Nin-ki-gal
(Queen of the Great Beneath)

Way of Enki (Ea)

Abode of Enki
King of All That is Below

Fig. 5. *The Babylonian conception of the universe.*

This is, of course, not the only ancient view of the world—the ancient Hebrews had their own vision of what the universe looked like. The Hebrew model of the universe is generally found in the first chapter of Genesis but can also be found in various references throughout scripture, especially the Psalms. It is a flat earth, anchored by great pillars, covered by a dome of sky, surrounded on all sides by water.[2]

2. See, for example, Genesis 1:6: "And God said, 'Let there be a dome between the waters, and let it divide the waters from the waters.'" For a more complete discussion of the creation accounts, see under the heading "The Poetry of Scripture" in chapter 7.

There are windows in the dome of sky to let the rains in and great fountains of the deep, which are the source of the seas (Gen 7:11; Isa 24:18). Affixed to the dome are the stars and traveling across the dome on their daily circuits are the sun and moon, referred to in the creation accounts as the "larger light" and the "smaller light" (Gen 1:14–16). And finally, above the dome is heaven, God's dwelling place in the creation.

There are a number of illustrations of this cosmology, but none better than artist Michael Paukner's rendering in Figure 6.

Fig. 6. *The Hebrew conception of the universe found in Genesis and the Psalms. (Illustration © 2009 Michael Paukner/Substudio.com. Used by permission.)*

The Hebrew version looks like the Babylonian conception—it imagines the earth as surrounded by a great sea—and is similar to other Near Eastern cosmologies that often saw the world as a disk covered by a dome of sky.[3]

A flat earth was not the only way the ancients understood the world. The Greeks believed that the world was round, and probably a sphere. Having traveled for trade throughout the ancient world, they knew that the angle of the North Star changed depending on how far north you were. They had also noted that the sails of a distant ship came into view before the rest of the vessel did. Their observations suggested that the world had to be spherical in shape.[4] The Greek mathematician and scholar Eratosthenes even used the assumption of a spherical earth to figure out how large the earth was by comparing the difference in the angles of the sun at two different places in Egypt on the same day.

As far as the rest of the universe beyond the earth was concerned, the Greeks looked to the system described by the Greek astronomer Ptolemy. Under Ptolemy's scheme, the sun, moon, and planets all orbited the earth, which remained unmoving at the center. It was a complicated system and the orbits of these heavenly bodies were not simple: from our perspective on earth, a planet's progress across the heavens appears to stop, move backward, and then move forward again. This apparent motion is called "retrograde motion" and is the result of the fact that both the earth and the planet observed are moving relative to each other (Fig. 7).

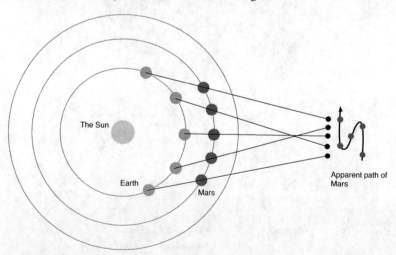

Fig. 7. *The apparent movement of Mars as seen from earth with its retrograde motion.*

3. To be fair to the ancients, that *is* what it looks like from our point of view.
4. Hawking, *Illustrated A Brief History*, 3.

If you insist that the earth is at the center of the system, however, the only way to explain the apparent backward motion of the planets is to conclude that each planet had something called an "epicycle"—a small orbit on its orbit. With this solution in place, the Ptolemaic universe took shape (Fig. 8).

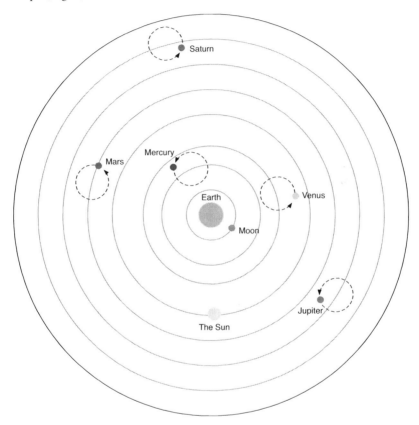

Fig. 8. *The Ptolemaic view of the universe, with the sun, moon, and planets orbiting the earth. The planets' orbits included "epicycles" to account for their retrograde motion as seen from earth.*

Sure, it's a little strange that the planets should take these curious little loop-de-loops on their way through the cosmos, but it (mostly) matched the observations of the planets' journeys across the heavens. And the universe had a comforting order to it: the sun, moon, and planets all on their courses, the stars affixed to the celestial sphere, and us, at the middle of it all.

There is one thing all the ancient cosmologies, from the Babylonians to the Greeks, had in common: the earth, whatever its shape, was *fixed*. So, whether the earth was flat and covered by a dome of sky or whether it was a sphere surrounded by concentric spheres of heaven, the earth was unmoving. Everything else in the heavens moved around the fixed earth.

And then along came Copernicus and Galileo.

In 1514, a Polish priest and astronomer, Nikolai Kopernik, better known to us by his Latin name, Nicholas Copernicus, put forward the idea that, rather than the sun, moon, planets, and stars orbiting the earth, it was the earth, along with the planets and stars, that orbited the sun. He developed this model because the Ptolemaic system could not account for all the motions of the planets as they were observed. In Copernicus's thinking, centering the planets on the sun explained the motion of the planets much better than centering them on the earth.

Perhaps fearing backlash from the church—which maintained that the biblical description was the correct one—Copernicus circulated his ideas anonymously at first and it was nearly a century before his idea was taken seriously. It would be through the work of two astronomers—the German Johannes Kepler and the Italian Galileo Galilei—that this acceptance would become possible.[5]

Galileo was particularly instrumental in helping to defeat the Ptolemaic model by undermining one of its chief assumptions: the idea there could only be one center to the system and that everything needed to orbit that center. Since it was clear that the moon orbited the earth, it could not be possible that earth itself orbited the sun—that was seen as too complex; better that the moon and the sun both orbit the earth. But when Galileo began using a new invention—the telescope—to observe the heavens, he discovered that Jupiter had a number of moons of its own. This observation made it clear that not everything had to orbit the earth directly, as the Ptolemaic model maintained. Once that stumbling block was removed, it became easier to accept the Copernican model because it was a far more elegant explanation of the heavens than the complicated Ptolemaic system. This, along with Kepler's proposal that the orbits of the planets were ellipses rather than circles, would ultimately provide a much better model of the cosmos than Ptolemy's. Later, Isaac Newton discovered, much to his surprise, that his theory of gravity was able to describe the motion of the planets in their orbits. Once Newton had provided the math and the physics to explain how the Copernicus-Galileo-Kepler model worked, the question was settled.[6]

5. Ibid., 6.
6. Ibid., 7.

That's not to say that the question was settled without resistance. The reaction to Copernicus's teaching was strong. There were all kinds of reasons for this, of course: the church wanted to defend the scriptures, or the teaching authority of the church, or the time-honored Ptolemaic system. But I don't think that's what was really going on.

The Copernican view of the universe was unsettling because, in that view, the earth was no longer unmoving. It was no longer stable or certain. It was in motion like everything else. The Ptolemaic worldview had not merely been explanatory—it had been *comforting*. And now that was being taken away.

When we look back at the Hebrew conception of the world, the really striking thing is the compact size of the universe: it's only a few thousand miles across, if that. It's very manageable. The Ptolemaic system was a little larger as it included the concentric celestial spheres in which the planets and the sun moved and the fixed sphere of stars beyond that, but it was still relatively compact. Even the Copernican cosmology did not do anything to disrupt that sense of scale: the sun might be at the center, but the stars were still fixed to the celestial sphere.

Even though our understanding of the relative positions of the earth, sun, and planets had changed, our sense of how large the universe was had not. The reason for this stability in the perceived size of the cosmos was the fact that the stars, unlike the planets, never changed position. Even considering the motion of the earth, the stars remained fixed, and suggested fixed, stable objects in a celestial sphere. But in the nineteenth century, with far more precise instruments available, astronomers noted that the earth's motion around the sun does, in fact, change the angle at which the stars appear to us. It's just not obvious to us with the naked eye because the stars are *really far away*. Suddenly now, with this recalculation, the size of the universe jumped from manageable to inconceivably vast, perhaps even infinite.

So, we started off with a small, manageable cosmos, consisting of a flat earth established on pillars with a dome of sky overhead, and moved to an unmoving spherical earth orbited by the planets and the fixed stars, then to an earth that orbited the sun along with the other planets, and finally to a sun that was one of countless stars, themselves adrift on a limitless sea of space.

The word had been knocked off its foundations and set adrift. And it was only going to get worse.

Chapter 15

A Warped and Uncertain Cosmos

IN THE MOVIE *ANNIE Hall*, the main character, Alvy Singer, played by Woody Allen, flashes back to a time in his childhood that showed that, even as a child, he was afflicted with a fair amount of existential angst:

Doctor: Why are you depressed, Alvy?

Alvy's mom: Tell Dr. Flicker.

(Young Alvy sits, his head down—his mother answers for him.)

Alvy's mom: It's something he read.

Doctor: Something he read, huh?

Alvy: *(his head still down)* The universe is expanding.

Doctor: The universe is expanding?

Alvy: Well, the universe is everything, and if it's expanding, some day it will break apart and that would be the end of everything!

Alvy's mom: What is that your business? *(turning back to the doctor)* He stopped doing his homework!

Alvy: What's the point?

Alvy's mom: What has the universe got to do with it? You're here in Brooklyn! Brooklyn is not expanding![1]

It's a scene meant to be an "even then they knew" kind of scene for the character, highlighting the neurosis that has plagued Alvy his whole life. But the subject of Alvy's anxiety is not arbitrary. The expanding universe is

---

1. IMDB, "Annie Hall (1977) – Quotes."

disquieting. It's a far cry from the "steady-state" universe, the fixed, eternal, "world without end" universe that had long been assumed to exist.

Prior to the twentieth century, people believed either that the universe had existed forever in an unchanging state or that it had been created at some point in the past more or less as it looked today. Perhaps this was due to a desire to believe in an eternal and unchanging world, a universe that was certain.[2] It would be troubling to learn otherwise.

That "steady-state" universe all changed in 1929 when astronomer Edwin Hubble discovered that every galaxy he could observe had a slight "red shift" to the light that was emanating from it. That is, much as the pitch of a siren moving away from you gets lower and lower because the sound wave is being stretched out, the wavelength of the light from these galaxies was being stretched out to lower and lower frequencies—toward the red end of the visible spectrum. These observations could only mean one thing: all of those galaxies were receding from us and from each other. The universe itself was expanding. Every galaxy in the universe was moving away from every other galaxy.

The implications of this observation would be world changing.

A Belgian priest and scientist named Monseigneur George Lemaître concluded that Hubble's data supported the idea that the universe was expanding, something that Einstein's theory of relativity had suggested but few had really considered. Lemaître proposed that these receding galaxies had expanded from an initial point, which he referred to as the "Cosmic Egg exploding at the moment of creation." The idea was derisively referred to by physicist Fred Hoyle as the "Big Bang." In fact, Lemaître's idea was not terribly popular with physicists, including Einstein, who remarked, "Your calculations are correct but your physics are atrocious." The idea that the universe was not a "steady state" was unnerving to many, not just to young Alvy Singer. And the idea of an expanding universe would only raise even more unsettling questions.

If the universe is expanding, where is it going? Will it expand forever? Will it reach a maximum and then begin a long process of collapse culminating in a "Big Crunch"? Or will it continue to expand forever and result in a universe that undergoes "heat death" in a cold, dark, empty cosmos that will continue on a time scale of inconceivable proportions? The fate of the universe is a topic of much debate in contemporary physics.

All of this talk of expanding universes, and the physics that made it possible, got started with the writings of an out of work professor named Albert Einstein. In 1905, while working as a Swiss patent clerk, Einstein

2. Hawking, *Illustrated A Brief History*, 9–10.

managed to publish four remarkable papers, the first one of which was enti-tled "On the Electrodynamics of Moving Bodies." This seemingly innocuous title belied the stunning propositions that were contained in the paper. In this astonishing stand-alone work was a new and striking theory that would come to be known as the *special theory of relativity*. And it would change the way we saw the world, especially the way we saw time.

To understand this new conception of time, it's helpful to use the same thought experiment that Einstein used involving passengers aboard trains. Consider the following. A passenger moving forward in a train has their velocity added to that of the moving train. For example, if I'm walking for-ward at five kilometers per hour in the train car and the train car is moving at 100 kph, then I am moving at a combined velocity of 105 kph relative to a stationary object, like a tree (Fig. 9).

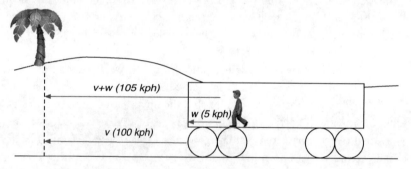

Fig. 9. *The velocity of the passenger is added to the velocity of the moving train relative to the tree on the embankment.*

If there's another train nearby moving at 150 kph, it is moving at 150 kph relative to the tree, 50 kph relative to my train, and 45 kph relative to me as I move forward in my own train (Fig. 10).

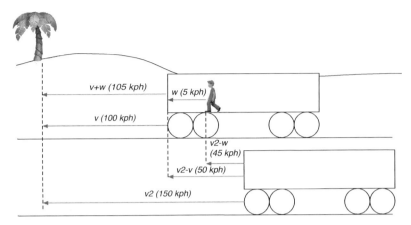

Fig. 10. *The second train travels at different relative velocities compared with the stationary tree, the first train, and the passenger moving on the first train.*

This is all pretty straightforward stuff. What Einstein demonstrated was that this common-sense understanding breaks down when light gets involved. If we substitute a beam of light for that second train, the light moves at the *same speed* relative to the tree, to my train, and to me. Einstein demonstrated that the speed of light (c) is a constant: it doesn't change. No matter how fast you're going toward it or away from it, the speed of light remains unchanged.[3]

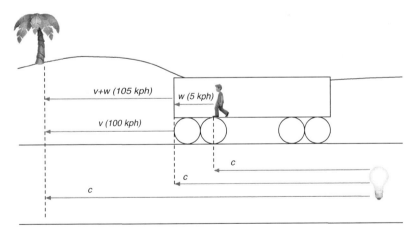

Fig. 11. *The speed of light (c) remains constant relative to the tree on the embankment, the moving passenger, and the moving train.*

3. Einstein, *Relativity*, 9–11.

The clearly counterintuitive nature of relativity is a little unnerving. We don't like it when the universe is at odds with our ordinary experience. How is it that the speed of light is constant with regard to both the stationary object (the tree) and the two moving objects (the train and the passenger)? It gets even stranger.

The same thing goes for the old-style word problem in math: a train leaving Chicago headed east traveling at 100 kph and a train leaving Buffalo headed west at 100 kph. They meet somewhere in Ohio, approaching each other at a combined velocity of 200 kph (100 kph + 100 kph = 200 kph). However, if we replace these trains with beams of light, those beams of light approach each other not at twice the speed of light, which is what we would expect from our experience with the trains, but rather at the speed of light. In relativity, $c + c = c$.

But how can that be? Math is math: if $1 + 1 = 2$, then $1c + 1c = 2c$, no? What Einstein demonstrated was that in cases involving such high velocities, *time itself* was not constant. In relativity, because the speed of light is always a constant, there is no other solution except to admit that time itself is a variable. Time is not absolute or certain.

Einstein demonstrated the implications of this phenomenon with another famous thought experiment known as the "twin paradox." In this paradox, there are two twins, say, 30 years old. One twin climbs aboard a space ship and travels to a star 10 light years away at velocities near the speed of light (Fig. 12). As far as she can tell, only a few months of time have elapsed as she is winging her way to Epsilon Eridani and back. However, when she returns, she discovers that 20 years have elapsed on earth and her young adult sister is now a middle-aged woman of 50.[4]

---

4. Hawking, *Universe in a Nutshell*, 11.

Fig. 12. *As a result of the dilation of time at high velocities, the spacefaring twin experiences less subjective time on her voyage than her earthbound sister. (Illustration © 2018 Kathleen Kimball. Used by permission.)*

The implications of this phenomenon of *time dilation* are striking: our perceptions of time are subjective. And not just the "watched pot never boils" or "time flies when you're having fun" kind of subjective—*actually* subjective. For the spacefaring twin, time has *actually* moved slower for her as a function of velocity under relativity than it has for her earthbound twin. This curious aspect of relativity has been confirmed through experimental observation. It has to be accounted for in the motion of our orbiting GPS satellites to account for the fact that our satellites are moving slightly faster through time than those of us on earth are.[5] Each of us, it turns out, has their own personal time and the time of any two of us only agrees when we are at rest with respect to one another.[6] There is no such thing as objective time.[7]

5. A satellite's higher relative speed would mean that time would move more slowly for the satellite than an earthbound observer. However, because the satellite is further away from earth's gravity than the earthbound observer, the net balance is that time actually moves slightly faster aboard an orbiting satellite than it does on the ground.

6. Hawking, *Universe in a Nutshell*, 9.

7. To be fair, at terrestrial velocities the differences are really, really small, so this fact is of limited use when you're late meeting someone for lunch.

It gets worse. Relativity goes on to say that it is impossible to say absolutely whether two events occur at the same time. To illustrate this, Einstein provides another thought experiment.

Lightning has struck two points on the railroad track (A and B), both of which are equidistant from a midpoint, M (Fig. 13). The light from the lightning strikes arrives at the midpoint M at the same time, indicating to an observer there that the lightning strikes at A and B were simultaneous. However, observers on a moving train, seated at a point corresponding to M (M'), because of their velocity on the train, will encounter the light from A earlier than that emitted from B. From their point of view, A happens *before* B.

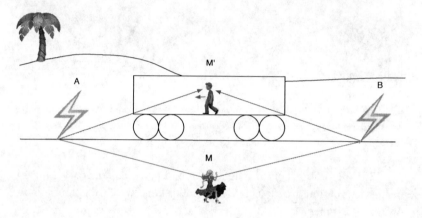

Fig. 13. *Because of the train's forward motion, the light from lightning strike A is seen by the moving passenger at M' before the light from lightning strike B, making it appear to the passenger as if A happens before B. However, from the point of view of the observer at M, the light from both A and B arrive at the same time, making it appear that the events are simultaneous.*

According to Einstein, events that are simultaneous with respect to the stationary observer are not simultaneous with respect to the train and vice versa. This is known as the relativity of simultaneity.[8] So do the lightning strikes happen at the same time or not? The answer is yes. And no. Relativity maintains that we cannot state in any absolute sense whether the two events were simultaneous or not.

It was not time alone that Einstein redefined. He had something to say about matter and space too. In his next paper (and fourth that year), entitled, "Does the Inertia of a Body Depend upon Its Energy Content?," he

8. Einstein, *Relativity*, 13–15.

put forward the idea that matter and energy were equivalent, concluding with the now famous equation: $E=mc^2$.

A few years later, Einstein incorporated gravity into relativity in his *general theory of relativity*, which posited that space and time were united in a continuum known as *space-time* that was not "flat" but "curved" by the effects of gravity.

All of this is to say that by the time we got to the first decades of the twentieth century, we'd come a long way from our small, manageable universe consisting of the earth and a dome of sky in which the stars were fixed objects. Now we inhabited a universe where *nothing* was fixed, not even time.

And that wasn't even the most disconcerting part.

Relativity made a huge impact on the twentieth century, so much so that *Time* magazine even went so far as to name Albert Einstein the "Person of the Century," given the indelible mark his work had on the science and, through the development of nuclear energy, the warfare of the twentieth century. But Einstein's influence has gone well beyond the impact he had in the realm of physics. What truly changed the world was the impact relativity had on so many other areas of thought. If velocity, time, and simultaneity were variable based on the observer's point of view, then perhaps everything else was relative too. Morality. Ideology. Culture. Religion. The question of relativity in these "social" aspects has been a matter of debate ever since. This kind of uncertainty terrified everyone—religious folks in particular.

Some philosophers take relativity a step further and argue that *all* truth is context specific, not just observable phenomena in the natural world. That is, it's not just whether two lightning strikes are simultaneous or or whether an object is in motion relative to a given frame of reference; it's that every single proposition of truth is dependent on context. Every single one. This theory of *strong contextualism* argues that universal truths can only be proved if you assume the existence of universal truths in the first place. Thus, they conclude that there are no absolute universal truths, independent of some context, and that there exists a context in which any given truth from one context is false in another.[9] Does your head hurt yet?

Relativity took the Copernican world, which had already been knocked off its Ptolemaic foundations, and warped it. And we were just getting started.

If relativity seems hard to wrap your mind around, quantum mechanics takes the counterintuitive weirdness to an entirely new level. Quantum mechanics is that branch of physics that describes the universe at the

---

9. Edmonds, "What If All Truth."

smallest, subatomic level. Its rules are quite different from those of relativity, which describes the large-scale universe quite well but comes up short in the subatomic realm. But that does not mean that quantum physics lacks the capacity to astonish just as much as relativity does.

In the early years of the twentieth century, the German physicist Werner Heisenberg made the astonishing claim that when it came to observing the behavior of subatomic particles, we were limited in what we could know. If we used high-frequency, short-wavelength light, that light would reveal where a particle was but would interfere with its momentum and trajectory. If we used low-frequency, long-wavelength light, we could identify its momentum, but not as precisely its location. Heisenberg noted that we could know *either* a subatomic particle's location (where it is) *or* its momentum (where it's going), but not both.[10]

This principle, known as the Heisenberg uncertainty principle, was not immediately accepted by most physicists. In fact, Einstein—whose work had helped to create quantum physics—rejected the idea that there was a fundamental vagueness or imprecision at the heart of the laws of the universe.[11] Einstein even spent the rest of his career attempting to disprove quantum physics, albeit unsuccessfully.

Was Heisenberg's claim as bad as it first seemed? Perhaps Heisenberg was merely making a statement of *epistemology*—that is, what we could *know* about subatomic particles—rather than making a statement about that particle's actual being. Einstein was willing to concede that we could not *know* both the position and momentum of a subatomic particle, but he maintained that surely these particles *had* both a position and a momentum. After all, how could they not? In recent decades, however, experiments have shown that subatomic particles simply cannot be described as simultaneously having position and momentum. The uncertainty principle does not just describe our ability to observe subatomic particles successfully; it describes a fundamental property of those subatomic systems.[12] The physics is clear: randomness, vagueness, and uncertainty are embedded in the physical laws of the universe, whether Einstein likes it or not.

But the weirdness of quantum mechanics was only beginning to be understood. The uncertainty principle leads us to even stranger phenomena. One such phenomenon is the possibility of *quantum tunneling*, an admittedly

10. Greene, *Elegant Universe*, 113.

11. The meaning of the German term that Heisenberg used, *Ungenauigkeit*, is better translated as "imprecision" or "vagueness" rather than "uncertainty." That being said, there remains an uncertainty because of the imprecision with which such information can be obtained.

12. Greene, *Elegant Universe*, 114.

unlikely—but *not impossible*—instance of an object passing through another solid object by virtue of its particles simultaneously "spilling out" through the solid object. It is very, very, very unlikely to happen, but it is something physicists describe as a *non-zero chance*, meaning it's *possible*. It would definitely explain all those missing socks in the laundry.

Even weirder than quantum uncertainty and the possibility of quantum tunneling are the results of experiments in quantum physics that defy not only expectation, but also intuition and basic common sense. In these experiments, photons or electrons are emitted toward a barrier with one or more slit openings in it. On the other side of the barrier is a phosphorescent screen that records the impact of each electron with a bright dot. If a beam of electrons is aimed at a barrier in which there is one slit carved, the wave will propagate through the slit in a predictable fashion, much like waves of water through a small gap in a wall, and will create an expected image on the screen opposite. (Fig. 14)

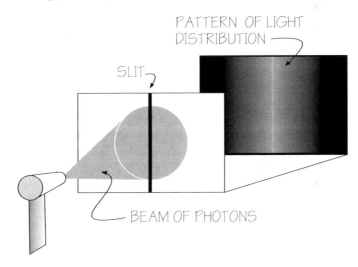

Fig. 14. *Light from a wave passes through a slit in a barrier, creating a distribution pattern on the film opposite.*

If a beam of electrons is aimed at a barrier in which there are two slits carved out, the wave spreads out as before, but this time, because there are two points of entry, two waves will be produced. The two waves will magnify each other where two crests intersect and diminish each other where two troughs come together. This creates what is known as an *interference pattern* and that pattern will be reflected in the image that results (Fig. 15).

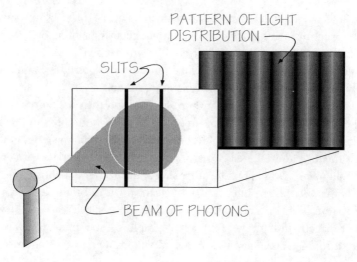

Fig. 15. Light from a wave passes through a pair of slits in a barrier, creating two sets of waves that interfere with one another and create an interference pattern on the film opposite.

Now, if instead of a beam of light or particles, *single* electrons or photons are fired one by one at a barrier in which there is one slit carved, a small band will appear on the plate opposite where the electrons have struck. The narrower the slit, the narrower the width of the band of electrons captured (Fig. 16).

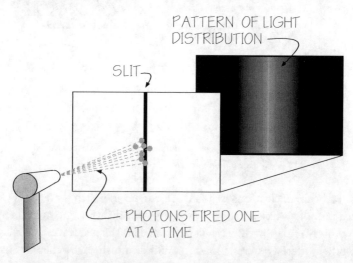

Fig. 16. Single particles, fired one by one, will create a single-band distribution pattern on the plate opposite.

However, if single electrons are fired one by one at a barrier in which there are two slits, a surprising thing happens. If the electrons are observed—that is, if light is shined upon them—they behave as you would expect them to and produce two bands on the photographic plate (Fig. 17).

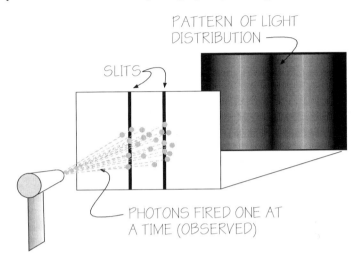

Fig. 17. *Observed photons (i.e., ones that have light shined upon them), fired one at a time produce two bands of light, as expected.*

However, if the electrons are unobserved, instead of seeing two bands on the plate opposite as one would expect, we get an interference pattern as we did with the plane wave of light (Fig. 18).

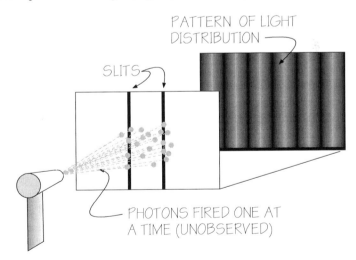

Fig. 18. *Unobserved particles, fired one at a time through one of two slits in a barrier, are expected to create two bands as in the experiment above. Instead, an interference pattern appears on the plate opposite as if a wave of particles had passed through instead.*

But how is this possible? The electrons are coming through one at a time; there is no reason for there to be an interference pattern. What are they interfering with? The surprising answer is that the electrons (or any subatomic particles, really) are behaving simultaneously like particles and waves, and are *interfering with themselves*. That is, each particle is behaving as if it went through *both* slits at the same time and interfered with *itself*.

It gets weirder. Physicist Richard Feynman proposed that the electrons are not simply behaving *as if* they had gone through both slits, but that the electron actually *does* go through both slits. Feynman argued that in traveling from the source to the phosphorescent plate, each individual electron actually traverses *every possible trajectory simultaneously*—perhaps even through distant points in the universe—on its way to the plate. In the aggregate, the paths this electron takes yield the same result as a *wave function*, the mathematical representation of probability.[13]

What this means is that the location of such an electron can only be stated as a function of *probability*, not certainty. That's a disquieting notion—disquieting enough to provoke Einstein to object, "God does not play dice with the universe!" It's disquieting because we tend to think of scientists as those who can provide us with the answers. These are, after all, the people in the white lab coats with the expensive microscopes and all the computers and equations. And the best they can do when asked for the position of a subatomic particle is say that it's *probably* over there. *Probably*?

This odd both/and nature of unobserved subatomic particles led some physicists to argue that until a subatomic particle interacted with or was observed by the outside world, it remained in a state of *quantum superposition*, meaning that the particle occupied multiple states simultaneously. At this point, its location was said to be *smeared* and could only be described through the probabilities of the wave function. Once observed or interacted with, however, this wave function "collapsed" and only one of the possibilities remained. Some physicists even argued that this had implications for the world of ordinary experience beyond the subatomic.

Not everyone was convinced that quantum physics was relevant to anything beyond the subatomic. In fact, the physicist Erwin Schrödinger reacted to this interpretation of quantum mechanics by trying to illustrate how bizarre this would be on a real-life scale through a now famous thought experiment:

> [To demonstrate how absurd this theory is] one can even set up
> quite ridiculous cases. A cat is penned up in a steel chamber,
> along with the following device (which must be secured against

13. Ibid., 110–11.

direct interference by the cat): in a Geiger counter there is a tiny bit of radioactive substance, so small, that perhaps in the course of the hour one of the atoms decays, but also, with equal probability, perhaps none; if it happens, the counter tube discharges and through a relay releases a hammer which shatters a small flask of hydrocyanic acid. If one has left this entire system to itself for an hour, one would say that the cat still lives if, meanwhile, no atom has decayed.[14]

Fig. 19. *In Schrödinger's example, the cat must be both dead and alive until someone looks into the box—a result he believed was absurd.*
(*Illustration © 2018 Kathleen Kimball. Used by permission.*)

Schrödinger pointed out that the mathematics of this experiment would claim that the living cat and the dead cat were "mixed or smeared out in equal parts"—that is, until someone looked, the cat would be both dead and alive. He accepted the idea that we could not know what was going on at the subatomic level, but the idea that the quantum *superposition* of the particle in question translated into the superposition of the cat (simultaneously alive and dead) was absurd to him. He concluded, "There is a difference between a shaky or out-of-focus photograph and a snapshot of clouds and fog banks," meaning, our unclear picture does not mean that reality is unclear, only that our ability to capture that reality is.

14. Schrödinger and Trimmer, "Present Situation in Quantum Mechanics."

Schrödinger was clear in his belief that one could not translate the quantum uncertainty at the subatomic level to macroscopic scale events; the idea that the cat was *both living and dead* until someone opened the chamber to check was ridiculous. However, since that time, some physicists have argued that the superposition of a cat being both alive and dead is real until the box is opened and we look for ourselves. Some double-slit experiments have even been performed with molecules with as many as 114 atoms, raising real questions about just where the boundary between the subatomic quantum world and the macroscopic "classical" world lies.[15] These experiments seem to suggest that the world, even on a real-life scale, can exist in a both/and superposition until it's observed. The universe, these physicists argue, allows for this kind of both/and state of affairs even in ordinary experience, such that reality is approaching the old joke: "Schrödinger's cat walks into a bar and doesn't."

* * *

In the end, our exploration of the natural world yields a world of uncertainty. Relativity defies our desire to declare any absolute frame of reference and even demonstrates that the experience of time is subjective. Likewise, quantum physics does not predict a single definite result for an observation; it predicts a number of different possible outcomes and the likelihood of each. Despite Einstein's objections to the contrary, God does indeed play dice with the universe. It seems that there is uncertainty written into the cosmos itself.

So, if you were looking to the nature of the universe for certainty and fixed answers, relativity and quantum mechanics suggest you were looking in the wrong place.

15. Moskowitz, "Largest Molecules."

The Inescapability of Uncertainty

In this part of the book we have seen that the certainty we seek cannot be found.

We saw that religious faith, often billed as a source of certainty, is nevertheless filled with uncertainty. The highly metaphorical nature of religious language—and of religious ritual as well—reveals religion to be a signpost pointing in the direction of some ultimate reality, rather than a perfect definition and description of that ultimate reality.

We saw that this embedded uncertainty in religion was not limited to religious language but could be found in all human language. We looked at the obstacles to communication, the challenges of translation, the fluidity of meaning, and the ambiguity of words and syntax. And we looked at the startling abundance of metaphor in language, revealing that language too is not a tool that perfectly describes the world we encounter, but is itself a signpost, pointing us toward that world. In any event, it is not a medium of perfect certainty.

We saw that language is not our only encounter with the world that is rife with uncertainty. Our senses too give us reason for uncertainty and doubt. The input of our senses must be interpreted by the brain, and because the brain prefers simplicity and coherence to complexity and inconsistency, it frequently "regularizes" the sensory inputs it receives from our senses, so that we can look at a dress and perceive it to be a different color from what our friends see. We can watch a man repeat a syllable and hear him saying one thing, then close our eyes and hear something else. We can be easily tricked and misdirected, or we can simply ignore information from our senses. Even here, there is uncertainty.

We have seen that the application of pure reason and the scientific method cannot deliver us from this tide of uncertainty. In fact, contrary to what most lay people understand, the scientific method does not eliminate our uncertainty. As a methodology, it deals primarily in probabilities, not in absolutes, and is in a constant process of undermining reigning assumptions. We saw that science does not eliminate uncertainty; it revels in it.

And finally, we saw that as we have grown in knowledge and come to progressively better understandings of the world we live in, we have also come to understand just how little we do know. And we have come to understand just how uncertain the world itself is.

We no longer inhabit a flat world covered by a dome of sky in a cozy and compact cosmos; we inhabit a mind-bogglingly immense universe, boundless and perhaps even infinite, in which no one frame of reference can be declared absolute and in which the very fabric of the universe teems with unpredictability.

Uncertainty, is not just a function of our metaphorical belief systems, our imprecise, uncertain human language, or a function of imperfect senses and skeptical scientific method. Uncertainty, it seems, is embedded into the very nature of the universe.

Uncertainty is inescapable.

PART III

The Uncertain Way Forward

The whole problem with the world is that fools and fanatics are always so certain of themselves, and wiser people so full of doubts.

—BERTRAND RUSSELL

So, what do we do with all of this?

Having seen that the world we live in, the medium we use to communicate about that world, and the systems we use to give meaning to our experiences of the world all contain unavoidable uncertainties, where do we go from here?

In this part of the book we will look at how embracing uncertainty is not only necessary, it is good. We will see that uncertainty can offer surprising benefits to religious faith, that doubt makes for a more meaningful faith, and that metaphor can help to build meaningful relationships across religious lines.

In the chapters that follow we will see not that the way forward is uncertain, but that uncertainty is the way forward.

Chapter 16

Theology in a Time of Metaphor

WHAT BECOMES OF RELIGION when religion is understood to be metaphor? Is it possible to bridge traditional religion and a metaphorical understanding of religion?

Undoubtedly there are many who would greet the departure of their religious certainty with feelings of loss. If you have for so long turned to your religious traditions to give you the certainty you crave, you may not easily accept the inherent uncertainty of religious faith. If I must accept that my religious traditions are full of uncertainty, have I not lost everything of value in my faith?

Quite the opposite.

In this chapter, we will look at the ways that seeing religion through the lens of metaphor shapes our understanding of scripture and theology, of what we can know, of the relative value of any theology, and of the role of mystery. In all of these, we will see that metaphor and uncertainty have much to offer a religious tradition and can give it new power and meaning.

Metaphor, Scripture, and Theology

This is all a slippery slope.

That's what you're thinking.

No doubt, there are many who might read this book and conclude that I am arguing that all bets are off when it comes to religion. I am not. But how do we know where metaphor ends and literal truth begins? When we read of Jesus walking on water are we talking fact or metaphor? When we talk about Jesus' resurrection from the dead are we talking fact or metaphor? When we talk about God altogether? Am I really arguing that all of those things are just metaphors? Should we abandon all belief in anything concrete?

No.

But is Jesus walking on water a metaphor? Maybe. Maybe not. The point I'm trying to make is not whether or not certain things are factually accurate, it's that given how poetic and metaphorical religion and religious language can be, we cannot have *certainty* about whether particular things are literal truth or metaphor. If a believer feels in their heart of hearts that Jesus walked on water, then, by all means, they should believe that. However, recognizing the uncertainty inherent in religion, a believer has to believe it with humility and can't assume that someone who does not believe the same is somehow lacking in mental or spiritual capacity. The uncertainties in religion help believers to understand that their claims on truth might not be as perfect as they imagine them to be. That can be unsettling, to be sure, but it can also be empowering.

First, even if the bulk of the scriptures were metaphorical that would not undermine the text. The text is able to communicate truth and meaning through metaphor. The Psalms say that God will raise us up on eagle's wings—does anyone assume that God has literal wings to carry us into the sky? Does that make such a statement less true for those who believe it? There is nothing preventing someone from believing that the scriptures are both God's word *and* metaphor. What are metaphors, after all, but words?

Second, embracing the metaphorical nature of the text allows the reader to explore the deeper message being pointed toward. Acknowledging the uncertainty of the scriptures—not knowing whether something is meant to be literal or metaphorical—may help to remind a person to look beyond the metaphor to the reality that is being pointed at. For example, whether or not Jesus actually walked on water, the story is not placed in the scriptures merely to provide an interesting narrative about something that happened one day on the Sea of Galilee; it was placed there to tell the reader something about Jesus. Even a story of Jesus walking on water goes beyond simple narrative to point past itself to the reality experienced in Jesus of Nazareth.

So here are two ways a conversation about scripture might go:

A: Did Jesus really walk on water?

B: Yes, he did; it's in the Bible. And if you don't believe that, you're denying God's word and are going to hell.

—or—

A: Did Jesus really walk on water?

B: I don't know. I like to believe he did. But in any event, what I think the story is telling us is something profound about Jesus . . .

The second way embraces the power of metaphor to point beyond itself to a deeper truth, a truth the faithful are called to seek out as part of a life of faith.

Some make the case that embracing metaphor is necessary to the future of faith. For example, theologian John Hick argues that Christians should keep the traditional claim that Jesus is an incarnation of God but should understand the claim metaphorically. Seeing traditional claims through the lens of metaphor, he argues, is necessary for the church to engage those who grew up in the church and who have become dissatisfied with its inability to reflect on its beliefs critically and thoughtfully. A metaphorical understanding of religious faith is also helpful in engaging with those outside the church who are drawn to religion through a deep spiritual hunger but who find the church's pat answers to spiritual questions unsatisfying.[1] Understanding the metaphors of a religious tradition helps that religion to engage with a changing world much more effectively than by holding on to traditional dogmas or literalist interpretations based on an ancient worldview.

Metaphor and What Can Be Known

The claim that religion is metaphor is not a claim that there is no underlying truth; it is a reminder that the truth we proclaim through metaphor is imperfectly known. As such, it stakes out an important middle ground in the question of what we can know.

There are those who argue that language should be used only to make objective statements about objective realities and truths. These *objectivists* believe that using metaphor is using words in their "improper senses" to stir emotions and, therefore, leads "away from truth and toward illusion."[2] Their belief is built on the idea that there is an objective reality independent of humanity that can be known, an idea that can be comforting in an uncertain world.

On the other side of the issue are the *subjectivists*, who argue that truth depends entirely on one's own perspective. It is an idea found at the heart of *postmodernism*, known for many things, but in the arena of philosophy and religion primarily known for one basic tenet: there is no absolute truth. It is not simply a rejection of the medieval idea that truth came through

1. Hick, *Metaphor of God Incarnate*, 13.
2. Lakoff and Johnson, *Metaphors We Live By*, 186–88.

divine revelation, or the modern idea that truth was known through human reason; it rejects the idea that there is an absolute truth *at all*.[3]

Between these two, metaphor offers a middle ground. Lakoff and Johnson see the use of metaphor as neither an objective nor a subjective kind of rationality, but as an *imaginative rationality*. Metaphor uses one of the most important tools that we have for trying to "comprehend partially what cannot be comprehended totally: our feelings, aesthetic experiences, moral practices, and spiritual awareness." In this way, metaphor does not need to deny the existence of truth, but it accommodates our inability to perfectly know what the truth is.[4]

The use of metaphor doesn't mean that there is no objective truth. It means that truth has to be conveyed in ways that people can relate to and understand. And in order to do that the truth has to be expressed in ways that appeal to ordinary human experience—through metaphor. Because it is impossible to separate metaphor from our experience of the world, we will never have certainty as to what that objective truth is. That is, the truth will always be expressed in terms that come from *our* experience—not from some objective reality.

Is there an ultimate truth? I like to think that there is. Of course, I cannot be *certain* that there is. I'm not alone in that; indeed, mathematicians and scientists and theologians have spent their lives looking for that ultimate truth, convinced that it exists. I will admit this: the postmodernists are right in saying that human beings will never *know* this ultimate truth with certainty. The statement that there is no absolute truth may not be true as a matter of *ontology*—that is, as a matter of the existence of things[5]—but it is likely correct as a matter of *epistemology*—that is, what can be known. The truth is out there; but so long as we're using metaphors to describe the ultimate reality of things, we will never be able to claim to have captured it perfectly.

Our understanding may be incomplete, our knowledge lacking. We may never be able to comprehend with fullness the nature of ultimate reality, and the metaphors that we use to talk about that ultimate truth are not the same as the truths they represent. But they are pointers *toward* that truth, and, in that capacity, they have great value to us.

3. It has been pointed out, of course, that the statement "There is no absolute truth" is itself a statement of absolute truth. It's an inherent contradiction that might show a fatal overreach in this approach of post-modernist philosophy.

4. Lakoff and Johnson, *Metaphors We Live By*, 193.

5. As noted above in chapter 15, however, there are those who argue that quantum uncertainty isn't just a matter of what we can know, it's a description of what actually exists.

The Value of a Metaphorical Theology

One objection to seeing religions as metaphorical systems is rooted in the fear of relativism. If everyone is just using metaphors for some unknown, ineffable mystery, then who's to say which one is *right*?

Perhaps we won't be able to. Perhaps we are denying ourselves the ability to reject one religion or another as *false*. (That may not be the worst thing.) But to do so would not be the same as saying that all metaphors for the ineffable were equally *valuable*. We might not be able to know whether the metaphor GOD IS A FATHER were *truer* than GOD IS A GIANT SEA SERPENT, but we might be able to discuss whether it were more valuable.

The same thing would be true of any religious metaphor: arguments about the truth of an unknowable reality would yield to arguments about the value of a metaphor. And the value of a metaphor could be determined by its implications for the here and now. Here's an example.

There are myriad views of the afterlife in religion, many of which are pretty detailed for an experience that no one has ever been able to document. There are two major views in Christianity, one of which is far more popularly held than the other. The more popular belief is that when we die our soul travels to another realm of either reward or punishment, where we live on in either non-corporeal bliss or in non-corporeal torment for eternity. The righteous dead can look down on the living from their perch in heaven.

The less commonly held belief is that when we die, we die. At some point in the future, we are raised to new, embodied life in a resurrection of the dead. The righteous live on forever and the wicked are annihilated in the lake of fire. The creation is renewed, the world is remade as the world of perfect peace and justice it was always intended to be, and God dwells with us in the renewed creation.

Which one accurately describes what happens after death? I have no idea. Perhaps neither. But I can tell you which one I think is more valuable, which one is more helpful. In my mind, that is clearly the second option.

I favor that view not because I have any idea what actually happens to us when we die or because that particular view is the older of the two. Rather, I favor this view because it is the more valuable—because of its implications for the here and now. For example, a theology of resurrection speaks to God's intention to renew and restore the creation rather than to abandon it. It speaks to the worthiness of the material creation. It has implications in terms of my theology of the body, in terms of the environment, of the other creatures with whom we share this world, and of questions of basic human dignity. All of these things are profoundly affirmed in a theology that looks forward to a resurrected, bodily existence here in a renewed creation, much more so than in a theology that looks toward the day when my immortal soul flees its prison of flesh and returns to the spirit world. In short, because of its implications, the metaphor THE BODY IS A WORK OF GOD is more valuable than THE BODY IS A PRISON.

The merits of a metaphorical theology are in the fruits it bears in the here and now. Does a metaphor prompt me toward love of neighbor, justice, and peacemaking? Does it compel me to meet people's real, material needs in the here and now? To the extent a metaphorical theology prepares me only for escape, for example, it is less meaningful to me than a theology that prepares me to engage fully with the world in the here and now. Appraising metaphors on their value might be a far more constructive approach, and far more relevant for those who use the metaphors.

Now, when it comes to the metaphors we use to frame religious ideas, we do not embrace arbitrary metaphors; we embrace those that make the most sense to us in accord with our deeper values and our judgments about the world we live in. Samuel Coleridge noted that the particular metaphors of the Bible, for example, were not merely shadows arbitrarily invented to stand in for universal truths, they were "consubstantial with the truths of which they are the conductors."[6] That is, they have *something* to do with both the ultimate truth being claimed and the way we experience that truth.

As Lakoff and Johnson point out, metaphors allow us to understand abstractions in language grounded in our concrete experiences of the world. That concrete experience is what makes the ideas and abstractions relatable and real. It is what provokes the "Ah! I know what you're getting at!" moment of realization and understanding. When the metaphor intersects with an individual's experience of the world, it takes on a power that helps the deeper truth not simply to be understood, but to be experienced. When we hear the metaphors of faith, they only make sense to us if they connect with our experience. A metaphor that connects with our experience has value and can be judged accordingly.

The uncertainty that a metaphorical theology reflects may not permit us to say that any given metaphor is right or wrong. In a way, all metaphors for God or the ineffable become permissible, but that doesn't mean that all of them need be affirmed as valuable. Or, to paraphrase St. Paul: *all metaphors are lawful but not all metaphors are beneficial.*

---

6. Adams, *Philosophy of the Literary Symbolic*, 71.

Embracing Humility

Nothing that I am writing should be interpreted as advocating that people abandon their cherished beliefs. Such beliefs speak a powerful truth to the believer and, in the believer, they are confirmed by an experience of the divine, of the ineffable. But it's precisely that ineffability that should give the believer some humility, especially because religious beliefs have to be understood in a different light than other truths that might be asserted.

Religious beliefs are not, for example, the same as scientific fact. In science, a scientist who performs an experiment and obtains a particular result will publish her results and invite others to follow. If there were no flaws in the scientist's experiments, then her results should be replicable and other scientists should be able to obtain the same results. After a while, a scientific consensus will emerge about what can be said with a greater likelihood and what cannot.

But it is not so with faith. God is not testable like a scientific theory. There is no laboratory where I can run an experiment on God, or that I can run once with God and once without God.[7] God is not an empirically measured phenomenon. God is an experience.

But since one person cannot receive the experience of another, except through language, our ability to communicate these experiences with certainty is limited. I might have a powerful experience of God that confirms all of my most deeply held beliefs, but I cannot give that experience to you so that you, too, will become convinced of what I believe. All I can do is tell you about it. My testimony relies on human language to express something that can only be understood through experience.

What so many believers fail to appreciate is that these experiences do not automatically translate through speech nor do they always convince. I

---

7. The main objection to pseudo-scientific theories like "intelligent design" is that they cannot be tested.

might have an incredibly powerful experience of the divine, but I should not expect that my experience alone will convince you. I would not expect your experience alone to convince *me*.

Where the spiritual enterprise differs as well from the scientific is that we have no agreed upon starting point. In a scientific paper, there will always be a section that defines the methodology used and the particulars of the experiment and will look something like this:

> Healthy male Sprague-Dawley rats (n = 22; 300–450 g; Charles River Laboratories, Wilmington, MA) were anesthetized with an intraperitoneal injection of a mixture of ketamine and acepromazine (72 and 4 mg/kg, respectively) and 0.01 mg/kg of subcutaneous buprenorphine for analgesia. Core body temperature was maintained at 370C with a warming pad (Harvard Apparatus, Cambridge, MA). The right and left femoral veins were cannulated with PE-50 catheters for intravenous (IV) infusion of the PFC and control solutions and the femoral artery was cannulated for blood sampling and arterial blood pressure and heart rate (HR) monitoring (Datascope Corporation, Montvale, New Jersey). Because pilot studies showed that rats breathing room air (21% oxygen) became hypoxemic, all animals were intubated and mechanically ventilated with a small animal ventilator (RSP1002, Kent Scientific Corp., Lichtfield, CT) using 40% oxygen and 60% nitrogen with settings adjusted to maintain normal blood gases ($PaCO_2$ of 35–45 mm Hg and $PaO_2 \geq$ 80 mm Hg). Pial microcirculation was accessed as described in Levasseur *et al.* [22]. Briefly, a rectangular craniotomy (~3 x 4 mm) was prepared in the right parietal bone and the dura was cut and reflected to the side to allow visualization and imaging of pial surface microvasculature. . . . [*and so on*][8]

The genetic line of the lab rats is provided; weight and anesthesia are detailed. Body temperature, the brand of warming pad used, the vein in which the catheter was placed, the brand of the blood pressure monitor, and the brand of intubator and ventilator are all provided, and more. In short, everything needed to replicate the experiment *exactly* is provided.

But let's say that I've had an experience of God. How does someone else even go about trying to replicate that? What do we even mean when we say, "I've had an experience of God"? It is not a statement like, "I had an experience with a zebrafish," where I could provide the specifics of that exact kind of fish and you could go out and replicate that experience. Even Soskice, who notes that science and religion make similar use of metaphor

---

8. Abutarboush, "Brain Oxygenation."

to describe things they don't yet know or understand, nevertheless admits that unlike science, religion does not afford us the opportunity to transfer another person's religious experiences.[9]

An experience of the divine is particular kind of experience not universally shared—how can such an experience be communicated? Although metaphors allow for partial communication of an experience that is not shared, without a shared experience, speakers cannot communicate meaning fully and adequately.[10] Because the only way to convey an ineffable experience of the divine is through metaphor, our ability to communicate that experience will only ever be *partial*.

However powerful the experience of the divine I might have, I cannot export that experience to someone else. All I can do is tell them what I have experienced and use the uncertain tool of metaphor to do so. Someone might hear what I say and agree that they've had a similar experience, but how can I know that we are describing the same reality? Can I take someone else's agreement with me as definitive proof that my experience is universal? If I cannot, shouldn't I have some humility when coming to conclusions about whether my experience represents universal truth, however true and powerful it might have been for me?

It is not only the impossibility of sharing experiences directly that leads us to humility—humility is necessary in helping us to understand our *own* experiences. Let's say I've had a powerful religious experience—how do I know whether it is appropriate to describe such an experience as an experience of *God*? How do I know that I am using the metaphor *God* correctly? For this I need to appeal to experience, to an interpretive tradition, and, most of all, to community.[11] Because appealing to community and authority requires humility, humility, then, is essential not only when claiming to possess religious knowledge, but also when seeking to *understand* it.

The community not only supplies the vocabulary with which an experience might be described (e.g., *God*), but can help a person determine whether that vocabulary truly is the word that should be used to frame that experience. It is the community that helps to determine that *God* might be more appropriate to use when someone says that their heart has been "strangely warmed" than it would be when someone says that they have been called to commit a genocide against a neighboring people. Having supplied the word *God* to refer to a particular experience, the community

---

9. Soskice, *Metaphor and Religious Language*, 138, 49.

10. Lakoff and Johnson, *Metaphors We Live By*, 224–25.

11. Soskice, *Metaphor and Religious Language*, 49.

can help to determine whether someone's use of the term fits within the accepted usage.[12]

The community is not just the arbiter of whether it's appropriate for a given metaphor in a given instance; it can determine whether a given metaphor for an experience of the divine is appropriate at all. Even were everyone to agree that the language for the divine was metaphorical, it wouldn't mean that all bets were off and that everything would be appropriate. There may be room for expanding current metaphorical models LIKE GOD IS A FATHER to GOD IS A MOTHER as attitudes about gender and the divine shift. But a model like GOD IS AN UNCLE is less likely to gain traction because, even though male, it does not speak to the experience of relationship that most people share. For that same reason, GOD IS A TOADSTOOL or GOD IS A LAWN CHAIR are also unlikely. Thus, the experience of the community and the community's reflection on its encounter with the divine is a check on the idea that a metaphorical understanding of religion would lead to a metaphor free-for-all.

But beyond the fact that experiences are not easily communicated, perhaps the greatest reason for humility is simply the immensity of what we're trying to comprehend.

The universe is immense. Just the part we can see is mind-blowingly huge. Now, if God is, by most religious accounts, *greater* than that, how on earth do we imagine that we've got God all worked out when the universe itself remains firmly beyond our ability to comprehend? This too is something we've been told before, and we don't have to go far to see it.

The book of Job is one of the more enigmatic books in the Hebrew Bible and for good reason: it's trying to be. The narrative tells the story of Job, a man who is described as "pure, right, and God-fearing" who suffers greatly in spite of being a pure, right, and God-fearing person. Throughout the text, his friends try to convince him he must have deserved the punishment; he insists that he is innocent and that God must not know that he is suffering. At the end of the narrative, God appears to Job from the whirlwind, and issues a withering rebuke to all the parties, and especially to Job:

> Where were you when I laid the earth's foundation? Tell me if
> you know. Who put its measurements—you know, don't you?
> Or who stretched out a line over it? What were its bases set on
> and who cast its cornerstone as the morning stars joyfully sang
> together and all the children of God shouted out? Or who shut

---

12. It is entirely fair to point out that not even the community's say-so is the ultimate guide. If it were, we would have no basis for criticizing the many instances where the community has approved of associating *God* with all manner of despicable acts.

the sea in with doors when it burst forth from the womb? When I set the clouds as the sea's garment and the darkness as its swaddling band and established a proscription for it and put bars and doors and said, "Up to here you can come but no farther, and here your proud waves are stopped"? (Job 38:4–11)

God goes on like this for the next *five chapters*, describing everything from the ordering of the heavens, to the weather, to the behavior of the animals, to the mysteries of the leviathan beneath the waves. In effect, God lays out God's power as creator of all that exists by way of framing this question to Job, "Who is this darkening counsel without knowledge?" God is saying, in effect, "I am the one who made the universe. Do you comprehend the universe? If not, then where do you get off claiming to understand my ways?" Job can only answer, "I have indeed spoken about things I didn't understand, wonders beyond my comprehension. . . . Therefore, I relent and find comfort on dust and ashes" (Job 42:3).

Job's answer is ours too. We are inclined to speak about things we don't understand. In the face of the immensity and incomprehensibility of what we seek to describe, we are left only with metaphor and indirect speech, and we're going to have to learn how to relent and find comfort in that.

It was the prophet Micah who reminded the people of Judah that what the Lord required from them was to "do justice, love covenant-faithfulness, and walk humbly" with their God (Mic 6:8). Of those three injunctions, the requirement to walk humbly is the one we often overlook. That's unfortunate, given that humility, both in our living and in our understanding, may be one of the most important elements of faith. If nothing else, understanding faith as metaphor helps us to live into the prophet's instruction to walk humbly and to accept the reality of our own smallness before the immensity of existence.

Embracing Mystery

If metaphor in religion should teach us anything, it is that at the heart of faith is a mystery. The metaphors themselves point to our inability to describe that mystery with anything other than poetry and symbol. Nevertheless, religion has not always done a good job of embracing mystery and symbol, and few are content let the mystery be. But we are not without hope: there are some success stories.

Of all the branches of Christianity, the one that seems the most able to deal with mystery is the Orthodox church. The Orthodox do not seem simply capable of dealing with mystery; they seem *comfortable* with it. At a recent service at a Greek Orthodox cathedral that I attended, the priest was giving his concluding homily in which he was reflecting on the brokenness of the world. He said that such brokenness prompts a number of questions: *Why does God allow evil? Why is there suffering? Why do bad things happen to good people?* And so on. And he remarked, "A perfectly legitimate answer to these questions is, 'I don't know.'" And he *left it at that.* He didn't say, "I don't know; but here's my theory . . ." He didn't give platitudes about everything being God's plan. He just said, "I don't know." It was beautiful. I know so many other churches—most of them Protestant—where they'd have an answer ready to that question.

So why do the Orthodox have a leg up when it comes to mystery? Looking through the Divine Liturgy of St. John Chrysostom, the main liturgy of the Orthodox churches, you notice a few things about the language. The liturgy includes the word *mystery* or *mysteries* a number of times. Adjectives like *incomprehensible, beyond compare,* and *ineffable* are found throughout. Perhaps it's the repeated exposure to such language that primes the Orthodox soul for mystery. Perhaps it's Orthodoxy's continued presence in the East, where more legalistic Western theologies never took root. Perhaps it's due to the church's visible embrace of symbol, icon, and sign. Whatever the reason, the Orthodox Christian communities really do have a leg up on the rest of Christendom.

It's not to say that mystery is not embraced elsewhere. Even among the text-certain Protestants, one community in particular seems to have tapped into this understanding of mystery: the emergent churches. The emergent movement is a loose association of communities and congregations seeking to reimagine traditional faith as a process of emergence rather than as one of arrival.[13] That is, they think faith is less about the destination than the process—thus *emergent.*

In the emergent church, ideology is seen as a kind of idolatry, in which God is reduced to an intellectual object rather than the usual physical one. Whereas the idolatries of the past sought to contain the divine in the form of wood, bronze, or gold, the idolatries of the present seek to contain the divine in doctrine, dogma, and theology.[14]

Looking at it this way, we can understand the contradictions and multiple definitions of God in the creation accounts that we explored in chapter seven as a biblical effort to teach us that no one definition can contain God. In a way, the poems of scripture are the first biblical injunctions against idolatry. As Peter Rollins puts it:

13. Rollins, *How (Not) to Speak of God,* 9.
14. Ibid., 12.

The Bible itself is a dynamic text full of poetry, prose, history, law and myth all clashing together in a cacophony of voices. We are presented with a warrior God and a peacemaker, a God of territorial allegiance and a God who transcends all territorial divides, an unchanging God and a God who can be redirected, a God of peace and a God of war, a God who is always watching the world and a God who fails to notice the oppression against Israel in Egypt.

The interesting thing about all this is not that these conflicts exist but that we *know* they exist. In other words, the writers and editors of the text did not see any reason to try and iron out these inconsistencies—inconsistencies that make any systematic attempt to master the text both violent and irredeemably impossible.[15]

The emergent church seeks to embrace these tensions rather than smooth them over with a systematic theology that attempts once and for all to capture God through the use of human reason. So, it seems the Orthodox don't have a leg up on *all* the other churches.

However, across all religious lines, it is the mystics who understand the importance of mystery best.

The mystical traditions have always had a different attitude toward the role of language in religion than their more traditionalist counterparts. Mystics are accustomed to taking a decidedly non-literal approach to the words of a sacred tradition. In the Kabbalistic mystical tradition of Judaism, for example, a passage from the *Zohar*—one of the main texts of Jewish mysticism—makes it clear that true meaning is not to be found in the words of the Torah:

> Rabbi Shim'on said, "Woe to the human being who says that the Torah presents mere stories and ordinary words! . . . [As angels put on a garment before entering the world], So this story of Torah is the garment of Torah. Whoever thinks that the garment is the real Torah and not something else—may his spirits deflate! He will have no portion in the world that is coming. . . . Woe to the wicked who say that Torah is merely a story! They look at this garment and no further. Happy are the righteous who look at Torah properly! As wine must sit in a jar, so Torah must sit in this garment. So look only at what is under the garment. All those words and all those stories are garments."[16]

15. Ibid., 13.

16. Matt, *Essential Kabbalah*, 135–37.

According to the *Zohar*, the true meaning of the scriptures lies in the mystical meaning *underneath* the written text. The written text is merely a garment that clothes the true Torah and allows it to endure—and allows the world to endure the Torah. True meaning does not reside in the words of the text.

That's a fairly extreme position when it comes to the relationship between the literal meaning of a text and its truth. Because of that position, some philosophers of religion see the mystics, of all theists, as realists who acknowledge both the presence and reality of God and the inability of human thought and speech to contain God.[17]

However, other philosophers of religion have a different take on mysticism. Logicians, for example, have long noted that there is an inherent *meaninglessness* to religious language. By that, they do not mean that the words lack meaning, but that in a system of logic, the propositions of faith cannot be either demonstrated or contradicted—that is, they cannot be shown to be either true or false. As such, as logical propositions they are considered to be *meaningless* or *nonsense*.

As religious philosopher Alfred Ayer puts it: "to say that something transcends the human understanding is to say that it is unintelligible. And what is unintelligible cannot significantly be described."[18] Therefore, if a mystic admits that the object of a mystical vision is something that can't be described, then the mystic has to admit that all talk about that vision is nonsense. Ayer is not particularly fond of mystics, and sees them as having forfeited, by their own admission, the right to speak about God. In effect, he follows Wittgenstein's admonition that "What we cannot speak about we must pass over in silence."[19]

But mystics do speak about God. All the time. They are driven to speak about God in spite of the impossibility of adequately doing so. Rudolf Otto noted that rather than respond with "unbroken silence" because of the inability to describe God, mystics tended to demonstrate a "copious eloquence" instead.[20] This "mystical compulsion" to speak is not limited to the mystics. As Peter Rollins notes, "That which we cannot speak of is the one thing about whom and to whom we must never stop speaking."[21]

If the experience of God, mystical or otherwise, is powerful, then individuals are bound to want to share it. But if the experience defies

17. Soskice, *Metaphor and Religious Language*, 152.
18. Ayer, "On the Literal Significance," 133.
19. Rollins, *How (Not) to Speak of God*, xiii.
20. Otto, *Idea of the Holy*, 2.
21. Rollins, *How (Not) to Speak of God*, xiv.

description, then all we are left with is approximation. And the language of approximation is poetry and metaphor.

It is interesting to note just how often the mystical traditions make use of formal poetry. For starters, take a look at this passage from Lao Tzu's *Tao Tê Ching* as translated by R.B. Blakney:

> There are ways but the Way is uncharted;
> There are names but not nature in words:
> Nameless indeed is the source of creation
> But things have a mother and she has a name.
>
> The secret waits for the insight
> Of eyes unclouded by longing;
> Those who are bound by desire
> See only the outward container.[22]

Here, in the very text of the *Tao Tê Ching* is a stunning admission: what we are calling *The Way* has no name. The text simultaneously attempts to talk about the source of creation and admits that it cannot be talked about. And a further mystical note: "Those who are bound by desire / see only the outside container." That is, those who are unenlightened see only the name and fail to perceive the nature behind it as those who are enlightened do.

Traditions such as these are very often up front about the inadequacy of language and the provisional nature of any name:

> Something there is, whose veiled creation was
> Before the earth or sky began to be;
> So silent, so aloof and so alone,
> It changes not, nor fails, but touches all:
> Conceive it as the mother of the world.
>
> I do not know its name;
> A name for it is "Way";
> Pressed for designation,
> I call it Great.[23]

"Pressed for designation, I call it Great." This is the challenge of the mystic: an encounter with the divine that cannot be adequately described, and yet, is so powerful that the individual feels compelled to say *something*. This paradox is at the heart of mysticism.

22. Lao Tzu and Blakney, 53.

23. Ibid, 77.

We do not see this paradox in Eastern mysticism alone. In the West, the mystical tradition that arose in the monasteries and convents of medieval Europe displayed this same tension between the indescribable and the need to speak out. Some of the great medieval mystics of the Christian tradition—Hildegard of Bingen, Catherine of Sienna, Julian of Norwich—experienced profound and powerful encounters with the divine that they attempted to describe in colorful and evocative language. They wrote, preached, and taught about their experiences, even though, given the time period and the strictures of the medieval Catholic Church, doing so would often get them into trouble. They stretched traditionally understood categories and definitions, such as when Julian of Norwich wrote of the Second Person of the Trinity as *Mother Christ*.[24]

Often these women mystics were accused of heresy or of other wrongs. They were frequently criticized for having dared, as women, to say *anything* at all and for not knowing their place. As a result, these women mystics were conflicted, torn between their desire to avoid conflict with church officials and their need to speak out about their powerful experiences.

Such is the lot of the mystic.

Although some philosophers of religion have argued that those who claim that nothing meaningful can be said about the divine should then refrain from saying anything—it's not that simple. The encounter with the divine leaves a person simultaneously overwhelmed, lacking in any way to adequately describe the experience *and* driven to attempt to do so anyway.

"Pressed for designation, I call it Great." Lao Tzu admits in the same breath that "Great" is what he calls the "something" that's there and that his own designation is inadequate. "The Way eternal has no name," he writes, embracing the paradox of having named the very thing he cannot name.

This same paradoxical tension can be seen in Christian mystical writings too, such as this passage from Gregory of Nazianus:

> God is Light,
> the Most High, the Unapproachable;
> God cannot be conceived in the mind
> or spoken by the lips.[25]

Or this from Simeon the New Theologian:

> What is this awesome mystery

24. Oden, *In Her Words*, 184.
25. McGuckin, *Book of Mystical Chapters*, 112.

that is taking place within me?
I can find no words to express it;
my poor hand is unable to capture it
in describing the praise and glory that belong
to the One who is above all praise,
and who transcends every word . . . .
My intellect sees what has happened,
but cannot explain it.
It can see, and wishes to explain,
but can find no word that will suffice;
for what it sees is invisible and entirely formless,
simple, completely uncompounded,
unbounded in its awesome greatness.
What I have seen is the totality recapitulated as one,
received not in essence but by participation.
Just as if you lit a flame from a flame,
it is the whole flame you receive.[26]

Here, the tension between having no words and speaking out is laid bare. And in the end, the tension is bridged with metaphor. In fact, Simeon the New Theologian seems particularly fond of metaphor as can be seen in this astonishing prayer where the metaphors come in a near-ceaseless torrent:

Come, true light.
Come, eternal life.
Come, hidden mystery.
Come, nameless treasure.
Come, Ineffable One.
Come, Inconceivable One.
Come, endless rejoicing.
Come, sun that never sets.
Come, true hope of all who wish to be saved.
Come, awakening of all who sleep.
Come, resurrection of the dead.
Come, Powerful One who ever creates and re-creates and transfigures by your simple will.
Come, Invisible One beyond all touch or grasping.

26. Ibid., 159–60.

Come, eternally Motionless One, ever active to come to us and save us who lie in hell.

Come, beloved name repeated everywhere, whose existence and nature we cannot express or know.

Come, eternal joy.

Come, untarnished crown.

Come, royal purple of our great King and God.

Come, jeweled belt of shining crystal.

Come, unapproachable sandal.

Come, imperial vestment.

Come, sovereign right hand.

Come, Lord, whom my miserable soul has longed for and longs for still.

Come, Solitary One, to this solitary, for as you see, I am all alone . . .

Come, for you have alienated me from all things and made me be alone in this world.

Come, you who have become my desire and have made me desire you, the Inaccessible One.

Come, my breath, my life.

Come, consolation of my poor soul.

Come, my joy, my glory, my endless delight.

For I must give you all my thanks for making yourself one with me in spirit.[27]

At first glance, it may appear that Simeon is praying for specific events to come—the resurrection of the dead, the awakening of all who sleep. But the poetic parallelism makes it clear that phrases like *endless rejoicing, awakening of all who sleep*, and *resurrection of the dead* are metaphors for the divine, epithets for the *beloved name repeated everywhere, whose existence and nature we cannot express or know.*

The most striking thing is that so many of Simeon's metaphors embrace paradox. In addition to the *beloved name* that we cannot express, we are confronted with other contradictions. For example, how does an "eternally Motionless One" *come* anywhere? It becomes clear that even *come* is a metaphor; after all, the infinite, ever-present one is already everywhere present and does not need to *go* anywhere. And yet the mystic feels compelled to call over and over again: "Come."

Through the use of metaphor, there is simultaneously a description and an admission that the description is inadequate. Metaphor helps to

---

27. Ibid., 178–79.

balance Rollins's "that which we cannot speak of" and "the one thing about whom and to whom we must never stop speaking." The mystics have long understood that metaphor is the *both/and* in response to the competing impulses of impossibility of description and necessity for speech.

What the mystics realize first and foremost, and what they demonstrate through their use of poetry, paradox, and metaphor, is that to encounter the divine is to encounter mystery. Religion is the response to the perception of that great mystery, the perception that there is something more to this reality than what can be perceived through ordinary experience, that there is some meaning behind it all.

Over the millennia, religious thinkers have struggled to identify that mystery. When all other words failed, they constructed poetry and metaphor to describe what could otherwise not be described, to point to what could not be comprehended, to say that the mystery is unknown but lies somewhere in *that* direction. Along *this* way.

* * *

Acknowledging mystery and embracing metaphor helps to prevent the fossilizing of sacred tradition. It serves as a reminder that sacred objects, rites, and texts are signposts guiding believers along the way.

Embracing faith as metaphor offers an alternative to doubling-down on a certainty and literalism that cannot be sustained. Embracing a metaphorical theology helps us to embrace our lack of understanding, to embrace our uncertainty, and, above all, to let the mystery be.

Chapter 17

On the Necessity of Doubt

Doubt is not the opposite of faith; it is one element of faith.

—PAUL TILLICH

DOUBT IS A PROBLEM for many people of faith, and it's a particular dilemma for Christians, especially those of us of the Protestant variety. Doubt is frequently cast as the opposite of faith, and the Protestant Reformation was, after all, driven by the principle that salvation was by accomplished by God's grace *through faith*. As a result, it is often the case that any admission of doubt is seen as a lack of faith, and no one wants to admit that. Doubt is frequently shunned and sometimes outright condemned.

In what was probably one of the most unusual first dates I ever went on, I went to a Maundy Thursday service at a church of a different denomination from my own. As the pastor broke the bread for Communion, he said—as is frequently done in many churches—that the Communion table was "the Lord's table," not our own. "How*ever*," he continued, "if you have any doubt as to your commitment to Christ, you should not partake of this meal because then you will be drinking the Cup of Judgment." Any doubt? *Any?*

That seemed like a tall order. For anyone. How could anyone *not* have doubt? I doubt a lot. The pastor's question seemed to me an absurdity. But it wasn't absurd for the people in the pews around me, I guess. They were certain. Or at least weren't about to admit otherwise. (That may explain why that first date never became a second date.) The rejection of doubt seems to be a core principle of faith for many.

But doubt and uncertainty are inescapable, as we have seen. People might try to double down on doctrinal purity, proper modes of worship, or pat answers to the difficult questions, but the reality is that the existential mystery still looms. Doubt and uncertainty remain. Having said that, we certainly do our best to deny that fact.

* * *

In the movie *The Naked Gun 2-1/2*, a car chase results in the villain crashing into a fuel truck, miraculously surviving, and crashing into a mobile missile launcher. Surviving that collision as well and now riding on the missile itself, he crashes into a fireworks factory. As the factory goes up in flame and its employees flee from the scene amid spectacular fireballs and fireworks, Lt. Frank Drebin makes his way to the front of the gathering crowd, turns to face them, and says, "All right, move on! Nothing to see here! Please disperse! Nothing to see here!"

Sometimes religion acts like a police officer standing in front of a crime scene, waving off would be spectators with a casual, "Nothing to see here!" Religion—bad religion, anyway—frequently places itself in front of the sea of doubt and insists to the faithful, "Nothing to see here!"

There are two problems with that approach. First, it's clearly a lie. As with a crime scene, there is most definitely something to be seen there and we all know it. The lie may be comfortable and may give us a sense of security—that we're not really in any danger—but we all know something is going on. Second, those insisting "There's nothing to see here" are standing with their backs to what is going on. Faith cannot stand with its back toward the void. It has to turn around and embrace it. Given the unavoidability of doubt, to stand with your back to it and deny its existence is folly.

But even more to the point, doubt is not simply unavoidable. It's *necessary*.

As I noted earlier, we often fall into the trap of equating faith with belief. But faith is not belief. Faith is trust. And there's an interesting thing about trust—it is not rooted in certainty. This is a truth that even our popular culture sometimes understands. In one of the best lines ever uttered on television, one character in *Battlestar Galactica* asks another, "How do you know you can trust me?," to which the other responds, "I don't; that's what trust is."[1]

How is it that the writers of a science fiction television series can articulate a truth that is seemingly so hard for religious folks to get? Faith is trust, and trust is not about certainty. Trust is about setting out in spite of uncertainty. Were we to have certainty, we could not trust. We would just simply know.

Understanding faith to be trust in the midst of unknowing can be transformative, not only in our relationships with the divine, but also with one another. By way of illustrating this, Peter Rollins invites us to reflect

1. This line is my favorite line of the entire series. As soon as I heard it, I knew it would preach.

on two different kinds of marriage commitments: one involving a couple who firmly believe that they will be happily married as long as they live and another who understand that their relationship will face various hardships in an uncertain future with no guarantees. Rollins argues that the second couple is the one making a commitment of faith:

> Here we can see that doubt provides the context out of which real decision occurs and real love is tested, for love will say "yes" regardless of uncertainty. A love that requires contracts and ab-solute assurance in order to act is no love at all.[2]

Faith has never been about knowing. It has never been about certainty. It has never been about belief. It has been about stepping into the unknown, about taking that leap.

This is not a blind leap. It is not a leap of ignorance. It is not a leap where we cover our ears and eyes and ignore what the world has to say. Instead, it's a leap in which we acknowledge what we don't know—we acknowledge our own limitations, our own gaps in understanding, our own fears, our own doubts—and we go anyway. A person of faith can acknowledge and even cel-ebrate the *dark night of the soul*—a time of profound doubt and alienation from God—seeing such a time not as a "darkness which conceals an enemy but rather the intimate darkness within which we embrace our faith."[3]

In chapter 2, I mentioned a tract entitled "How to Know for Sure You Are Going to Heaven." As a reminder, here is one of the statements from that tract:

> We're learning more and more about everything and yet we seem to know less and less for sure. However, one of the char-acteristics of the first followers of Jesus was their certainty. They didn't guess . . . or hope . . . or wish. They knew for certain. They were even willing to die for that certainty![4]

It's a nice sentiment, I suppose, but it shows a lack of understanding about the concept of *knowing* in the biblical tradition. In the Hebrew/Aramaic tradition of the disciples, the word that is translated as "know" (יָדַע *yada*) does not mean intellectual comprehension of an idea; it means "knowledge by experience."[5] If the early disciples "knew" their salvation, it was because they had experienced it in Jesus and in the community he had created. They

---

2. Rollins, *How (Not) to Speak of God*, 36.

3. Ibid., 37.

4. Kennedy, "How to Know."

5. This explains how Adam and Eve conceived a child after Adam "knew" his wife (Gen 4:1).

had not simply been handed a tract that they came to believe. They had had an experience of faith.

In addition, the disciples did not display certainty—they displayed *faith*. The biblical record makes it clear that even after Jesus' resurrection, "some doubted" (Matt 28:17). It was not their absolute certainty that propelled them from one end of the Mediterranean world to the other, it was their faith—their *trust* in God—in spite of their doubts.

I am always perplexed by statements such as the one found in this tract. What bible is this individual reading that he concludes the disciples were paragons of absolute certainty? Has he not read the story of Doubting Thomas? After all, it's a story that has a lot to teach us about the role of doubt in faith:

> When it was later on that day, the first day of the week—with the door locked where the disciples were out of fear of the Jewish leadership—Jesus came and stood in the middle of them and says to them, "Peace be with you." And after saying that, he showed them his hands and his side. Then seeing the Master, the disciples rejoiced. Then Jesus said to them again, "Peace be with you: as the Father has sent me, so I am sending you." And saying this, he breathed [on them] and says to them, "Receive Holy Spirit. If you forgive the sins of anyone, they're forgiven them; if you retain them, they're retained."
>
> But Thomas, one of the Twelve who was called "the Twin," was not with them when Jesus came. Then the other disciples were telling him, "We've seen the Master!" But he said to them, "Unless I see the holes of the nails in his hands, put my finger into the nail holes, and put my hand into his side, I won't believe it." Eight days later, the disciples were again inside and [this time] Thomas was with them. With the door shut, Jesus comes and stands in the middle of them and said, "Peace be with you." After that, he says to Thomas, "Bring your finger here and see my hands and bring your hand and put it into my side; don't be unfaithful, but faithful. Thomas answered and said to him, "My Lord and my God!" Jesus says to him, "Do you have faith because you've seen me? Happy are those who do not see me and yet are faithful." (John 20:19–31)

On that first Easter Sunday, the disciples are all huddled together and afraid when, suddenly, Jesus appears among them. He breathes the Holy Spirit on them and tells everyone, "If you forgive the sins of anyone, they're forgiven; if you retain them, they're retained." Well, he tells everyone but

Thomas because Thomas, for some reason, isn't there.[6] But when he does return and the other disciples all tell him that Jesus has appeared to them, he says, "Unless I see the holes of the nails in his hands, put my finger into the nail holes, and put my hand into his side, I won't believe it."

It is hard to imagine our reaction being any different. Or the reaction of the other disciples, for that matter. These were the ones, after all, who'd scattered and fled when Jesus had been arrested, who'd betrayed or denied him, who'd been hiding out in an upper room for three days. It's safe to say that had it been Peter, James, John, or anyone else, who'd been absent that day the response would have been the same.

But it was Thomas who wasn't there and so he gets to go through history known as Doubting Thomas. Even when Thomas comes to believe, it's only because he's had proof. Without the proof, he'd still have his doubts, and, as we noted earlier, doubts are a source of embarrassment for "faithful" people.

But there's something interesting to note about Thomas. Thomas isn't even his real name; it's his *nickname*. *Thomas* (תְּאוֹמָא *Ta'oma*) is just the Aramaic word for "twin." As Simon Peter is "the Rock," Thomas is "the Twin."

All of which raises an interesting question: whose twin is he? It stands to reason that Thomas must be somebody's twin. Even if *twin* is just meant to suggest that he really looks like someone else, who is the person that he looks like? It's unusual to call someone *twin* or *look-alike* and not say who it is he is a twin to or who it is he looks like.

But then again, the group Thomas belongs to isn't just any old grouping of friends. This group is a master and his disciples. If one of the members of that group is called *the Twin* and his twin is unspoken, it's likely that it's got to be the master. That is, Thomas is Jesus' *twin* or *look-alike*. Now, if true, this would explain why Judas needed to identify Jesus to the temple guard in the garden—because there was another man there who looked a lot like him.[7]

But let's consider the implications of Thomas being Jesus' twin. If Jesus is the model of perfect faith, and his twin is Thomas, who models doubt, then what we understand is that faith and doubt are not antitheses—they're twins. As the poet Kahlil Gibran said, "Doubt is a pain too lonely to know that faith is his twin brother."[8] Faith and doubt are paired together. Bound up

---

6. Where on earth is Thomas by the way? This is one of the great unexplored mysteries of the scriptures.

7. It also bears noting that Judas does not simply say to the temple guard, "Oh, he's the tall, blond, blue-eyed, white guy—you can't miss him."

8. Gibran, *Jesus the Son of Man*, 92.

in relationship. Just as you cannot have just one twin, you cannot have faith without its twin, doubt. Like a yin and yang, the two go hand in hand.

Faith, doubt, and uncertainty are inextricably linked. In a paraphrase of the question and answer posed earlier, we might say: *How do we really know that we can have faith in God? How do we really know that life has meaning and purpose? How do we really know that there is hope for us and for peace and justice in this world? How do we really know that there is more to this life than what we can see?—We don't; that's what faith is.*

Some years ago, I was part of a staff retreat at which our facilitator asked us to come up with a motto or self-description in six words. Most were relatively prosaic. Mine was: *I know not; still I believe.* I'll admit, I was pleased with that one. I've even thought of using the Latin translation—*Nescio; adhuc fideo*—as my family motto should I ever get a family crest.

Mottos like that are supposed to be bold and it'd certainly be a bold one; after all, what risk is there in putting your trust in certainties? What courage is required to commit oneself to a path that is easy and predictable? Setting out into the unknown is a much bolder statement of faith than traveling familiar and safe paths at home. Relying on certainties may be easier but doing so cannot create a vibrant and robust faith or a meaningful life. It can only create a comforting illusion because as we have seen, uncertainty is unavoidable. We do not know. In some cases, we *cannot* know. Still we believe. Still we trust.

Faith is at its best when it embraces doubt, its twin. In embracing uncertainty, faith does not wind up depleted, but enriched. When we stand at the edge of the abyss of unknowing, we can turn our backs to it and pretend it does not exist, or we can stretch our arms wide and embrace it. When we embrace our unknowing, we find that faith is not lost in the profound depths but becomes profound itself. In embracing the emptiness, both faith and life become filled.

Chapter 18

Drinking of One Wine

EMBRACING UNCERTAINTY HELPS US to embrace humility, mystery, and our own doubt. But even more significantly, it helps us to embrace each other.

Seeing religion as a metaphorical system full of uncertainty gives us the tools to bridge the divides between people of different religions or among people of the same religion divided by doctrine and dogma. This approach can go a long way toward establishing not simply religious tolerance, but genuine and meaningful coexistence.

It was a strategy employed by the great medieval Islamic mystic and theologian Abu Hamid al-Ghazali as he sought to address the issue of theological intolerance within Islam. At the time, various schools of thought within Islam were accusing one another of كفر *kufr* "unbelief"— that is, of heresy or apostasy. Al-Ghazali noted that frequently these schools defined *unbelief* as meaning "that which contradicts the teaching of one's own school." That is, the Ash'arites considered *unbelief* to be a rejection of Ash'arite thought; the Mu'tazilites considered unbelief to be a rejection of Mu'tazilite thought and so on. Al-Ghazali countered that, Islamically speaking, *unbelief* means "to deem anything the Prophet brought to be a lie"—in other words, denying the existence of those things that the Prophet Muhammad said exist.[1]

Al-Ghazali noted that there were five different ways that something might *exist*:[2] including *ontological existence* (ordinary, actual existence),

---

1. al-Ghazālī, "Decisive Criterion," 92.

2. The five total are: (1) *Ontological existence* (ذاتي dhātī)—ordinary, actual existence. The real, concrete existence of things in the world, external to senses and the mind; (2) *Sensory existence* (حسي hissī)—that which is perceived by the senses, but has no existence outside the world of the eye; waking visions and dreams; (3) *Conceptual existence* (خيالي khayālī)—the physical image of something normally perceived through the senses, but removed from the senses; the conjuring up in one's mind of an image of something one has seen; (4) *Noetic existence* (أقلي 'aqlī)—a thing's possession of a function, without positing any physical image; for example the concept of "the ability to seize and strike"

conceptual existence (conjuring an image of something in one's mind), and *analogous existence*.[3] By *analogous existence*, al-Ghazali meant something that does not exist literally, but there is something analogous to it that does exist. For example, some Islamic theologians maintain that it is logically impossible for God to feel anger, so *anger* is used as an analogy to some attribute of God that has the same result. In this way, the *anger of God* would not exist *ontologically*, that is, in actuality, but as it relates to some attribute of God that does exist, the *anger of God* would be said to have *analogous existence.*

Al-Ghazali argued that if you claim something to exist in any of these ways, you are still claiming that it exists *in some way*. If you claim that the Prophet was simply trying to deceive people, then you are claiming something to be a *lie* and are an *unbeliever*. Otherwise, if you claim that something has to be understood figuratively, you cannot be considered an *unbeliever*, even if you deny its *literal* existence.[4]

According to al-Ghazali, to interpret something in a figurative sense is not to deny it; on the contrary, those who engage in allegorical or metaphorical interpretation affirm its existence as an *analogous* reality. He pointed out that even those schools of thought that frowned on figurative interpretation and that were more literal-minded used figurative interpretation when they deemed it necessary. "Every party, even those who go to extremes in holding to the apparent meanings of texts," he wrote, "finds itself compelled to figurative interpretation."[5]

Al-Ghazali's point is clear: if *unbelief* is defined by denying the existence of the things that the Prophet says exist, then while different schools may disagree about whether to take a passage literally or metaphorically, they are all affirming the object's existence *in some way*. This beautiful reflection preserves a commonality in the midst of great theological diversity. In this way, whether particular objects or events are literally or figuratively interpreted, all believe in some manner of existence for those objects or events. No one need be branded an unbeliever as long as existence is affirmed *in some way*. This line of reasoning could even be extended beyond divisions within individual faith communities to relationships among and between different religious communities.

---

could be said to be a *noetic hand*; and (5) *Analogous existence* (شبهي *shabahī*)—a thing itself does not exist, but something analogous to it that possesses some quality or attribute peculiar to it does exist. Ibid., 94.

3. Ibid., 94–96.

4. Ibid., 101.

5. Ibid., 103.

Historically speaking, one faith's engagement with other faiths has not gone well, especially in the monotheistic traditions where the existence of only one God presumes the existence of only one truth. Religions are frequently seen as making competing truth claims whereby if one is true then the other must be false. But we would never make that assumption with things we clearly understood to be poetry or metaphor.

If you were to ask someone to describe the feeling of love and they said that love was *tumbling headlong through a field of fragrant wildflowers*, you would be considered unstable if you were to respond, "No, it isn't, you fool! Love is *being drunk on the sweetest wine!*" And yet, that is precisely how some people respond to different metaphors of faith. We respond with criticism, and frequently with anger, when someone uses different language to describe the encounter with the divine. Our failure to appreciate the metaphorical nature of religion, to appreciate the *poetry* of faith, prevents us from engaging with other faiths in a constructive way.

When we look at our own religions as merely making literal truth claims and propositions, then competing religions are making competing and contradictory truth claims and, therefore, must be rejected or opposed. But if we look at religions as different metaphorical systems attempting to describe the same underlying ineffable reality, then our understanding of different faiths is transformed.

For example, what would it mean for Christians to see the Jewish concept of *chosenness* not as a legal declaration of privilege over and against non-Jews but as a metaphor of intimacy and responsibility? What would it mean for Muslims and Jews to view Christian claims of Jesus' sonship as a metaphor of intimacy in relationship rather than as a literal claim of divine paternity (and thus an affront to monotheism)? What would it mean for Christians to see Muslim claims about the Qur'an in the same light of their own claims about Jesus being the *Word of God*, understanding it to be a special revelation that reveals God's own mind? Instead of seeing inherent contradictions, we might see different metaphorical systems, attempting to grasp what ultimately cannot be fully comprehended by the human mind.

By doing so, we could see other religions as fellow travelers along a road of understanding, each employing the metaphors that help that community to grapple with the ultimate mystery of being. One tradition might use the metaphor of a royal covenant with a people to understand the presence of the divine in the world. Another might use the metaphor of a father and son to explain its encounter with that ultimate reality through a flesh and blood human being. Another tradition might use the metaphors of the spoken and written word itself to explain a powerful revelation of the divine to a people in need of guidance. Still another might understand the ultimate reality through many different metaphors all seen as avatars or manifestations of the one all-encompassing reality.

Understood this way, you might understand yourself to be an adherent of a religion not because you are convinced it is true to the exclusion of all others, but because you feel that its metaphors resonate with you more powerfully than others. A friend of mine who is a convert to Islam from Christianity told me, "It's not that I rejected Christianity or disbelieved it; it was that Islam made more *sense* to me." By that, he meant that the metaphors and conceptualizations of that faith resonated with him more deeply. As a student of religion, there is much that I admire and appreciate in religions other than my own; sometimes, I am profoundly moved by insights that other religions have to offer. And yet, beyond all theological argument and apologetics that I could use to defend my own tradition, the deeper reality is that the metaphor, imagery, and models of Christianity *work* for me in a fundamental way. This is a sentiment echoed by religious historian and author Reza Aslan, who invokes a Buddhist metaphor to describe his understanding of the different faith traditions:

> I'm a person of faith, and the language that I use to define my faith, the symbols and metaphors that I rely upon to express my faith, are those provided by Islam because they make the most sense to me. The Buddha once said, "If you want to draw water, you don't dig six 1–ft. wells, you dig one 6–ft. well." Islam is my 6–ft. well. But I recognize that I am drawing the same water that everyone around me is.[6]

Our religious traditions are those "6–foot wells" we dig with our metaphors. We seek to gain access to that deep water at the heart of existence, but the only way we can dig through the earth and rock of unknowing and incomprehensibility is with the shovels of metaphor. We might all be using different tools, but the deep ground water we seek is the same.

The recognition that different religions are different metaphorical systems does not mean we need to affirm all metaphors as equally valuable—not all metaphors *within* a tradition are equally valuable—but it does require us to see those who employ them as fellow travelers down a road of seeking. If we can do this, we might spare ourselves and others the needless suffering that can happen as a result of our inclination to see the differences rather than the common ground in religion. We do not need to continue to reenact the sins of the past.

Almost every year, I take a group of university students on a week of service-learning to the Eastern Band of the Cherokee Nation in western North

6. Luscombe, "Is Reza Aslan Anti-Christian?"

Carolina. There we have occasion to learn about Cherokee history (including the long history of oppression and suffering), culture, tradition, politics, and faith. On one such trip, we were speaking with Bo Taylor, an expert in native dance and music at the Museum of the Cherokee Indian. He is also a committed Christian who continues to embrace traditional Cherokee spirituality as well. He told us a story, which I will paraphrase as follows:

> When the white men first came to our lands, they saw us singing songs to the sun and they said, "Ah, they're sun worshipers!" Then they saw us dancing around the fire and singing songs and said, "Ah, they're worshiping the fire!" And so they thought that we were savages and heathens. But that's only because they never stopped to ask us what we were doing. Because if they had, we would have told them that there is only one Great Spirit who is the Creator of all things. The Creator has an emblem in the sky: the sun, the fire that burns in the heavens. That fire also burns on the earth and is a sign of the Great Spirit in our midst. And we know that that fire burns within us giving us life: the first thing that happens after you die is that the fire goes out and the body grows cold. Now, let me ask you, have you ever heard of a fire in the heavens, the fire that dwells on earth with us, and the fire that dwells within?

Of course, at this point, all the Christians in the room sheepishly admitted that this was one way of understanding the Trinity. We said as much. Bo continued:

> We had the same religion that you had. We just used different names. But you never stopped to ask us. You just assumed we were heathens and savages and that we needed to be forcibly converted to your religion. But we'd already had it.

In chapter 8, I discussed the problem of those who do not look past their religion's metaphors to the reality they point to—those who "mistake the finger pointing at the moon for the moon." Bo's story is the perfect illustration of what happens when we confuse our metaphors for the reality they point to. Both sets of metaphors, the traditional Christian articulation of the Trinity and the Cherokee sun and fire, point to an ineffable reality beyond ordinary experience. But in this case, the white evangelists could not distinguish between the metaphors they employed and the reality those metaphors pointed to. As a result, they were incapable of seeing another set of metaphors pointing to the same reality they were purporting to proclaim.

One of the biggest obstacles to interfaith understanding is an inability to perceive each other's metaphors *as* metaphors rather than literal claims.

(As demonstrated above, it's hard enough to do this in one's own religion.) This obstacle is created by our need for certainty and our unwillingness to admit any uncertainty in religious faith. But an openness to uncertainty allows us to see the metaphors in our own faith traditions, and an awareness that one's own tradition is rich with metaphor is essential in understanding the metaphorical nature of other traditions. With that understanding, we are able to see that all the religious traditions are about a deeper purpose of unraveling and exploring mystery.

In that enterprise, we are united. To seek meaning and purpose. To encounter the great mystery of existence. To stare into the void together and in so doing, find greater fellowship and common life. It is a sentiment expressed so beautifully by the poet Rumi, here in this translation by Coleman Barks:

> A learned man once said, for the sake of saying *something*,
> "There is a tree
>
> in India. If you eat the fruit of that tree, you'll never grow
> old and never die."
>
> Stories about "the tree" were passed around, and finally
> a king sent his envoy
>
> to India to look for it. People laughed at the man. They
> slapped him on the back
>
> and called out, "Sir, I know where your tree is, but it's far
> in the jungle and you'll need
>
> a ladder!" He kept traveling, following such directions and
> feeling foolish, for years.
>
> He was about to return to the king when he met a wise man.
> "Great teacher, show me
>
> some kindness in this search for the tree." "My son, this is
> not an actual tree,
>
> though it's been called that. Sometimes it's called a *sun*,
> sometimes an *ocean*, or
>
> a *cloud*. These words point to the wisdom that comes through
> a true human being, which

may have many effects, the least of which is eternal life!
In the same way one

person can be a father to you and a son to someone else,
uncle to another and nephew

to yet another, so what you are looking for has many names,
and one existence. Don't

search for one of the names. Move beyond any attachment
to names." Every war

and every conflict between human beings has happened because
of some disagreement about

names. It's such unnecessary foolishness, because just
beyond the arguing there's a long

table of companionship, set and waiting for us to sit down.[7]

What Rumi refers to as *names* we understand to be metaphors—words pointing beyond themselves to the ineffable mystery behind. To one, the experience of the ineffable is a tree, to another the sun, to another the ocean. Each name is pointing beyond itself to the great mystery.

The names we use are often the products of our cultural backgrounds. Philosopher and theologian John Hick argues that our awareness of the ultimate reality is shaped by concepts we take from our cultural context, which, in turn, shape how we perceive that ultimate reality. We start with particular foundational concepts, such as a *Deity* (a personal "Eternal One") or *the Absolute* (an impersonal concept), and develop our metaphorical understandings from there. Even these starting points, these foundational concepts, are *already* an interpretative framework for an encounter with the divine.[8]

Our religious expressions are a function of our cultural experience and presumptions. Even our encounter with the "Eternal One" as either personal (*God*) or impersonal (*Truth*) is a conditioned by culture. And so, the ultimate reality is filtered through the different religious traditions, none of which can claim to possess a perfect understanding of that ultimate reality free of the lenses of human culture and our own mental biases.

7. Rūmī and Barks, *The Soul of Rumi*, 46–47.
8. Hick, *God Has Many Names*, 52.

Awareness of the cultural contexts of our religious metaphors also has consequences for the religious communities' relationships with one another. Again, Rumi makes it clear:

A man gives one coin to be spent
among four people.
The Persian says, "I want

angur." The Arab says, "*Inab*, you
rascal." The Turk,
"*Uzum!*" The Greek,

"Shut up all of you. We'll have *istafil*."
They begin
pushing each other, then

hitting with fists, no stopping it. If a
many-languaged
master had been there,

he could have made peace and told
them, *I can give each of*
you the grapes you want

with this one coin. Trust me. Keep
quiet, and you four
enemies will agree.

I also know a silent inner meaning that
makes of your
four words one wine.[9]

Here, the "many-languaged master"—that is, a mystic who understands the poetry and metaphor of faith—could have resolved this conflict by helping the four to understand that what they call by different names is the same reality.

But there is an even deeper experience lying beyond the revelation that we are all seeking to describe the same underlying reality. Out of the ordinary grapes of our understanding, with the right secret we can make a wondrous new wine.

9. Rūmī and Barks, 51.

This wine, this deeper essence lying beyond the names can only be experienced, not communicated.[10] Even were all the religions of the world to agree on the same term—*God, Being, Universe, Truth, Way*—the essence of that ultimate reality would still lie beyond the realm of definitions and could only be found in the realm of experience. That experience of that secret wine is what the traveler is called to experience. Once again, we are invited not to stop at the sign but to follow the sign to where it leads. But first, we have to realize that all of our signs are pointing in the same direction, that we're all seeking the same grapes.

But in the meantime, if we can get to the point where we can see others as speaking different words for the same idea, perhaps can get closer to having our experiences become one wine for all.

10. Aslan, *No God but God*, 208.

Ending

The Certainty of Uncertainty

So, we now come back to the question raised at the beginning of the book: is absolute certainty possible?

Over the course of this book, we have seen that uncertainty is everywhere. Uncertainty is a factor in our religion, both in the ineffable nature of the subject matter and in the metaphorical systems used to grapple with those ineffable experiences. Uncertainty is a factor in our language, whether in the obstacles to communication that we all struggle with or in the imprecision with which metaphors of our ordinary speech are vested. It is written into the very fabric of the universe, whether in the unnerving relativism of Einsteinian space or in the weird counterintuitive workings of quantum physics.

The conclusion to all of this is that in our great human attempts at understanding we never obtain perfect certainty, we never fully identify absolute truth, we only point in its direction. What we have is the finger pointing at the moon, not the moon.

Now, to be perfectly honest, there are things I can be fairly certain of. I can be certain that I am typing on a well-worn and much-loved MacBook Pro. I am certain that there is a stack of books to my left and an empty cup of coffee to my right. Of these things I am absolutely certain and reasonably so.

But those things are not matters of great consequence. However useful to me the existence of that MacBook Pro beneath my fingertips is to the writing of the book you are now reading, it is not one of the great claims of truth that help give meaning to life. Indeed, I have never spent a night wracked by doubt as to whether there was truly a laptop beneath my fingers while I believed myself to be typing on one.

Rather, there seems to be a sliding scale of uncertainty in inverse relationship to the significance of the thing to be known. The more meaningful and significant something is, the less, it seems, we can be certain about it:

Is there a laptop under my fingers?—Yes, I am absolutely certain.

Is it plugged in?—I think so. Yes, there's the little green light.

Will my car still be there?—Yeah, should be. I remember locking it.

Will I get home safely tonight?—Likely, but you never know.

Will I get my dream job?—Maybe, it depends.

Should I vote for candidate X?—I guess so. I think X will be a good leader, but often I'm wrong.

Will this policy be helpful or harmful?—It seems like it should be helpful, but there are always unintended consequences.

Does N. love me?—I think so. But you never truly know someone else's heart.

Is there a God?—I believe so, but I can't prove it, and sometimes I'm not sure.

Does life have any meaning?—Beyond what we give it, I don't know.

This is just a sampling. Within each of those questions is a whole series of other questions that also reveal their own uncertainties in various degrees. The fact of the matter is that with the biggest, most meaningful questions— the questions of life, love, and faith, the ones that really *matter*—there are no answers that can be given with absolute certainty.

This sliding scale works across the three endeavors we have looked at so far in this book: the aspects of science, language, and religion that we can speak about with certainty tend to be the ones that are not as significant. Physics is very predictable for slow-moving objects on a manageable scale in relatively flat space but breaks down at the point where the universe comes into being. Language is fairly precise in the lens of simple description—*There is a dog in the yard*—but less so when it comes to questions of emotion and meaning that require poetry and metaphor—*I breathe in the warm sunset and it becomes ice in my veins; the cheery song of evening a dirge in my ears.* And religion has plenty of questions it can answer easily—*Friday prayers begin at 12:30* and *The grape juice for communion is in the sacristy*— and questions that require poetry and metaphor to even begin to address—*I don't know why there is suffering, but we believe God takes suffering into God's own being and is not separated from it.*

In spite of all of that, there are some people in our world who are very certain about the answers to these more unknowable questions, and they're the ones causing all the trouble. It is rare that people who are unsure or who brook a fair amount of doubt are the first ones off on the crusade. Skeptics rarely lead the Inquisition or attempt to set up the caliphate. Mystics rarely are the ones calling for the purging of the heretics and the excommunication of those who express unorthodox views.[1] Those who embrace unknowing are rarely the ones mocking others' beliefs (or lack thereof) in online forums with words like *fairy tale* or *blasphemy*. They are rarely the ones decrying their political opponents as *un-American* or *traitors*. No, those are the acts of the certain. These are the acts of those who long to know for sure.

The desire to know is a powerful one. One I understand very well. If I have not already made it apparent, I am something of a know-it-all. I love to learn and share that knowledge with others—whether they want it or not. One of my least endearing traits is my tendency to supplement a conversation (frequently one I am not a part of) with some tidbit or piece of information I find interesting. The college students I work with are usually tolerant enough of this only because they are either too nice, too impressionable, or too young to know that they should be annoyed by this obnoxious behavior.

But one of the net effects of my know-it-all-ism is that I can't stand the idea of not knowing something. The idea that some information remains forever hidden drives me crazy. I want to *know* the answer. I become frustrated with revelations that are drawn out and, while I love the ongoing mystery of well-crafted entertainment like *Lost*, I have slight anxiety that I might die before the mystery is revealed.[2] Forget the problem of whether George R. R. Martin dies before he finishes *A Song of Ice and Fire*—what if *I* do? How will I ever know if Daenerys Targaryen rides her dragons to defeat the White Walkers?

And so, I understand the desire for certainty. I understand the desire for knowing. I have that same desire; I want those things. I am not writing this book because doubt and uncertainty are easy for me; I write it because they're hard for me. I am good at preaching them, but deep down, I long to be sure. To be certain. To know.

But this one thing I have come to know: such certainty is impossible. In response to those big questions of life—the meaning of life, the existence

---

1. To be fair, the mystic al-Ghazali did call for the execution of some heretics, but not on the basis of what they had believed, but because they, as mystics, should have known better than to reveal mystical knowledge to ordinary people, who would not understand the complexities of the mystery therein and could do great damage to religion.

2. For a long time, my perfect vision of heaven has been getting to learn all the things that I didn't know in life. I always figured eternity was about right for that task.

of God, the purpose for all things, the length of days we're allotted—we simply cannot have any answers with certainty.

That may turn out to our advantage.

The Usefulness of Uncertainty

It turns out that uncertainty can be extremely beneficial to us and may be at the root of what makes us successful. Successful people will often say that they learned far more from their failures than their successes. This is not just a trite sentiment used at high school and college graduations; it's a recognition of the fact that being reminded of our lack of knowledge can be the biggest factor in figuring out what success is. As Jamie Holmes points out in his insightful book *Nonsense: The Power of Not Knowing*, failure reminds us that we might not have understood business/marketing/design/ministry/education/studying/the electorate as well as we had thought. It forces us to revisit old certainties and to impose ambiguity on things we thought we understood well.[3] Holmes argues that our relationship with ambiguity and uncertainty should not be limited only to learning how to avoid the pitfalls of certainty or manage our anxiety about unknowing but should involve recognizing the benefits of embracing ambiguity and uncertainty.

In recent years, Holmes notes, the value of failure has come to be appreciated much more, especially in Silicon Valley where it has come to be seen as a "badge of honor"—part of the process of trial and error. "Originality requires venturing out into the unknown," he writes, "dwelling in uncertainty, and learning from missteps." Failure has also been seen as an essential ingredient in new theories of teaching, as educators reappraise the role that failure can play in helping students to learn.[4]

From business to science to education, uncertainty and ambiguity are no longer seen as obstacles to success, they are seen as foundational *for* success. As innovation in science and industry are deemed essential to the health of the economy in a technological age, embracing uncertainty is a necessary requirement for any forward-thinking society. The option of retreating into our citadels of certainty is tempting, but the way forward is along the way of uncertainty.

We're just not going to have the certainty that we crave—whether it's by the nature of the universe, the metaphorical nature of our language, the systems of meaning we construct, or the pragmatic realities of science, business, innovation, and a forward-thinking society. It is not our lot to be certain.

3. Holmes, *Nonsense*, 159.
4. Ibid., 162, 68.

And that's okay.

Because while we may not be able to have the certainty that we crave, there is something that we *can* have that is much deeper, more meaningful, and more powerful.

The Faithfulness of Uncertainty

The philosopher Miguel de Unamuno argues that some of the most meaningful experiences are the result of uncertainty. He writes that when we pair the despair of the "tragic sense of life"[5] with what he calls a "vital skepticism," we receive "holy, sweet, saving uncertainty, our supreme consolation." [6] To explain what he means, Unamuno refers to a story in the gospel of Mark, of a man who asks Jesus to heal his son from possession by an evil spirit. When Jesus heals his son, the man declares: "Lord, I believe! Help my unbelief!" Unamuno points out the apparent contradiction: he believes, so why does he ask Jesus to rescue him from his lack of trust? Unamuno continues: "This contradiction is precisely what lends the profoundest human value to the cry from the heart of the possessed boy's father. His faith is a faith based on uncertainty."[7]

Unamuno argues that a faith built on uncertainty is "the most robust" faith. Faith is not a rational belief in a theoretical idea; it's trust in a person who assures us of something.[8] In order to claim this "robust faith," we have to become comfortable with our doubt and our unknowing. Our uncertainty should not be seen as a problem, but as a badge of honor, making plain to us and all the world that our faith is genuine.

This point was made very clear a few years ago with the publication of some private papers belonging to Mother Teresa. They did not contain the usual unsavory details that are in so many celebrities' diaries, but there was an unexpected revelation. The collection contained a letter sent to a priest with a heartfelt, and anguished, confession:

> Now Father— since [19]49 or 50 this terrible sense of loss—this loneliness—this continual longing for God—which gives me pain deep down in my heart—Darkness is such that I really do not see—neither with my mind nor with my reason—The place of God in my soul is blank—There is no God in me—When the pain of longing is so great—I just long and long for God—and

5. See, ch. 1., p. 3.

6. Unamuno, *Tragic Sense of Life*, 131.

7. Ibid., 133.

8. Ibid., 205.

there is that I feel—He does not want me—He is not there— . . .
God does not want me— Sometimes—I just hear my own voice
cry out—"My God" and nothing else comes—The torture and
pain I can't explain.[9]

Mother Teresa, the author of this letter of anguish, was perhaps one of
the most visible examples of Christian service for decades. She admits to
being in what is referred to as a *long dark night of the soul* and to wrestling
with profound doubt and uncertainty. The pain she feels in these letters is
real and her doubts are real. "What do I labor for?" she wonders. "If there
be no God, there can be no soul. If there is no soul, then, Jesus, you also
are not true."[10] In another letter she offers a colleague comfort, assuring
him that "Jesus has a very special love for you," but concluding, "as for me
the silence and the emptiness is so great that I look and do not see, listen
and do not hear."[11]

These letters were not written at the end of her life after a long period
of spiritual exhaustion. They were written in the middle of her decades-long
career working with the poor in the slums of India—that is, she continued her work with the poor in the midst of severe doubt and loss of faith.
And she would continue it for decades after she felt she had lost her faith
altogether.

Well, on second thought, perhaps it's not right to say she lost her faith.
She may have lost her *belief*—she no longer knew whether the things she
believed in were true—but she did not lose her *faith*. Her faith continued in
her commitment to move forward with the work of loving and caring for
other people *in spite* of her unknowing.

Mother Teresa was not a perfect individual—there is plenty of information available that makes her human failings clear—but she might be
an important model for us anyway. We may not all be deep in the pits of
despair, in the middle of the *long dark night of the soul* as she was, but we all
have to deal with our own share of doubt and uncertainty. We are all in that
place of not knowing, in that uncertainty about whether what we believe—
from religious truth to political truth to interpersonal truth—is true. To us,
Mother Teresa models a faithful response in the middle of doubt: get up and
go to work anyway. In this way, she is an exemplar for us. Perhaps she and
Thomas are the patron saints of doubters.

A faith that required certainty could never have been robust enough to
have sustained Mother Teresa during her years of doubt and unknowing. A

9. Rollins, *Insurrection*, 77.

10. "Struggles of a Pious Leader."

11. Symon and Kohlmorgen, "5 Lost Documents."

faith built on certainty cannot lead a person to *trust* in any meaningful way. Such a faith would have to exist in some kind of bubble in order to ignore all the evidence of uncertainty in the world. And it would not be a faith that would challenge the believer, a faith that prompted reflection and wonder, or a faith that required standing face to face with mystery. It would ignore all of those things in favor of certainty. No, a faith built on certainty is not robust—it's an accessory to a life that is comfortable with disengagement from the real world. A faith built on trust, however, engages with the real world, messiness and all.

Living a life of faith in the midst of doubt and uncertainty isn't easy, but nothing bold, nothing meaningful, nothing life-changing ever is.

Love and Uncertainty

There is one final model for us as we consider a faithful response in a world of uncertainty. That model is built on one of the most common metaphors in Christianity: GOD IS LOVE. This metaphor is so often quoted—to the point of being a cliché—that perhaps we've lost sight of what it might be telling us. For in this metaphor is a model of relationship: we relate to an experience of God as we relate to an experience of love.

Think about a relationship with someone you love. Imagine this person says to you, "I love you." On what basis do you claim to know that this is true? "She said it." People say lots of things; they don't always turn out to be true. "He is really caring toward me." How do you know that he's not just going through the motions and every day is looking for a way out? "I saw the look in her eyes." Can this look be measured by an ophthalmologist and charted to ensure that your beloved is still in love day after day?

Love is not a measurable phenomenon such that you can perform an eye exam or take a blood sample to find out whether someone really, truly loves you. You can make an argument that love can be identified (as I frequently have) by what a person *does* rather than what a person says, but even so, all we have is data. We don't have *certainty*.

And so, we can *believe* that someone loves us, taking into account their words, their deeds, and that look in their eyes, but can we ever *know* to the point where we can stop worrying and comfortably count on the affections of our beloved? Probably not.

But in love, knowledge and belief are beside the point. Love is trusted in. Relied upon. In other words, when our beloved tells us we are loved, we *trust* in that love.

And when we trust in love, we open ourselves up to something wonderful. When we experience the world through the lens of love, we see it in a new way: colors are brighter, music is sweeter, flowers more fragrant, and food is more flavorful. Love is transformative not just to the relationship between the lover and the beloved, but to the way they both encounter the world.

And so it is with faith.

We do not have faith because we know for certain or because we possess beliefs alone. We have faith in response to an experience we cannot define and cannot claim to fully know. The experience is even exceedingly difficult to describe. But that experience impels us to respond in faith: trusting that the world is more than a series of random events, cold and indifferent to our struggles and longings. We have faith that evil, injustice, and oppression will not triumph, but that liberation, justice, and good will.

We cannot *know* or be certain in our beliefs about these hopes, nor can we prove our hope in God without appealing to things we already believe.[12] In the end, our ability to know or to be certain about faith are beside the point, just as much as they are beside the point when it comes to love. What matters is the trust.

For when we live lives of faith, it is just as powerful a statement as choosing to trust in someone's love. It has a way of transforming not just the one doing the trusting, but the way that person encounters the world.

When we open ourselves up to lives of faith, we do not do so in the absence of doubt, we do so despite our doubt. We, as with the case of love, make the choice to *trust*. And as in the case of love, doing so is transformative. The very act of trusting creates a kind of power of its own.

Taking a leap of faith is far more rewarding than all the certainties we attempt to store up for ourselves. A faith that acknowledges unknowing and doubt, *because of* the doubt and unknowing, is more meaningful than any unthinking, unquestioning faith could ever be.

In the midst of powerlessness and alienation, the decision to trust is itself a powerful statement of faith. More powerful than the ability to recite chapter and verse or to declare assent to all the ancient creeds or to be able to defend doctrine and dogma. Powerful enough to offer hope, to build community, to stand up to injustice, and to proclaim a way of living that models something other than the power structures of the world. And it is testimony to a faith that is capable of defeating the greatest enemy of all.

---

12. I've always been mystified by believers who attempt to demonstrate proof for their beliefs to outsiders by saying, "It's in the Bible!" Appealing to the Bible only works if you already believe in God.

Uncertainty and Vanquishing Fear

There are two great poles of human emotion: the first is love, the other fear. Although most people would be inclined to pair love and hate, on reflection it becomes clear that everything good comes from love—peacemaking, trust, generosity—and everything evil—anger, hate, greed—comes from fear. We live in a world caught between these two poles.

Fear is the great enemy. It is the tool that terrorists use to achieve political aims. It is the tool that politicians use to get you to vote for them ("Vote for me or they're going to take your guns!!!" "Vote for me or they're going to take away your prescription drug benefits!!!"). It is the tool that marketers use to get you to buy their products, terrifying you about the prospect of thinning hair or off-white teeth. It is the tool that media outlets use to get you to watch their broadcasts ("There's a product in your kitchen right now that can kill you . . . Details at 11!"). And fear—fear of freedom, existential isolation, meaninglessness, and the "core terror" of death—compels us toward certainties, control, domination, and defensiveness.

And this is why faith is such a powerful antidote to fear: because it is love lived out. Faith in God (or whichever metaphor you choose to define that ineffable reality),[13] like faith in love, is not grounded in certainty. It is not grounded in knowing or believing. It is not grounded in an ability to describe reality in simple propositions. It is grounded in trust.

Claiming faith in the midst of doubt and uncertainty is fearless. It is standing face to face with the void and daring to step into it. As an embodiment of love, a faith willing to embrace uncertainty and doubt is the most powerful antidote to fear. This faith is not the easy, wide road of seeking power, control, and certainty that so many others take. But the more people who take this path, perhaps the more well-worn it will become, the more visible and available it will be to others caught in the same trap of fear and existential anxiety.

This is a faith certain of uncertainty: fearless, open, and honest. Willing to admit what it does not know and to go forward with the work of faith regardless. Engaging one another in integrity and openness, reaching across religious and ideological lines with humility and respect.

It is a faith free from the chains of certainty and rigidity, free from the shackles of literalism and judgmentalism, that can liberate us from those same prisons. A faith that acknowledges—and *embraces*—the certainty of uncertainty is a faith that can eliminate narrow religious and political

---

13. Atheists, agnostics, and skeptics can live "faithful" lives too, if they engage with their ultimate realities (nature, the universe, etc.) with the same measure of humility and mystery that I have been encouraging theists to do.

thinking, a faith that can drive out the need for simplistic answers and extremist ideologies, a faith that no longer sees the world as *us* versus *them* but sees all as fellow travelers, a faith that can eliminate the divisions based on creed, doctrine, and ideology.

It is a faith that can change the world.

Bibliography

Abutarboush, R., S. H. Mullah, B. K. Saha, A. Haque, P. B. Walker, C. Aligbe, G. Pappas, et al. "Brain Oxygenation with a Non-Vasoactive Perfluorocarbon Emulsion in a Rat Model of Traumatic Brain Injury." *Microcirculation*, January 22, 2018.

Achenbach, Joel. "The Age of Disbelief." *National Geographic*, March 2015.

Adams, Douglas. *The Hitchhiker's Guide to the Galaxy*. New York: Pocket, 1981.

Adams, Hazard. *Philosophy of the Literary Symbolic*. Tallahassee: University Presses of Florida, 1983.

Al-Ghazālī, Abū Hāmid Muhammad b. Muhammad b. Muhammad. "The Decisive Criterion for Distinguishing Islam from Masked Infidelity: Annotated Translation of Faysal Al-Tafriqa Bayna Al-Islām Wa Al-Zandaqa." In *On the Boundaries of Theological Tolerance in Islam: Abū Ḥāmid Al-Ghāzalī's Fayṣal Al-Tafriqa Bayna Al-Islam Wa Al-Zandaqa.*, edited by Sherman Jackson, 83–141. Karachi: Oxford University Press, 2002.

Ali, Abdullah Yusuf. *The Holy Quran: Text, Translation & Commentary*. Lahore: Sh. M. Ashraf, 1983.

Alston, William P. *Divine Nature and Human Language: Essays in Philosophical Theology*. Cornell Paperbacks. Ithaca, NY: Cornell University Press, 1989.

An, Kirkland. "Do Muslims and Christians Worship the Same God? College Suspends Professor Who Said Yes." *Washington Post*, December 17, 2015.

Aquinas, Thomas. "Whether Faith Is More Certain than Science and the Other Intellectual Virtues?" In *Certainty*, edited by Jonathan Westphal, 10–12. Indianapolis: Hackett, 1995.

Aslan, Reza. *No God but God: The Origins, Evolution, and Future of Islam*. New York: Random House, 2011.

Augustine. "Three Things True and Certain." In *Certainty*, edited by Jonathan Westphal, 8–9. Indianapolis: Hackett, 1995.

Ayer, Alfred. "On the Literal Significance of Religious Sentences." In *Religious Language and the Problem of Religious Knowledge*, edited by Ronald E. Santoni, 129–35. Bloomington: Indiana University Press, 1968.

Barnstone, Willis. *The Poems of Jesus Christ*. New York: Norton, 2012.

Bellos, David. *Is That a Fish in Your Ear?: Translation and the Meaning of Everything*. New York: Faber, 2011.

Brock, Sebastian P. *The Luminous Eye: The Spiritual World Vision of Saint Ephrem*. Kalamazoo, MI: Cistercian, 1992.

Brown, Francis, S. R. Driver, Charles A. Briggs, Edward Robinson, and Wilhelm Gesenius. *A Hebrew and English Lexicon of the Old Testament, with an Appendix Containing the Biblical Aramaic.* Oxford: Clarendon, 1952.

Brueggemann, Walter. *The Prophetic Imagination.* Philadelphia: Fortress, 1978.

Buber, Martin. "Meaning and Encounter." In *Religious Language and the Problem of Religious Knowledge,* edited by Ronald E. Santoni, 182–85. Bloomington: Indiana University Press, 1968.

Buechner, Frederick. "Christian." Accessed November 15, 2015. http://frederickbuechner.com/content/christian.

———. *Now and Then.* Cambridge; Hagerstown: Harper & Row, 1983.

Burton, Robert Alan. *On Being Certain: Believing You Are Right Even When You're Not.* New York: St. Martin's, 2008.

Button, Katherine S., John P. A. Ioannidis, Claire Mokrysz, Brian A. Nosek, Jonathan Flint, Emma S. J. Robinson, and Marcus R. Munafò. "Power Failure: Why Small Sample Size Undermines the Reliability of Neuroscience." *Neuroscience* 14 (May 2013) 365–76.

Campbell, Joseph, and Eugene C. Kennedy. *Thou Art That: Transforming Religious Metaphor.* Kindle ebook. Novato, CA: New World Library, 2002.

Caris, E. M. "10 Tiny Miscommunications with Massive Consequences." *Listverse,* March 2, 2014. Accessed November 3, 2015. http://listverse.com/2014/03/02/10-tiny-miscommunications-with-massive-consequences/.

Chomsky, Noam. *Language and Problems of Knowledge: The Managua Lectures.* Cambridge, MA: MIT Press, 1988.

Coolidge, Frederick L., and Thomas Wynn. "Numerosity, Abstraction, and the Emergence of Metaphor in Language." In *The Evolution of Language: Proceedings of the 8th International Conference (Evolang8), Utrecht, Netherlands, 14–17 April 2010,* edited by Andrew D. M. Smith, 74–82. Singapore: World Scientific, 2010.

Corn, David. "Ben Carson: The World Was Created in 6 Days. Literally." Mother Jones, September 24, 2015. Accessed November 10, 2015. http://www.motherjones.com/politics/2015/09/ben-carson-creationism-six-days.

Crombie, I. M. "The Possibility of Theological Statements." In *Religious Language and the Problem of Religious Knowledge,* edited by Ronald E. Santoni, 83–116. Bloomington: Indiana University Press, 1968.

Davies, Oliver, and Fiona Bowie, editors. *Celtic Christian Spirituality: An Anthology of Medieval and Modern Sources.* New York: Continuum, 1995.

Dawkins, Richard. *The God Delusion.* Boston: Houghton Mifflin, 2006.

Debonis, Mike, Robert Costa, and Rosalind Helderman. "A Vacuum at the Top for House GOP." *Washington Post,* October 9, 2015.

Debonis, Mike, Robert Costa, and David A. Fahrenthold. "'I'm Not the One': How McCarthy Became a Bystander on His Big Day." *Washington Post,* October 9, 2015.

Descartes, René. "Meditations I and II and from Meditation VI." Ch. 4 in *Certainty,* edited by Jonathan Westphal, 13–27. Indianapolis: Hackett, 1995.

Deutscher, Guy. *Through the Language Glass: Why the World Looks Different in Other Languages.* New York: Metropolitan, 2010.

———. *The Unfolding of Language: An Evolutionary Tour of Mankind's Greatest Invention.* New York: Metropolitan, 2005.

Edelman, Gerald M., and Giulio Tononi. *A Universe of Consciousness: How Matter Becomes Imagination,* New York: Basic, 2000.

Edmonds, Bruce. "What If All Truth Is Context-Dependent?" *SSRN*, March 10, 2001. doi:10.2139/ssrn.259850. http://www.researchgate.net/profile/Bruce_Edmonds/publication/2530464_What_If_All_Truth_is_Context-Dependent/links/00b7d5295f6bc0d071000000.pdf.

Edwards, Paul. "Being-Itself and Irreducible Metaphors." In *Religious Language and the Problem of Religious Knowledge*, edited by Ronald E. Santoni, 146–155. Bloomington: Indiana University Press, 1968.

Eilperin, Juliet. "Obama Weighing Authority on Guns." *Washington Post*, October 9, 2015.

Einstein, Albert. *Relativity: The Special and General Theory*. Lexington: Emporium, 2013.

Fischer, Steven Roger. *A History of Language*. Edited by Jeremy Black. London: Reaktion, 1999.

Floyd, Shawn. "Aquinas: Philosophical Theology." *Internet Encyclopedia of Philosophy*. Accessed October 22, 2015. https://www.iep.utm.edu/aq-ph-th/.

Frenkel, Edward. *Love and Math: The Heart of Hidden Reality*. New York: Basic, 2013.

Frick, Frank S. *A Journey through the Hebrew Scriptures*. Belmont, CA: Wadsworth, 2003.

Fromkin, Victoria, and Robert Rodman. *An Introduction to Language*. New York: Holt, Rinehart and Winston, 1983.

Gibran, Kahlil. *Jesus the Son of Man: His Words and His Deeds as Told and Recorded by Those Who Knew Him*. New York: Knopf, 2002.

Giles, Steve. *Theorizing Modernism: Essays in Critical Theory*. New York: Routledge, 1993.

Gillman, Neil. *Sacred Fragments: Recovering Theology for the Modern Jew*. Philadelphia: Jewish Publication Society, 1992.

Gordon, Bryan, director. "Affirmative Action." *Curb Your Enthusiasm*, season 1, episode 9. HBO, 2000.

Greenberg, Jeff, Sheldon Solomon, and Tom Pyszczynski. "Terror Management Theory of Self-Esteem and Cultural Worldviews: Empirical Assessments and Conceptual Refinements." In *Advances in Experimental Social Psychology*, edited by P. Zanna Mark, 61–139. Academic Press, 1997.

Greene, Brian. *The Elegant Universe: Superstrings, Hidden Dimensions, and the Quest for the Ultimate Theory*. New York: Vintage, 2000.

———. Interview with Stephen Colbert. *The Late Show with Stephen Colbert*. CBS, November 11, 2015.

Griffith-Jones, Robin. *The Four Witnesses: The Rebel, the Rabbi, the Chronicler, and the Mystic*. San Francisco: HarperSanFrancisco, 2000.

Gove, Philip Babcock, editor. *Webster's Third New International Dictionary of the English Language, Unabridged*. Springfield, MA: Merriam-Webster, 1993.

Harper, Douglas. "God." *Online Etymology Dictionary*. Accessed September 2, 2015. https://www.etymonline.com/word/god.

Hashimoto, Takahashi, Masaya Nakatsuka, and Takeshi Konno. "Linguistic Analogy for Creativity and the Origin of Language." In *The Evolution of Language: Proceedings of the 8th International Conference (Evolang8), Utrecht, Netherlands, 14–17 April 2010*, edited by Andrew D. M. Smith, 184–91. Singapore: World Scientific, 2010.

Hawking, Stephen. *The Illustrated A Brief History of Time*. New York: Bantam, 1996.

———. *The Universe in a Nutshell*. New York: Bantam, 2001.

Hick, John. *God Has Many Names*. Philadelphia: Westminster, 1982.

————. *The Metaphor of God Incarnate: Christology in a Pluralistic Age*. Louisville: Westminster John Knox, 2006.

Hitchens, Christopher. *god Is Not Great: How Religion Poisons Everything*. New York: Twelve, 2007.

Holmes, Jamie. *Nonsense: The Power of Not Knowing*. New York: Crown, 2015.

Hume, David. "Of the Academical or Sceptical Philosophy." Ch. 6 in *Certainty*, edited by Jonathan Westphal, 33–38. Indianapolis: Hackett, 1995.

Ibeji, Mike. "Becket, the Church and Henry II." BBC, February 2, 2011. Accessed November 3, 2015.http://www.bbc.co.uk/history/british/middle_ages/becket_01. shtml.

IMDb. "*Airplane!* (1980) - Quotes." Accessed March 21, 2018. http://www.imdb.com/ title/tt0080339/quotes.

————. "*Annie Hall* (1977) - Quotes." Accessed September 15, 2015. http://www.imdb. com/title/tt0075686/quotes.

————. "*Guardian of the Galaxy* (2014) - Quotes." Accessed November 4, 2015. http:// www.imdb.com/title/tt2015381/quotes.

————. "*Zoolander* (2001) - Quotes." Accessed September 15, 2015. http://www.imdb. com/title/tt0196229/quotes.

Jacobellis v. Ohio. 378 U.S. 184 (1964).

Jalāl al-Dīn, Rūmī, and Coleman Barks. *The Soul of Rumi: A New Collection of Ecstatic Poems*. San Francisco: HarperSanFrancisco, 2001.

"Joseph Campbell Quotes." BrainyQuote.com, Xplore, Inc., Accessed April 21, 2018. https://www.brainyquote.com/quotes/joseph_campbell_141385.

Kahneman, Daniel. *Thinking, Fast and Slow*. New York: Farrar, Straus and Giroux, 2013.

Kellenberger, James. *The Everlasting and the Eternal*. New York: Palgrave Macmillan, 2015.

Kenneally, Christine. *The First Word: The Search for the Origins of Language*. New York: Viking, 2007.

Kennedy, James D. "How to Know for Sure You Are Going to Heaven." Edited by Crossway/ATS. Garland, TX: Crossway, 2001.

Lakoff, George, and Mark Johnson. *Metaphors We Live By*. Chicago: University of Chicago Press, 2003.

Lao Tzu and Raymond Bernard Blakney. *The Way of Life. A New Translation of the Tao Tê Ching*. Translated by Raymond Bernard Blakney. New York: New American Library, 1955.

Lazic, Stanley E. "The Problem of Pseudoreplication in Neuroscientific Studies: Is It Affecting Your Analysis?" *BMC Neuroscience* 11/5 (2010) 1–17.

Leibniz, G. W. "On the Method of Distinguishing Real from Imaginary Phenomena." Ch. 5 in *Certainty*, edited by Jonathan Westphal, 28–32. Indianapolis: Hackett, 1995.

Livio, Mario. *The Golden Ratio: The Story of Phi, the World's Most Astonishing Number*. New York: Broadway, 2002.

————. *Is God a Mathematician?* New York: Simon & Schuster, 2009.

Luscombe, Belinda. "Is Reza Aslan Anti-Christian? The Author of Zealot Explains His Views on Faith and Historical Scholarship." *Time*, July 30, 2013. Accessed November 15, 2015. http://ideas.time.com/2013/07/30/is-reza-aslan-anti- christian/.

MacIntyre, Alasdair. "Is Religious Language So Idiosyncratic That We Can Hope for No Philosophical Account of It?" In *Religious Language and the Problem of Religious Knowledge*, edited by Ronald E. Santoni, 47–51. Bloomington: Indiana University Press, 1968.

Martland, Thomas R. *Religion as Art: An Interpretation*. SUNY Series in Philosophy. Albany: State University of New York Press, 1981.

Matt, Daniel Chanan. *The Essential Kabbalah: The Heart of Jewish Mysticism*. San Francisco: HarperSanFrancisco, 1995.

McDonald, J. H., translator. *Tao Te Ching*, by Lao Tzu. 1996. Accessed March 30, 2018. http://www.wright-house.com/religions/taoism/tao-te-ching.html.

McFague, Sallie. *Metaphorical Theology: Models of God in Religious Language*. Philadelphia: Fortress, 1982.

McGrath, Alister E. *Christian Theology: An Introduction*. Chichester: Wiley-Blackwell, 2011.

McGuckin, John Anthony. *The Book of Mystical Chapters: Meditations on the Soul's Ascent, from the Desert Fathers and Other Early Christian Contemplatives*. Boston: Shambhala, 2003.

McKenna, Kristine. "ART: Picture Imperfect: For Maverick Duane Michals, a Photo Is Worth Far Less than a Thousand Words When the Questions Are about the Very Meaning of Truth." *Los Angeles Times*, March 14, 1993. Accessed April 17, 2018. http://articles.latimes.com/1993-03-14/entertainment/ca-543_1_duane-michals.

McPherson, Thomas. "Positivism and Religion." In *Religious Language and the Problem of Religious Knowledge*, edited by Ronald E. Santoni, 52–66. Bloomington: Indiana University Press, 1968.

"Mokusatsu: One Word, Two Lessons." Unclassified per (b) (3)-P.L. 86-36. https://www.nsa.gov/public_info/_files/tech_journals/mokusatsu.pdf.

Moore, G. E. "Certainty." Ch. 9 in *Certainty*, edited by Jonathan Westphal, 58–80. Indianapolis: Hackett, 1995.

Moskowitz, Clara. "Largest Molecules Yet Behave Like Waves in Quantum Double-Slit Experiment " Live Science, March 25, 2012. Accessed May 21, 2016. http://www.livescience.com/19268-quantum-double-slit-experiment-largest-molecules.html.

Mounce, William D. *The Analytical Lexicon to the Greek New Testament*. Grand Rapids: Zondervan, 1993. Accordance Bible Software.

National Geographic. "An Experiment in Gravity." Segment of "The Lives of the Stars," *Cosmos: A Space Odyssey*, season 1, episode 9, 2014. Accessed March 21, 2018. http://channel.nationalgeographic.com/u/kc-onOO8EE9geYP33xt37H 1YPdkbuu2wq9CrtLn3VwCgOlRZzXuN9Dus05C0-Z_RYrX3egEOcMeqrvp-pSqTEoRtlo4/.

National Research Council (U.S.), Committee on Defining and Advancing the Conceptual Basis of Biological Sciences in the 21st Century; National Research Council (U.S.), Board on Life Sciences; and National Academy of Sciences (U.S.). *The Role of Theory in Advancing 21st-Century Biology: Catalyzing Transformative Research*. Washington, DC: National Academies Press, 2008.

Nhất Hạnh, Thích. *Old Path, White Clouds: Walking in the Footsteps of the Buddha*. Berkeley, CA: Parallax, 1991.

Oden, Amy. *In Her Words: Women's Writings in the History of Christian Thought*. Nashville: Abingdon, 1994.

Otto, Rudolf. *The Idea of the Holy: An Inquiry into the Non-Rational Factor in the Idea of the Divine and Its Relation to the Rational.* Translated by John W. Harvey. London: H. Milford, Oxford University Press, 1923.

Pagitt, Doug. *A Christianity Worth Believing: Hope-Filled, Open-Armed, Alive-and-Well Faith for the Left Out, Left Behind, and Let Down in Us All.* A Living Way. San Francisco: Jossey-Bass, 2008.

Partridge, Eric, Paul Beale, and Eric Partridge. *A Concise Dictionary of Slang and Unconventional English: From a Dictionary of Slang and Unconventional English by Eric Partridge.* New York: Macmillan, 1990.

Pinker, Steven. *Language, Cognition, and Human Nature: Selected Articles.* New York: Oxford University Press, 2013.

———. *The Sense of Style: The Thinking Person's Guide to Writing in the 21st Century.* New York: Viking Adult, 2014.

———. *The Stuff of Thought: Language as a Window into Human Nature.* New York: Viking, 2007.

Plato. "Knowledge and Opinion." Ch. 1 in *Certainty,* edited by Jonathan Westphal, 1–7. Indianapolis: Hackett, 1995.

Platts, Mark de Bretton. *Ways of Meaning: An Introduction to a Philosophy of Language.* Boston: Routledge and Kegan Paul, 1979.

Quirk, Tom. *Mark Twain and Human Nature.* Columbia: University of Missouri Press, 2007.

Reagan, Michael. *The Hand of God: Thoughts and Images Reflecting the Spirit of the Universe.* Kansas City, MO: Andrews McMeel, 1999.

Reid, Patrick V. *Readings in Western Religious Thought.* New York: Paulist, 1987.

Robinson, B. A. "Humorous Quotations from Church Bulletins and Similar Sources." Accessed November 4, 2015. http://www.religioustolerance.org/ch_bull.htm.

Robinson, Neal. "Ibn Al-'Arabi, Muhyi Al-Din (1164–1240)." *Islamic Philosophy Online.* Accessed September 22, 2015. http://www.muslimphilosophy.com/ip/rep/H022.

Rollins, Peter. *How (Not) to Speak of God.* Brewster, MA: Paraclete, 2006.

———. *The Idolatry of God: Breaking Our Addiction to Certainty and Satisfaction.* New York: Howard, 2012.

———. *Insurrection.* Nashville: Howard, 2011.

Romero, Oscar A., and James R. Brockman. *The Violence of Love.* Farmington, PA: Plough, 1998.

Rosenblum, Lawrence D. "The McGurk Effect." Accessed January 5, 2016. http://www.faculty.ucr.edu/~rosenblu/VSMcGurk.html.

Rubenstein, Richard E. *When Jesus Became God: The Epic Fight over Christ's Divinity in the Last Days of Rome.* New York: Harcourt Brace, 1999.

Santoni, Ronald E. *Religious Language and the Problem of Religious Knowledge.* Bloomington: Indiana University Press, 1968.

Saussure, Ferdinand de, and Roy Harris. *Course in General Linguistics.* New York: Bloomsbury Academic, 2013.

Schrödinger, Erwin, and John D. Trimmer. "The Present Situation in Quantum Mechanics: A Translation of Schrödinger's 'Cat Paradox Paper.'" Accessed October 31, 2015. http://www.tuhh.de/rzt/rzt/it/QM/cat.html#sect5.

Sheppard, Richard. "The Problematics of European Modernism." Ch. 1 in *Theorizing Modernism: Essays in Critical Theory*, edited by Steve Giles, 1–51. New York: Routledge, 1993.

Siegel, Ethan. "The Most Important Equation in the Universe." *Forbes*, April 17, 2018. https://www.forbes.com/sites/startswithabang/2018/04/17/the-most-important-equation-in-the-universe/.

Smith, Andrew D. M. *The Evolution of Language: Proceedings of the 8th International Conference (Evolang8), Utrecht, Netherlands, 14–17 April 2010*. English. Singapore: World Scientific, 2010.

Smith, Leonard A. *Chaos: A Very Short Introduction*. New York: Oxford University Press, 2007.

Soskice, Janet Martin. *Metaphor and Religious Language*. Oxford: Clarendon, 1985.

Stace, W. T. *Time and Eternity: An Essay in the Philosophy of Religion*. Princeton: Princeton University Press, 1952.

"Struggles of a Pious Leader." ABC News, August 24, 2007. Accessed November 23, 2015. http://abcnews.go.com/WN/story?id=3521905.

Symon, Evan V., and Matthew Kohlmorgen. "5 Lost Documents That Shatter Your Image of Famous People." Cracked, December 2, 2013. Accessed November 23, 2015. http://www.cracked.com/article_20712_5-lost-documents-that-shatter-your-image-famous-people.html.

Tegmark, Max. *Our Mathematical Universe: My Quest for the Ultimate Nature of Reality*. New York: Knopf, 2013.

"Test Your Awareness: Do the Test." March 10, 2008. Accessed March 21, 2018. https://www.youtube.com/watch?v=Ahg6qcgoay4.

Tillich, Paul. "Symbols of Faith." In *Religious Language and the Problem of Religious Knowledge*, edited by Ronald E. Santoni, 136–45. Bloomington: Indiana University Press, 1968.

"Top 20 Most Frequently Asked Bible Questions." Got Questions Ministries, Accessed November 22, 2015.

Traugott, Elizabeth Closs. "'Conventional' and 'Dead' Metaphors Revisited." In *The Ubiquity of Metaphor: Metaphor in Language and Thought*, edited by René Dirven and Wolf Paprotté. Amsterdam: John Benjamins, 1985.

Trueblood, Elton. *The Predicament of Modern Man*. New York: Harper, 1944.

Tsialas, Vasilios. "[B-Greek] Etymology of Αγια/Agia." April 30, 2008. Accessed October 29, 2015. http://lists.ibiblio.org/pipermail/b-greek/2008-April/046462.html.

Tumulty, Karen. "With Echoes of the Presidential Race, an Angry Insurgency Takes No Prisoners." *Washington Post*, October 9, 2015.

Unamuno, Miguel de. *The Tragic Sense of Life in Men and Nations*. Translated by Anthony Kerrigan. Princeton: Princeton University Press, 1977.

Underhill, James W. *Creating Worldviews: Metaphor, Ideology and Language*. Edinburgh: Edinburgh University Press, 2011.

The United Methodist Hymnal: Book of United Methodist Worship. Nashville: United Methodist Publishing House, 1989.

Warren, William F. "Babylonian and Pre-Babylonian Cosmology." *Journal of the American Oriental Society* 22 (1901) 138–44.

Whinfield, E. H., translator. *Masnavi i Ma'navi—Teachings of Rumi: The Spiritual Couplets of Maulana Jalalu-'D-Din Muhammad i Rumi*. Ames, IA:

Omphaloskepsis, 2001. Accessed March 20, 2018. https://archive.org/stream/MasnaviByRumiEnglishTranslation/rumi_masnavi_djvu.txt.

Wigner, Eugene P. "The Unreasonable Effectiveness of Mathematics in the Natural Sciences." *Communications on Pure and Applied Mathematics* 13/10 (1960) 14.

Wiseman, Richard. "Colour Changing Card Trick." Quirkology, November 21, 2012. Accessed March 21, 2018. https://www.youtube.com/watch?v=v3iPrBrGSJM.

Wright, Sylvia. "The Death of Lady Mondegreen." *Harper's Magazine* 209/1254 (November 1, 1954) 48. http://proxyau.wrlc.org/login?url=https://search.proquest.com/docview/1301534666?accountid=8285.

Yalom, Irvin D., and Ben Yalom. *The Yalom Reader: Selections from the Work of a Master Therapist and Storyteller*. New York: Basic, 1998.

Zukin, Cliff. "What's the Matter with Polling?" *New York Times*, June 21, 2015, published electronically June 30, 2015. http://www.nytimes.com/2015/06/21/opinion/sunday/whats-the-matter-with-polling.html.

Subject Index

Scriptural Index